The Insider's Guide to Book Editors and Publishers

1990–1991

How to Order:

Quantity discounts are available from the publisher, Prima Publishing & Communications, P.O. Box 1260JH, Rocklin, CA 95677; telephone (916) 624-5718. On your letterhead include information concerning the intended use of the books and the number of books you wish to purchase.

U.S. Bookstores and Libraries: Please submit all orders to St. Martin's Press, 175 Fifth Avenue, New York, NY 10010; telephone (212) 674-5151.

The Insider's Guide to Book Editors and Publishers

1990–1991

Jeff Herman

Prima Publishing & Communications
P.O. Box 1260JH
Rocklin, CA 95677
(916) 624-5718

Production by Robin Lockwood, Bookman Productions
Typography by Recorder Typesetting Network
Interior design by Judith Levinson
Cover design by The Dunlavey Studio

Prima Publishing & Communications
Rocklin, CA

Library of Congress Cataloging-in-Publication Data
Herman, Jeff, 1958–
The insider's guide to book editors and publishers / Jeff Herman.
—1990–1991 ed.
p.   cm.
ISBN 1-55958-016-X—ISBN 1-55958-015-1 (pbk.)
1. Editors. 2. Editing 3. Publishers and publishing.
I. Title
PN162.H44   1990
070.5′025—dc20   89-39347
CIP

90 91 92 93 RRD 10 9 8 7 6 5 4 3 2 1

Printed in the United States of America

I dedicate this book with love to
my parents, Robert and Doris Herman

And, with love and empathy,
to people who write books.

Acknowledgments

I am fortunate to have many friends and colleagues who helped me create this book in indispensible ways, and I intend to thank as many of them as possible. In alphabetical order, they are Deborah Adams—a soon to-be-famous writer and a special friend; Mr. Jan Barry—a man of principle and a pro; Dianna Booher—a pleasure and honor to work with; Julian Block—who can make complexities seem easy; Gene Busnar—a truly talented and dedicated writer; Ben Dominitz—the best publisher a writer could have; Laura Glassover—the lady who actually makes everything happen; Richard Laermer—a talented journalist and wordsmith, he personifies the word "writer"; Anne Mayer—who could write a book about enthusiasm and charm; The Nameless Lady—this whole thing was her idea; Gerry Nicosia—I admire his passion and dedication to the truth; Pete Mueller—a perceptive, hilarious kind of guy; Karen Romer—one of the best PR agents in the business; Michael Sedge—an excellent writer and an irrepressible entrepreneur; Robert Shook—an esteemed friend and mentor; Jeff Slutsky—the proverbial idea man and a good buddy; John Talbot—a very fine person and a credit to the business.

In addition, I received significant editorial and research assistance from Mr. Jamie Forbes, Nancy Kricorian, and Rita Pazniokas.

Contents

Introduction

If you are an unagented writer, the biggest obstacle standing between you and a publishing contract is getting your work read by an editor. You may have written the next *Grapes of Wrath*, but if you don't know whom to submit it to or how to do it, you will only end up with sour grapes. This book was written to give you, a writer without an agent, a fair chance.

This book contains publishing industry information never before released. It provides the elusive names and specialized interests for hundreds of book acquisition editors at more than 150 publishing houses, information that will help you target your submission to the editor most likely to be interested in your topic.

I urge you to carefully read and reread everything in this book. There is a right way and wrong way to do things in the book business, and second chances are few and far between. In addition to the names of the people you want to reach, *The Insider's Guide* has chapter after chapter of valuable advice written by industry experts on everything from how to develop marketable book ideas and submit unagented, unsolicited submissions to a complete model nonfiction book proposal and an extensive glossary of book industry terms. Unlike its closest competitor, *The Insider's Guide* goes into great detail on practical matters like query letters, ghostwriting, humor writing, taxes, and worldwide sales. With the information in *The Insider's Guide,* you can develop a book idea, make a successful submission to an acquisitions editor, negotiate a bigger advance, and prepare for a publicity tour.

Do follow the advice in this book. It may sound harsh, but ignorance is rarely tolerated by harried editors. Unagented writers do get published not only because their work has merit, but because they know how to reach the editor they need most. This book will give you the savvy to make a sale.

Please note, *The Insider's Guide* does not list all of the editors at all of the houses. Many top editors were intentionally left out, as they are the least accessible for aspiring writers. Other editors requested that they not be included, and I have honored their requests. The publishing industry is noted for its high turnover; a handful of editors listed here will have changed houses or left the publishing scene altogether by the time this book is published. We recommend that prior to sending any submission you call to confirm that the editor is still on board. To keep the book as current as possible, *The Insider's Guide* will be revised annually.

You hold in your hands the advantage that you need for a successful unagented, unsolicited submission. Use it well, and feel free to write me with any comments, compliments, or additions. Best wishes.

Jeff Herman

The
Insider's Guide
to Book Editors
and Publishers

1990–1991

The Book Acquisition Process:
Why a Few Get Published While Most Don't

JOHN TALBOT

Do you really have to know someone in order to get published? Do you have to have an agent? Or is it just blind luck, like a lottery? Happily enough for aspiring authors, the answers to the above questions are "no"; "no, but it helps"; and "of course not."

There are more books being published now than ever before, although the odds are still long against any given manuscript getting published. Surprisingly enough, though, the reasons many manuscripts are returned often have less to do with quality than with whether or not the editorial and marketing needs of a particular house are being met. In other words, there's a lot of good material out there; what separates the published from the unpublished is often that the published manuscript has somehow found its way into the appropriate house at the right time. Although it sounds like there's a great deal of luck involved in that—and there sometimes is—getting published is more often than not the result of a well-planned submission strategy by the author. The few who get published have often done just a little bit more homework than most, ensuring that the factors they can control in the submission process fall in their favor.

John Talbot is an editor with Berkley Publishing Group.

Corporate editorial offices receive stacks of submissions each day. Some come from agents or through solicitations, but many, many more come unsolicited and without agents. And a surprising number of these over-the-transom submissions do get published each year. What follows are a few simple suggestions to help you get an unsolicited manuscript past any initial screening and into the hands of an editor. These suggestions can't guarantee publication, but they can go a long way toward that first, all-important step in the process—getting a fair, attentive reading.

Once your material is ready and as strong as you can make it (I'll spare you my long-winded theories on that vast subject), there are two basic parts of the submission process to consider. The first is simply mechanical: how to make your manuscript as clean and easy to read as possible. The second is strategic: making sure your manuscript gets into the hands of the right editor at the appropriate publishing house.

To illuminate these goals, let's look at the acquisition process from an editor's viewpoint. Editors are always on the prowl for any good material. Not only do they simply love books, but their earnings are indirectly tied to the number of books they work on and the success of these books. So the more good material bought, the better. This means, as writers, editors are potential friends and, if you contact them in the proper way, they should be willing to review your material.

Every corporation has a slightly different system, but a simplified view of the acquisition process is this: Unsolicited manuscripts addressed to specific editors are sent directly to that person and read by that editor or his or her assistant; manuscripts with no addressee are assigned by subject or parceled out by volume. If the reading on a submission—which can take a few weeks—is favorable, the submission may be passed on for another opinion and/or discussed at an editorial meeting. After the second opinion or after the meeting, a decision is made on whether to make an offer.

Sounds simple, right? There are, however, some potential roadblocks. Unsolicited manuscripts are put in big piles, called slush piles, to be read later. Editors and their assistants read these submissions when time permits, but admittedly—since their first obligation must be to authors already under contract— the response time can be a few months. Manuscripts in slush piles or out on readings can get shuffled, SASEs lost, or queries separated from the submission. Material without an addressee, or addressed to someone no longer with the company, is likely to get a slow response or slip into the bowels of a slush pile because it's not assigned to anyone and therefore cannot be directly accounted for.

Other more devious ways of working into the nether reaches of a slush pile are submitting material with signs of carelessness: shoeprints on your query letter, spaghetti stains on the envelope, pencil text and crayon drawings, and so forth. And submitting proposals to the wrong people—a sports proposal to a cookbook editor, for example. A couple of other ways to sabotage your submission are cold-calling editors and trying to sell a manuscript over the phone, repeated demands for a reply only days after a manuscript has been mailed, and requests for detailed critiques.

As an aspiring professional, your goal is to get your material read and acted on before it sits too long, disappears, or works its way down into the slush pile. Editors often have only a few moments to decide if they want to read something; a professional-looking manuscript with a strong query letter is the most likely candidate for that reading. Give an editor a manuscript in his or her particular area of interest and expertise, presented in a clear, clean format, and your chances of a favorable reply will increase tenfold. Note that these are all factors you yourself can influence or control.

In addition, your manuscript should meet these general standards and formats. It should be typed on white $8\frac{1}{2}'' \times 11''$ paper. The paper should be of medium-to-heavy thickness and nonerasable. Lines should be double-spaced, and the pages should have generous margins. The type should be letter quality, as crisp and clear as you can possibly make it. Though choice of typeface is a matter of personal style, choosing something standard and large—say, Courier 10—is wise; anything that's easy on the eyes will probably be appreciated.

Number your pages consecutively from beginning to end rather than renumbering each section or chapter, and put your last name on the top righthand corner of each page. Make sure your address and phone number are on both the manuscript and your cover letter. Send your material unbound; binders and folders are more of a hindrance than a help while reading, and usually end up broken off.

SASEs are optional. Most of the larger companies will return your material even without an SASE, and there's a school of thought that says an SASE makes a rejection easier and thus more likely to happen. Don't send loose stamps; they'll probably end up getting separated, and you may pay for the swift return of someone else's manuscript.

Make sure you have extra copies of your material. This saves time if your manuscript is lost, and enables you to quickly respond to a request for another. You'll also feel better knowing you've got backup copies; as soon as you find a publisher, they may come in handy.

In formulating your submission strategy, there's no better substitute for the knowledge gained by researching your prospective publisher. A few minutes of fact checking—for correct addresses, editors' names, publishing guidelines, and specialties—can really get your manuscript in the right door and avoid a lot of headaches. In addition to the help you'll find in this book, the latest *Literary Market Place*—also known as the *LMP*—will have all the other necessary information. Your library should have a copy. Various writing magazines can also help with updated information, as do the annual Writer's Digest books (see Suggested Readings).

Your first task is to learn which houses publish in your specific area. Look at the spine of the books you like to read and of those most similar to what you're writing. Check the copyright page and update that information with the *LMP* or a phone call. If you're writing Westerns, you don't want your novel to end up in the hallways of a house that publishes only romance or science fiction. Remember that the bigger publishing houses have various imprints—essentially publishing houses within publishing houses—that specialize in different types of books. Get to know a couple of the imprints that publish your kind of material, and send it there. Be careful of multiple submissions when you do this, though; fewer corporations are controlling more imprints than people know, with the result that three submission letters from one author can all end up on the desk of one editor—an amusing but embarrassing occurrence.

Once you've picked the right house, you need to find a specific editor to address your submission to. The listings in this book should be helpful, but if you're still not sure, a brief phone call to double-check is okay. You want to learn which editor covers the kind of books you write, and you want to make sure that editor still works at the house you have listed, since—as with other industries—editors are changing jobs more frequently than ever. Never send your material with no addressee. A submission without a name is no one's responsibility, and, since it won't be logged to a specific editor, will be difficult to track. To Whom It May Concern letters just don't get much attention.

Another approach is to send your material directly to assistant or associate editors. Most of these people do the preliminary reading anyway, and they may be flattered to have submissions sent directly to their attention rather than to that of their boss. Chances are you'll find an attentive, appreciative reader among the assistants and associates. You might also send material higher up—to executive editors and editorial directors. Though these people rarely read unscreened or unsolicited material, they will assign it to appropriate editors.

Cover letters should be brief and businesslike—one page or less. State concisely who you are, what the manuscript is, and why you're sending it to a particular person. Include any pertinent biographical information—previous publications, personal experience in the area, unusual qualifications. A resumé is sometimes helpful for nonfiction, particularly if you're a specialist in your writing area. Make sure the date on your submission letter is current, and send out fresh copies when necessary.

Although these are easy things to overlook, an editor won't want something that has plainly been making the rounds for months. Be brief and to the point, not chatty, and remember to sign the letter. The quality and thoughtfulness of a cover letter are usually indicative of what lies behind it.

Simultaneous submissions are fine if they're kept within reason, and as long as you mention you're doing so in your cover letter. Sending your manuscript to three or four houses can save time and push an editor to respond faster. Be aware, though, that there are still a few people who refuse to read multiple submissions, and that no one reads the more obvious mass mailings.

Some general advice to keep in mind: Know your market and know who publishes your kinds of books. As much as "writing what you know," try writing what you read; tailor your manuscript to your own tastes and desires as a reader. If you're a compulsive thriller reader, you should probably be writing thrillers as opposed to horror novels. Don't worry about following trends; by the time they become apparent it's too late to latch on, and editors are looking elsewhere. And don't worry about writing the most original manuscript ever published. If you've never read a futuristic Western sci-fi romance thriller, don't feel you're the person who has to get the first one published. Strong writing in any genre is what matters most. The same story can be told a hundred times if it's done right, and if, in its voice and many details, it's really yours.

How to Develop Marketable Book Ideas

Anne Mayer

One evening, my husband and I went to a Chinese restaurant. After we had finished our meal, the waiter brought us some fortune cookies. I picked up a cookie and opened it, wondering what mysterious fortune the gods would reveal to me. My fortune read: "You have an extraordinary ability to think up marketable ideas." This story is absolutely true, and the fortune made me feel quite encouraged, particularly since I had recently sent off the last chapter of my first book to my editor. Being a published writer since I was 16, more years ago than I care to count, I can tell you that ideas for books are everywhere, but you have to be willing to work hard at tuning into the world around you in order to recognize a good book idea when it hits. You may be inspired by a fortune cookie, a conversation with a friend, or some tiny newspaper clipping, but unless you've been constantly analyzing popular trends and keeping on top of subjects the public wants to know about, or know more about, a marketable idea may slip right by you.

Cultivate Your Curiosity

The major path toward that possible first book forks in many directions. In other words, when scouting for ideas you must be

Anne Mayer has written dozens of articles for top-circulation magazines and is the author of the forthcoming book *The Burned-Out Parents' Guide to Sex* from Price Stern Sloan.

open to anything and everything. To begin with, explore your own feelings, your passions. What are you most concerned about right now? What issues or trends or events seem to haunt you? What subject do you know so much about that friends will often come to you for advice and insights? What less familiar topic has such a grip on you that you are champing at the bit to explore it further?

Next, ask yourself what other people seem to be most curious about. What is driving them, causing them to feel angry or worried or excited? Good places to tune into what people are talking about are parties, movie theaters (that is, people's reactions to a movie they have just seen), restaurants, grocery stores, bookstores, museums, beauty salons, and elevators. I'm not saying, of course, that you should walk right up to people and ask them what they are thinking or feeling. I am saying that by merely tuning into people around you, by listening peripherally, you just might pick up on something that excites you, too. Developing peripheral hearing is an art and requires lots of concentration, but it's worth it.

Another art worth developing is the ability to make connections. For example, you may hear a group of mothers discussing a specific topic that catches your attention. The mothers are wondering if sons who form a close relationship with their fathers grow up to be stronger, more self-assured men. The next day, you read in the newspaper about a study conducted on this very subject, along with interviews of some highly successful businessmen who attribute their huge success to the close relationship they had with their fathers. Click! A connection light goes on in your head, and you figure this topic is worth further investigation. If you can imagine yourself as a private eye of facts and feelings, you will make a good start toward tracking down ideas. My husband always calls me his walking encyclopedia, for example, because I am always telling him about some interesting story or fact I read about somewhere. Naturally, I take this as a compliment.

BE A MEDIA JUNKIE

If you want to get a feel for the pulse of America, read, listen, and watch. The *New York Times, USA Today,* the *Wall Street*

Journal and the *Christian Science Monitor* are virtual gold mines for ideas. Don't just skim the front page, however. You have to dig deeper than that and look at various inside sections, all the while keeping your sixth sense open to anything. The very first thing I grab from my Sunday edition of the *New York Times* is the Book Review section. I check out the best-seller lists first. If you make a practice of reading between the lines, you'll soon discover these lists are excellent barometers of national tastes and interests, as well as emerging trends and concerns. Other good sources are popular magazines, such as *People, Cosmopolitan, Glamour, Woman's Day, Psychology Today,* and *American Health.* Local newspapers and magazines are also excellent sources, as well as the newsletters of various organizations, such as a parent support group, a health club, or a business networking system.

When you are driving your car, listen to the radio. Change the channel from your music station and focus on local radio talk shows. If it is a call-in program, listen to the concerns people are calling about. Keep a small notepad and a pencil in the glove compartment, so you can write down any information that sounds interesting the first chance you get.

In fact, never be without a good notepad and pen when tuning into popular news shows, such as *Good Morning America, 60 Minutes, 20/20, The Today Show, Donahue,* or *Entertainment Tonight,* as well as news specials. These shows tend to focus on what's hot in popular trends, people, and issues.

USE THE LIBRARY

Make libraries your second home if you have not done so already. Take a look at *Publishers Weekly,* the publishing industry's trade magazine. More commonly known as *PW,* this publication is an indispensable tool because it gives you the inside scoop of the kinds of books publishers are interested in. It will give you a chance to test your idea to see if it is original, or encourage you to find a new angle on a familiar idea, or help you decide whether or not to pursue your idea at all. *PW* features and columns that would be most helpful to you are "News of the Week," "Trade News," "Bookselling and Merchandising," the bestseller list, and the ads and new title announcements. You can subscribe to *PW*, but a yearly subscription is expensive, about $97 for 51 issues. Most libraries, however, subscribe to *PW*. Just ask your librarian.

If you want an even more comprehensive idea of the subjects that are finding their way into books, and become inspired yourself—or if you have an idea that is haunting you and you want to check out competitive books on the market—look through *Books in Print (BIP)*, an annual reference guide published in ten volumes that lists every book in print in the United States. The volumes are categorized by title, author, and subject.

TEST-DRIVE YOUR IDEA

Is your book idea one that only interests you or a handful of people, or might it excite thousands or millions? Is it an idea that can develop into a book that will stand the test of time, or will it have a short life? Does your idea have the proper perspective, or is it too broadly focused? Does your idea have the strength to be developed into a book, or is it merely a magazine article? One good way to find the answers to these questions is to write an article on the subject. If your article generates enough interest among the editors and readers of the publication in which it appears, and if you feel you can write a lot more on the subject, you may be onto something. A friend of mine published an article in a popular woman's magazine several years ago. The editors were so excited by it that the managing editor found her an agent. The agent liked the article, which my friend turned into a book proposal, which turned into a book two years later. Having a published article on her subject actually helped sell her book proposal. If you are concerned that someone might steal your idea if it appears in a published article, one way to help protect yourself would be to ask the editor of the publication to state in your author's bio, usually at the end of the piece, that you are currently working on a book on this subject. At least this will give you a bit of a headstart over other curious writers.

BE PERSISTENT

The only way to know if your idea has possibilities is to keep testing it. If one magazine isn't interested in an article on your particular subject, try another magazine, and another. Magazine editors are people, too. They have good days and bad days, and you may have hit them on a bad day.

Submitting a magazine article on your idea is optional, of course. If you have checked out the book market and are convinced you have an idea worth pursuing, then find out everything you can about how to write a good book proposal and write the best one you possibly can. And work hard at finding a catchy title for it. Book editors are busy people who read many book proposals every day, so you will want to come up with something that will catch their attention. Who knows? Maybe you and an excited book editor will one day make a literary connection.

CHAPTER 3

An Introduction to Literary Agents

JEFF HERMAN

In a way, literary agents are like stock or real estate brokers—they bring buyers and sellers together, help formulate successful deals, and receive a piece of the action (from the seller) for facilitating the "marriage."

More specifically, agents search for talented writers, marketable nonfiction book concepts, and superior fiction manuscripts to represent. Some agents also seek poetry, plays, and teleplays. Simultaneously, agents are cultivating their relationships with publishers.

When an agent discovers material she thinks she can sell to a publisher, she signs the writer as a client, works with the writer to perfect the material to maximize its chances of selling, and then submits it to one or more appropriate editorial contacts.

The agent has the contacts. Many writers don't know any appropriate editors; even if they do, the typical agent tends to know many more and also knows which editors like to see what material. A dynamic agent achieves the maximum exposure possible for the writer's material, which greatly enhances the odds that the material will get published—and for more favorable terms.

Having an agent gives your material access to the powers-that-be who otherwise might be inaccessible. Publishers assume that material submitted by an agent has been screened and is much more likely to fit their needs than the random material swimming in the slush pile.

If and when a publisher makes an offer to publish the material, the agent acts in the author's behalf and negotiates the advance (the money paid up front), royalties, control of subsidiary rights, and many other important and marginal contractual clauses. The agent acts as the writer's advocate with the publisher for as long as the book remains in print or licensing opportunities exist.

The agent knows the most effective methods for negotiating the best advance and other contract terms and is likely to have more leverage with the publisher than you.

There's more to a book contract than the advance and the royalty schedule. There are several key clauses you may know nothing about but would accept to expedite the deal. Negotiating any deal can be intimidating if you don't know much about the territory; ignorance is a great disadvantage during a negotiation. An agent, however, understands every detail of the contract and knows where and how it should be modified or expanded in your favor.

Where appropriate, an agent acts to sell subsidiary rights after the book is sold to a publisher. These rights can include serial rights, foreign rights, dramatic and movie rights, audio and video rights, and a range of syndication and licensing possibilities. Often, a dynamic agent may be more successful at selling the subsidiary rights than the publisher would be.

No agent succeeds in selling every project she or he represents. Some projects, especially fiction, are marketed for a long time before a publisher is found (if ever). What's important is that you feel sure the agent continues to believe in the project and is actively trying to sell it.

For his or her work, the agent receives a 10 to 15 percent commission against the writer's advance and all subsequent income relevant to the sold project.

Although this is a noticeable chunk of the income from your work, the agent's involvement should net you much more than you would have earned otherwise. The agent's power to round up several relevant publishers to consider your work opens up the possibility that more than one house will make an offer, which means you will be more likely to get a higher advance and have more leverage regarding the contract clauses.

The writer-agent relationship can become a rewarding business partnership. An agent can advise you objectively about the direction your writing career should take. Also, through his contacts, an agent may be able to obtain book-writing assignments you would never have gotten on your own.

There are many ways to get an agent; determination will be one of your most important assets. The best way to gain access to potential agents is by networking with fellow writers. Find out who they use and what's being said about whom. Maybe some of your colleagues can introduce you to their agents or at least allow you to use their names when contacting their agents. Most agents will be receptive to a writer who has been referred by a current and valued client.

Literary Market Place (R. R. Bowker), *Writer's Market* (Writer's Digest Books), and *Literary Agents of North America* (Author's Aid Associates) list names, addresses, and specialties of agents. You can also write to the two major agent trade associations, the Independent Literary Agents Association and the Society of Author's Representatives (see Appendix A), and request a current copy of their membership lists. Membership in either organization implies that the agent meets specific performance requirements and professional standards.

The universally accepted way to establish contact with an agent is to send a query letter. Agents are less interested in oral presentations. Be sure the letter is personalized; nobody likes generic, photocopied letters that look like they've been sent to everyone.

Think of the query as a sales pitch. Describe the nature of your project and offer to send additional material (enclose a SASE). Include all relevant information about yourself—a resumé if it's applicable. If you're querying about a nonfiction project, many agents won't mind receiving a complete proposal. But you might prefer to wait and see how the agent feels about the concept before sending the proposal.

For queries about fiction projects, most agents prefer to receive story synopses; if they like what they see, they'll request sample chapters. Most agents won't consider incomplete fiction manuscripts, basically because few publishers are willing to.

If you enclose a SASE, most agents will respond, one way or another, within a reasonable period of time. If the agent asks to see your material, submit it promptly with a polite note that you would like to hear back within four weeks on a nonfiction proposal, or eight weeks on fiction material. If you haven't heard from the agent by that time, write or call to determine the status of your submission.

You're entitled to circulate your material to more than one agent at a time, but you're obligated to let each agent know that you are doing so. (Some agents won't consider multiple submissions.) If and when you do sign with an agent, immediately notify other agents still considering your work that it's no longer available.

At least 200 literary agents are active in the United States, and their perceptions of what is and isn't marketable will vary widely, which is why a few or even several rejections should never deter writers who believe in themselves.

Some agents charge a fee simply to evaluate your work (most don't), regardless of whether or not they choose to ultimately represent it. *Writer's Market* and *Literary Agents of North America* identify those agents who charge fees.

When an agent eventually agrees to represent your work, it's time for the agent to begin selling herself to you. Just as when you're seeking employment, you don't have to work with an agent simply because she wants to work with you.

Do some checking before agreeing to work with a particular agent. If possible, meet the agent in person. Much can be learned from in-person meetings that can't be acquired from telephone conversations. See what positive or negative information you can obtain about the agent through your writers' network. Ask the agent for a client list and permission to call clients for references. Find out the agent's specialties.

Ask for a copy of the agent's standard contract. Most agents today will want to codify your relationship with a written agreement; this should equally protect both of you. Make sure you are comfortable with everything in the agreement before signing it. Again, talking with fellow writers and reading books on the subject are the best ways to acquire a deeper understanding about industry practices.

When choosing an agent, follow your best instincts. Don't settle for anyone who doesn't seem reputable, or who isn't genuinely enthusiastic about you and your work.

Agents aren't for everyone. In some instances, you may be better off on your own. Perhaps you actually do have sufficient editorial contacts and industry savvy to negotiate good deals by yourself. If so, what incentive do you have to share your income with an agent? Of course, having an agent might provide you the intangible benefits of added prestige, save you the trouble of making submissions and bargaining, or act as a buffer through whom you can indirectly negotiate for tactical reasons.

You might also consider representing yourself if your books are so specialized that only a few publishers are potential buyers. Your contacts at such houses might be much stronger than any agent's could be.

Some entertainment/publishing attorneys can do everything an agent does, though there's no reason to believe that they can necessarily do more. A major difference between the two is that the lawyer may charge a set hourly fee or retainer instead of a commission, or any negotiated combination thereof. In rare instances, writer-publisher disputes might need to be settled in a court of law, and a lawyer familiar with the industry then becomes a necessity.

The plusses and minuses of having an agent should be calculated like any other business service you might retain—it should benefit you more than it costs you. Generally speaking, the only real cost of using an agent is the commission. Of course, using the wrong agent may cause you more deficits than benefits; but then you will have at least learned a valuable lesson for next time.

Your challenge is to seek and retain an agent who's right for you. You're 100 percent responsible for getting yourself represented, and at least 50 percent responsible for making the author-agent relationship work for both of you.

CHAPTER 4

A Business Approach to a Writing Career

ROBERT L. SHOOK

At some point, writers disenfranchised themselves from the world of business. I am not sure why it occurred, but I suspect it was based on the premise that people in the art world are not supposed to engage in commercial activities to promote their work.

Of course nothing is further from the truth. Nothing is so sacred about the art of writing that it is above being identified with business. Lest we forget, in our free-enterprise system, *profit* is not a dirty word.

I have a strong suspicion that writers, like painters and musicians, avoid the marketing aspect of their careers simply because they are afraid of rejection. To avoid having their work turned down, they rationalize with statements such as, "I refuse to compromise my artistic standards," "I am an artist, not a peddler," and so forth.

Fortunately, prior to beginning a full-time writing career, I spent 17 years in sales, during which time I learned to deal with rejection by pounding the pavement day after day. My livelihood was, in part, dependent on my ability to pick myself up after getting a no, and confidently approach the next call with vigor and enthusiasm. When a prospect did not buy a life insurance

Robert L. Shook has authored more than 20 books, including the bestsellers *The IBM Way* and *Mary Kay on People Management,* both titles from Harper & Row.

policy from me, I assumed he was rejecting my product, not me. And other leading salespersons think the same way. "He doesn't want a computer"; "She isn't interested in buying a new car"; "They don't like this house." The buying decision is an impersonal one.

Those of us in the art world, however, tend to take rejection personally: A painting, an audition, and a manuscript are not merely products, they are extensions of our very beings. The publisher is not rejecting my manuscript, he is rejecting me!

A professional writer must not think this way. He or she must realize that publishers reject manuscripts for a variety of reasons. They might not be interested because a similar book is already listed in their catalog. Or, most commonly, manuscripts submitted by unpublished writers may be rejected because publishing firms are understaffed and, consequently, have no time to read them. There are a host of reasons why they reject well-written, publishable manuscripts. When one of mine is rejected, I assume: "They simply do not understand. They do not recognize its quality and marketability. But so what? Another publisher will."

Marketability is an essential area that a writer must address. One of the most common mistakes novice writers make is that they do not clearly identify who will buy their book after it is published. They ignore the fact that books are, after all, products, and that successful products must have an identifiable market. Since publishing firms are businesses, like other profit-making companies, they must be bottom line–oriented if they are to survive. Therefore, publishing firms have a vested interest in buying manuscripts that will generate a decent return on their investment. This happens only when their published books generate decent sales.

Knowing that publishers are market-driven business firms, I approach them with a strong sales presentation that emphasizes the ready market for my manuscript. Over the years, I have discovered that editors are overworked people with little time to spare. Typically, a meeting to sell a manuscript is allotted only about 20 minutes. I have observed that many authors spend 19 minutes of their conversation with an editor talking about the contents of their manuscripts. They then devote 60 seconds to the book's market. I reverse these numbers. I spend no more than one minute describing my manuscript, and the next 19 minutes covering who is the market for my book and how we can best reach these buyers.

For example, when my last book, *Honda: An American Success Story,* was in manuscript form, I met with four publishers during an eight-hour visit to New York. Each of them got the same pitch. I described the book briefly as follows:

Honda is America's largest seller of foreign automobiles. The company was founded in 1948, and it is the largest Japanese company to be founded after World War II. Although Honda is considered a maverick company in Japan, as a result of a series of unique management innovations, it is the most successful Japanese company doing business in America. When the company announced it would manufacture automobiles in central Ohio, its dealers protested: "Don't make cars in the U.S. Americans are not capable of producing quality products. By making them here instead of in Japan, you will put us out of business." Honda managers replied: "We will manufacture automobiles in America, and they will be the same quality as in Japan. We believe Americans are equally as capable as the Japanese." Honda opened its plant in Marysville, a small farming community in central Ohio and, for the most part, hired farmers who had never set foot in any factory. After its first year of manufacturing cars here, independent studies have confirmed that the Hondas made in the United States are the same quality as those manufactured in Japan, proving that America does not have a labor problem. Our labor force is capable of being productive and making quality products. Instead, we have a management problem. My manuscript contains specific revealing management innovations that American manufacturers must learn from if America is to enter the twenty-first century as an industrial world leader.

So much for my conversation about the contents of the book. Read the above description aloud and time it. It takes less than 60 seconds. The publishers could read the manuscript to learn more. For the next 19 minutes, I then educated them about why managers in every business would have a strong interest in reading the book. I also stressed how the more than one-thousand U.S. Honda dealers would be interested in purchasing these books to use as premiums. And Honda automobile and motorcycle owners would also be potential book buyers. I even discussed various ways to promote the book through the media to generate publicity. My concluding remarks were: "When you publish a Robert Shook book, you get (1) a well-written manuscript, and (2) Robert Shook, the super salesman, who will work closely with you to sell the book. I firmly believe that every writer has an obligation to sell the book as well as write it. And I promise you I will not let you down in the selling end of this deal."

Three out of the four publishers made offers to buy the manuscript. It was rejected by one because I stated I wanted the book to be released within six months to coincide with a Honda dealership convention in New Orleans, and the publisher was unable to meet my deadline.

To gauge a book's marketability, a nonfiction writer must address this question: "Will the book's reading audience be willing to spend $20 for a hardcover book and set aside two to four nights to read it?" A writer must also remember that many subjects are appropriate topics for a magazine article, but not a book. A person might invest a couple of dollars in a magazine and spend 20 to 30 minutes reading an article on pipe smoking or knock-offs on Rolex watches. But an entire book? I doubt it.

I am certain that many fine writers fail to evaluate the market for a book prior to writing their manuscript, and as a consequence are unable to find a publisher. Discouraged, they give up and never attempt to write another manuscript. These writers may very well possess wonderful writing skills—and yet they will go to their graves with many unpublished books inside them. It doesn't have to be that way.

How to Succeed at Ghostwriting and Collaboration

GENE BUSNAR

If you're looking for a writing career with a never-ending source of opportunities, you might want to consider ghostwriting or collaborating. I've learned that there's an almost inexhaustible supply of would-be coauthors who are convinced they're sitting with a bestseller—be it a unique personal experience, a revolutionary new way of growing tulips, or some secret of the universe that's going to improve our lives.

Far too many of these unheralded giants are driven by an inflated sense of their own vision and self-importance. But fortunately, quite a few potential collaborators out there actually do have commercially viable nonfiction book ideas. All they need is a professional writer to take care of a few minor details, which can be paraphrased as follows:

- I have the ideas, but lack the writing skills.
- I don't have the time to write the book myself.
- I don't have an agent or book-publishing contacts.

Now, if these were the only reasons people needed collaborators or ghostwriters, this business would be a lot simpler.

Gene Busnar has ghosted or collaborated on some 15 successful books, including the forthcoming title from Villard Books, *Have I Got a Match for You: Secrets of an International Matchmaker.*

Anyone with a great story or a wonderful idea for a how-to book could hire a professional writer simply to put everything in proper literary form. In theory, the book's content—its very soul—already exists, so the writer's job should be relatively simple.

Unfortunately, matters usually don't turn out that way. Professional ghosts and collaborative writers are expected to know what book companies are buying at any given time and to anticipate the inherent problems in a particular book idea—especially if it's being sold in proposal form.

A publisher or agent may come to you with a fully conceived project by an articulate, promotable coauthor, but this is relatively rare—especially when you are in the early stages of your career.

There have been times when I've had to reshape an idea, change the principal's voice and language, and find a better title for the book. If you happen to possess these skills, coauthors shouldn't be that hard to find. But first, you have to get some publishing credits under your belt.

If you haven't yet published a book, try writing articles for magazines and local newspapers. But don't expect your first assignments to pay well. Think of them as vehicles that can propel you to a higher level.

You may be able to short-circuit the steps most authors go through by coming up with an innovative book concept and putting together a proposal that indicates you can deliver the goods. But it's logical to assume that the skimpier and less relevant your credits, the more you'll be expected to prove before people will treat you with consideration—much less shell out serious bucks for your effort.

Maybe you've heard inspirational stories of people who struck it rich on their first try, but such cases are rare. The vast majority of successful nonfiction writers work extremely hard at improving their craft and building their business.

Frankly, I think it's ridiculous to enter the difficult and competitive field of ghostwriting and collaboration unless you possess the necessary talent. So before you go any further, it might be worthwhile taking a few minutes to think about some of the issues of the question, Do you have what it takes?

1. What experience do you have (professional or otherwise) as a writer?
2. Have you ever received feedback about your writing from an agent or editor?
3. What was the thrust of that feedback?
4. Have you ever won any contests or received any writing awards? List them.
5. Have you worked with a teacher or mentor who encouraged you to pursue a professional writing career?
6. Are you open to constructive criticism of your writing?
7. Can you think of an instance where such criticism helped you to improve your writing?
8. Do your writing talents fit into a commercial category?
9. If not, are you willing to take steps to present them in more commercial ways?
10. What about your writing sets it apart from or makes it superior to that of your competitors?

If you honestly feel you have the talent, you may be off to a running start. But remember, even the greatest talent doesn't guarantee success.

For present purposes, I've chosen to focus mostly on the business aspects of collaboration and ghosting—since many talented new writers need help in these areas. It's a truism that many fine writers aren't good at business, but that's not surprising. Most people enter this field because they like to write—not because they expect to get rich.

If money is the primary motivation, you'd be better advised to pursue a career in law, copywriting, or any number of more financially lucrative fields. Still, if you're going to succeed—or at least survive—you'd better accept the fact that business and marketing skills are at least as important as literary talent. This is especially true in collaborative and ghostwriting work—fields that require a good deal of negotiation and personal interaction.

If you want to write just for pleasure, that's one thing. But the moment you decide to earn money at your craft, you become a businessperson. If you want to be successful professionally, start thinking of yourself not just as a writer but as someone who's in the business of writing. Here are four suggestions to help point your career in that direction:

1. Take a business-minded approach.
2. Present yourself powerfully.
3. Position yourself advantageously.
4. Price your services for profit.

TAKE A BUSINESS-MINDED APPROACH

Don't make the mistake of thinking that because you're good, clients will find you. You've got lots of competitors out there who are aggressively pursuing work, so you can't afford to be too relaxed. It's part of your job to make potential clients aware of you. These include not only cowriters, but agents and editors who can direct projects your way.

Most successful nonfiction writers do many things to generate work and develop new contacts. No matter where you are in your career, you might want to consider devoting more time and energy to the following activities:

- Joining professional societies and attending their meetings
- Associating with as many agents, editors, and potential collaborators as possible
- Staying in touch with peers who have similar interests
- Signing up for relevant courses, lectures, and seminars—especially those conducted by reputable people in your field
- Reading trade publications
- Keeping up with economic and other trends that influence the writing business

Ultimately, your success as a writer can hinge as much on how creative you are in your business as it does on your actual work. That's why it's essential that you understand and assume responsibility for the business side of your writing career as early as possible.

PRESENT YOURSELF POWERFULLY

Whenever you submit a manuscript, proposal, or resumé to an editor, agent, or potential collaborator, it's essential to look at those presentation materials from the other person's point of view. When you present your work to people in a position to buy your services, you're selling yourself as well as your writing.

Professionalism in your work and manner communicates that you are someone people ought to take seriously—even if they don't buy the immediate project. The creation of a professional image includes looking like a pro:

- Having appropriate and well-organized materials
- Demonstrating dependability and promptness
- Being willing to accept critical feedback and rejection

Of all these factors, an openness to criticism and tolerance for rejection may be the most difficult. Here especially, you need to imagine for a moment how you'd feel if you were an agent or an editor. One of the toughest things is telling others that their work doesn't measure up—whatever the reason.

Criticism and rejection can be even more difficult when you're on the receiving end. Still, when you communicate a willingness to accept constructive criticism, you invite feedback that can help you make valuable refinements in your presentation. At the same time, you let people know they're dealing with a confident professional—one who has a genuine interest in meeting their needs.

POSITION YOURSELF ADVANTAGEOUSLY

One key to presenting yourself professionally is giving potential clients a clear-cut picture of what you do. Since they have the option of choosing the writer who best fills their specific needs, it's your job to see to it that you occupy that particular niche in their minds. In advertising, this concept is called positioning. It's a principle that applies especially well to the business of writing.

Positioning saves your prospects a good deal of time. You can assume that anyone who's in a position to give you paying work has certain requirements and categories in mind. It's your job to meet those criteria. If you don't, someone else will.

Many good writers are capable of collaborating or ghosting in a number of areas. Unfortunately, that's not what most agents and editors want to hear. Their lives are already too cluttered with superfluous people and irrelevant information. If you present them with all your credentials at once, they may find it difficult to remember anything about you.

Once you have an idea of what specific clients are looking for, you can provide only information that is most relevant at the time. The best way to make that determination is to research potential clients before you approach them.

Let's say, for example, you want to ghostwrite political autobiographies, and you're trying to interest an agent who specializes in that area. He asks you to send some samples of your work. How do you decide which materials to include and which to leave out?

As a rule, the best presentations are the most concise ones. That's why it's best to present only what relates to the job at hand. As you develop more of a relationship with agents and editors, you can make them aware of your other skills. But be careful not to clutter their minds with too much material.

If you tell an agent who perceives you as a political writer that you also have skills in the medical area, he may file that information away for future reference. But if a call for a medical writer comes in, he's most likely to go with someone who has positioned herself primarily in that area.

Of course, there are exceptions to the rule. For example, an agent may not be able to get the medical writer she wants at that particular moment. Going down her list, she may remember you had some background in that area and, suddenly, she's dialing your number.

PRICE YOUR SERVICES FOR PROFIT

You may have never thought about it, but in most professions, pricing is determined by positioning and perception rather than by any objective measure.

Have you ever wondered, for example, why your car mechanic charges $25 to $50 an hour, while your attorney can charge $200 an hour?

The reasons for this huge difference in pricing can't be measured in any real terms, but the fact is, nobody would pay $200 an hour to get his car fixed. And if an attorney asked for a mere $50 an hour, you'd probably question the person's competence.

Unfortunately, pricing guidelines in the book-writing business are not nearly so well established as in lawyering or repairing cars. That's why it's essential to establish yourself as a business-person who puts a high value on your hours.

Personally, I see no objective reason why the services of a good writer should be worth less than those of a mediocre attorney. But because writing is thought of as a so-called glamour profession, people sometimes expect you to work for nothing—especially when you start out. It's your job to let them know that you're in this business for profit—not glamour.

I'll never forget how offended one celebrity became when I told him that I actually expected to get paid—and paid well—for working with him on his book proposal. This made a profound impression on me, and I've since made it a policy to regard people who take this attitude as a threat to my very survival.

In writing—as in any business—there are times when it may be worthwhile to accept a low-paying project. Just make sure that you have a clear idea of what's in it for you and what to ask for when the price is wrong.

Here are six compensating factors that can offset a low price or can be used as negotiating points in deciding whether or not to accept a particular project.

1. The prominent appearance of your name on the cover and in all publicity for the book
2. A generous allowance for expenses and supplies
3. Greater creative freedom
4. A larger portion of the advance up front
5. A better deal on subsidiary or ancillary rights
6. A larger number of author's copies of the book

Most writers take on work for a combination of three reasons: to make money, to be creative and expressive, and to build credibility that will hopefully lead to making more money.

Once you accept these as the general business goals of collaboration and ghostwriting, it behooves you to look for projects that are fulfilling, well paying, and career-enhancing.

If you can find a project that meets all three of these criteria, go for it. If a project allows you to achieve any two of these goals, it's certainly worth considering. One out of three would be a marginal call at best. But if the project doesn't satisfy any of these three tests, the decision is simple: Forget it and move on to something more rewarding.

How Writing a Nonfiction Book Can Promote You, Your Product, and Your Business

DIANNA BOOHER

Now that the majority of white-collar professionals have college degrees, what do they do to distinguish themselves from their peers? They publish-or-perish because that mandate has spread from the academic environment to the corporate setting. Publishing has become the new pastime for those who are already there and those who are still nowhere.

The Rich and Famous. The likes of Lee Iacocca, Victor Kiam, Donald Trump, John Scully, and Harvey Mackay have turned publishing into power. Publishing has added pizzazz to their already prestigious corporate careers.

The Average Joe Professional. Each week five to ten callers to my office express their publishing plans this way:

- I'm a lawyer, and our firm is working on a really interesting case. We're thinking of doing a book on it. Can you tell me how to go about it?

Dianna Booher is president of the Houston based Booher Writing Consultants. She has authored more than 20 books, several of which have been selected by major book clubs.

- I've got a manuscript about real estate equities that I've just finished on my PC. As a stockbroker, I don't know much about publishing. Do I just take it to a publisher or a printer, or what?
- My boss is really after me to get a book published on this new anticorrosion process our company will be marketing next year. It was originally a technical paper, but I guess I'll have to change the approach a little bit for the general reader, don't you think?
- I'm a gynecologist who's developed a new technique for laser surgery, and the hospital wants to get some PR out of it. I've got 20 pages dictated. Can you people help me turn it into a book?
- I've got a small catering business and I want to do a cookbook. It'll be a giveaway to corporate customers.

The Competitive Corporations.   Publishing has also become the competitive edge in the corporate world. Corporations interested in enhancing marketing efforts for their products and services (à la *The Other Guy Blinked: How Pepsi Won the Cola Wars* and *Odyssey: A Journey of Adventure, Ideas, and the Future*) are putting big money behind the publishing efforts of their employees. According to an *Inc.* magazine article (April 1988), mention of a company's name and product or service is now worth measurable dollars—dollars these companies are willing to pay their employees in bonuses or professional PR people for their publishing efforts.

Whichever category you fall into—the rich and famous, the average Joe or Josephine, or the competitive corporations, the timing for getting your ideas into book form couldn't be better. That third-party endorsement from a major publisher says to the world that "somebody out there," some objective editor, thinks what you have to say is worthwhile and that people would pay money to hear/read it. Corporations underscore the credibility factor when they pay their employees bonuses and give them high visibility for their publishing efforts—whether books or journal articles.

Nothing enhances your credibility or brings recognition—from colleagues, from your own management, from customers and clients—like publishing a book on your subject of expertise. In fact, this principle has even worked its way into our language. To establish someone's credibility, we say, "He wrote the book."

Money may be no less important to you than to Tom Peters and Ken Blanchard, who top the list of those who have turned their business acumen into books and in turn have turned those books into more business. Not only do you receive nice royalty checks from the book sales, you often find that subrights sales fatten the pot: software, video, and audio rights; fees for excerpts reprinted in national magazines and journals; premium sales; sales of spin-off products such as T-shirts, buttons, posters, calendars, and other paraphernalia; and fees for consulting and speaking engagements.

So how do you make the most of publishing your book when your purpose is to promote yourself, the product or service, and your business? First, negotiate with your publisher an excellent discount schedule for your own purchase of the book for resale or promotional activities. Then, proceed as follows.

Tell everybody in your business community about the book.

Generate press releases on amusing, informative, unique, or thought-provoking research you've done for the book. Those late-night radio talk shows and little-known regional publications readily grab informative tidbits and statistics (as opposed to hype) to provide their audiences with useful information. Your message may reach just the specialized audience that will be interested in learning about how your firm can meet their needs.

Give copies to current clients to show your gratitude for their past business and to build loyalty for a long-term relationship. How can they take their business elsewhere when you keep supplying them with complimentary $29.95 hardcover books?

Give copies to prospective clients to gain their attention. Direct mail—no matter how clever the opening line and packaging—is still discarded by many secretaries before the boss even gets a look. Secretaries, however, don't generally discard free books. Give people a nice hardcover book, and they'll read your accompanying letter to learn the why, what, and how of your other products and services.

Give copies to individual "champions" inside a prospective client organization so that they, in turn, can present you and your ideas in the best way possible to their decision makers who can hire you or your firm for other projects.

Answer inquiries about your product or service with the routine brochure—and a free book. What better proof that you're a recognized expert on the subject? You've outdone the competition immediately in your willingness to be transparent about what you can really do for the client or customer.

Give copies to people who can refer you to others who need your product or service. It's one thing for a colleague to say to a friend over lunch: "If you're ever interested in someone who designs excellent employment-compensation packages, I know someone you should talk to." It's a far more impressive referral for a colleague to say to a friend over lunch: "If you need someone to design employment-compensation packages, I've got a book on my shelf that you need to see—this guy also consults on the side. . . ."

Mail copies to associations and meeting planners who are looking for speakers—an instant badge of credibility for a recognized expert. Then when you land a speaking engagement, give the audience a quality talk, and you'll end up with back-of-the-room book sales and leads for other business ventures. And those products will be passed along to other decision makers who can use your services. Although these pass-on audiences themselves might not have heard you speak, you're obviously an expert if you wrote a book, right? That book in hand is often as good as "being there."

Prestige, money, new business, recognition—all are valuable and reasonable to expect as a result of publishing and promoting your nonfiction book.

What Every Writer Should Know About Research

GERALD NICOSIA

The most important thing to know about research is that you've been doing it all your life. Every time you pick up a telephone directory, or call information, or ask a stranger on the street, "Where's a good restaurant in this neighborhood?" you're doing research. As a writer, you simply have to refine these tools and learn where more of them are.

Every professional writer and historian should at some point take a course in the use of libraries. Every library has a reference desk and shelves of reference books containing everything from home-run statistics for the major leagues in 1919 to how many writers live in each state in the Union. There is, almost literally, a reference book on every subject imaginable (and if there isn't one, you should consider writing it, as 5,000 libraries across the country will immediately order any significant reference book they don't already have).

Understandably, many nonscholarly writers have an aversion to libraries. But you have to learn to use them because there is too much material that others have gathered before you that you

Gerald Nicosia is the author of *Memory Babe: A Comprehensive Biography of Jack Kerouac* from Grove Press, and the forthcoming *Home to War: A History of the Vietnam Veterans' Movement*, to be published by W. W. Norton.

cannot afford to ignore. The other side of the coin is that your reluctance to lock yourself up in a library all day may serve a useful literary instinct. That is, the best material for a writer is the freshest material—the stuff no one has seen or heard before. This is where your detective instincts will come into play.

Learn to use your mouth! As a researcher, it is the most valuable tool you have. Don't be afraid to ask anyone even the most outrageous questions. (How do you think Barbara Walters became a millionaire?) People are far richer sources of information than any library—every person has millions if not billions of facts and memories stored in his or her brain. Tap that. Of course you will be most effective if you find the right people to ask. You cannot simply go up to your local news vendor and ask which approach to quantum mechanics is most valid in an Einsteinian universe. For such a subject you will want to ask questions of physicists and writers who are most familiar with Einstein.

How do you find the people you need to talk to? Here's where reading comes in to start you on your path. Read a few books on your subject; underline or take notes on the most prominent names. There are biographical dictionaries of authorities or celebrities in every field; these biographical dictionaries will tell you if such-and-such a person is still alive, where he or she now lives and works, and so forth. If the person is listed as having some affiliation with Princeton University, for example, you write in care of Princeton. If the person is no longer there, the folks in charge will usually be kind enough to forward your letter, or to let you know where the person has moved. And don't be cheap about the telephone! It will often save you time, because there are lots of people in this world (unfortunately) who will not answer a letter, even if it is their job to do so. Dialing for long-distance information (area code plus 555-1212) is probably the most frequently used research tool in my own bag of tricks.

You will naturally be ahead of the game if you are writing about a subject with which you have some familiarity. If you know a few of the people in the field (as I did for my book on

Vietnam veterans because a few of my friends had been veteran activists), you already have a list of contacts to interview and to call upon for further names. Anytime you speak with someone, even if that person draws a blank on your particular subject ("I'm sorry, but I never met a Vietnam veteran"), don't forget to ask if he or she knows anybody else who might be of help. Usually people do. ("Well, my neighbor down the block was a Marine in Vietnam.") Even more importantly, after you finish conducting an interview, ask that person for as many names and addresses of possible interviewees as he or she can provide. If Person X has been working with Vietnam veterans for 20 years, you can bet X has a list of useful sources a mile long. One person will lead you to a dozen others, and each of those dozen will lead you to a dozen more. What you'll find, before long, is that you actually have more potential sources on your list than you can possibly reach or use.

This brings me to my last point—the danger of overresearching. You have to know when to quit; at some point, usually around a third of the way into your work, you have to start discriminating. At first, you may want to talk to anyone you can find who seems to have something pertinent to say. But eventually you're going to find that your time is getting scarce and your ears are getting weary. It's time to start making the hard decisions. Do I really need to talk to Joe Blow and Joan Schmoe about their views on the theory of relativity when I've already interviewed Carl Sagan and ten other prominent physicists? It may well be that Blow and Schmoe can add a few humorous and poignant points, but they're not going to completely overturn the facts and figures I've already accumulated. Hence, unless, I have a lifetime trust fund to live off of in my beach house in Aruba, I think I'll just pass on those interviews and get back to my typewriter—which is, of course, where the most important part of the work takes place.

You never want to gather more material than you can reasonably handle and assemble. Otherwise, you will be struggling so hard to make sense of your piles of data that you will never find the story line that is so important in hooking a reader into any book. You have to have a sense of how all this material falls and fits together: the narrative thread, the overview, the larger structure. I always like to have more material than I can use so that I can pick out the most interesting, startling, and original stuff for my book, but I don't want to have so much that I can't handle it or make sense of it.

A safe estimate would be to gather about twice as much as you finally put into the finished manuscript. Gathering ten times as much as you need is definitely taking too big a risk. The in-between area will be defined by how good a head you have for holding facts and figures and by the amount and quality of tools—computers, card indexes, and the like—you possess to help manage the material.

Just remember: You already know more than you think you do, and research is just finding the person or book that will tell you what you don't know.

(But please, don't everybody call me at once.)

By the way, I haven't mentioned the world of computers basically because it's not a source I use very much (for whatever old-fashioned reasons). But you should certainly check into all the computerized data banks that exist now in almost every field of study and human activity (just as you should be aware of the millions of issues of magazines and newspapers that are stored in tiny alcoves of most libraries on microfilm). Librarians and computer wizards can help you in this regard.

Now, happy hunting!

CHAPTER 8

How to Use Your Time as a Writer Effectively

RICHARD LAERMER

The foremost thing any writer should remember is, take your time. To the novice that may sound like odd advice. To professionals, it's our standing credo. As a freelancer whose articles appear in a few dozen completely distinct newspapers and magazines, I know how quick work can result in sloppy writing. Tiny errors are intensely irritating to editors. You don't want to annoy your only overseers.

If you spend a moment each day or night (depending on your schedule) organizing exactly what you want done during the time set aside for writing, you'll eradicate haphazard habits.

Now that you've decided to slow down, figure out where you'll be able to write best. For many authors and authors-to-be, working at home can often be too restraining, and an office can be money-draining. I once took a tiny space with a nonwriter friend and found I was always searching for excuses to go home. I realized—this takes a test—that I was more comfortable with the sounds of my own place. (Most cities have part-time rentable cubbyholes that writers can rent alongside other writers. In New York, it's called The Writers Room.)

If you decide working at home is for you, set aside a space that is yours alone. Nothing else can go on in that corner except

Richard Laermer is a working journalist who covers New York City. His books include *Native's Guide to New York* and the forthcoming *Bargain Hunting in Greater New York,* both from Prima Publishing.

your precious thoughts. Ideally, it'll be a room and not part of a room. No matter how small, a *private* writing space is crucial. (Dirty laundry can get in the way.) Just as doctors recommend a regular late-night routine to get a restful sleep, writers sense that to keep the muse or thought process in shape, they need a routine. Try to keep loud posters and garbage from cluttering your mental space. It should be just you and your paper—or word processor.

If you decide to forgo home in place of an outside office, make sure it isn't so large that you spend too much time figuring out what to do with it. ("Here's where I'll keep the plants. Here's where I'll rent a desk out. . . .") And don't take a closet, either. You can get just as much done in your bathroom.

Once you're settled in, be sure there's a phone nearby. As any writer will attest—even self-professed phone snobs—when you're alone for a spell, it helps to have a way out: The phone suffices as an escape hatch, a way to contact humanity.

There is also a flipside to the phone. When the world knows there's a time when you won't have anybody looking over you, they perceive you as being free. So free that you'll stop whatever you're doing, whenever, to chat. It is crucial to invent a way to screen your calls, and an answering machine can do that. If you're popular, or in touch with someone who can give you work, keep the volume up a bit.

Make it clear to friends and admirers that their generous stop-over visits are to be preceded by a check-up call. Writers new to working alone laugh at this—they can't imagine that a friend stopping by could be a pain. Ah, but then they see that no one thinks they're busy! One of the most common experiences for any at-home writer is fights with friends when they exclaim, "You're not working!"

During the start-up phase, wordsmiths find they need to support themselves in another way to stay solvent. If you're a reporter, you'll discover that freelance jobs do not come automatically. If you're a fiction writer—plays, novels, screenplays, short stories, porno—you'll desire stress-free time to find your muse. Getting a job can help, especially if you're broke, and there are a multitude of ways to find one.

One way is to write newsletters, business brochures, or even letters, part-time or full, for a company or individual who needs your expertise. You could work in someone's office as a public relations or ad-copy person, and even rent space from them for your own work; or maybe act as writer-for-hire, which sounds glamorous but is terribly difficult (you're always on call).

Problems arising from word jobs include being too worn out afterward to do your own writing. You get home and turn on Vanna White. That's not why you're a writer in the first place.

Mindless labor is often the answer. Word processing or proof-reading pays $12–$30 per hour, depending on your abilities, and secretarial/receptionist work pays fairly well, too. There is also phone sales, but make sure you aren't toiling in a pressure cooker. Or you might take part-time jobs through temp agencies, where the money's great but there are no benefits. These jobs—labor that is not intensive and can be forgotten when you walk away—are usually generous about your taking time off to meet a personal deadline; and they often offer flexible shifts.

So now that you've got money, freedom, space, peace of mind, a schedule, and that all-important credo ("take your time"), problems will still arise.

What do you do if you have two writing gigs going simultaneously? You're doing a report for a publishing house because you like it; you appreciate the respect granted you by the editors there, and you know it pays well. But you're also rewriting a play that is likely to go into production soon.

You can't eagerly do both. The commonsense approach is to tell the publishing house you're sorry but you can't meet their deadline. Then you're free to happily rewrite your second act, the one that's giving you sleepless nights because you can't figure how to kill off an evil character. You need more quality time, you tell your gainful employers.

The publisher, however, depends on you and has readily helped you when you were desperate. To turn your back on him/her could result in the loss of rent money, or elicit bad vibes between you and the editors. You think, "Well, pretty soon I won't need him/her." Except that, even in the best-case scenario, if your play succeeds you will need to write another one. Between hits, what'll you do? Probably work in publishing.

This situation exemplifies the mind-set of writers, most of whom juggle their own happy freedom with the inherent need for security. Most people think it's easy to roll out of bed, slap some water on your face, turn on Mr. Coffee, and sit in a chair and write. ("And you get *paid* for it?") Most people do not see that you need something to write, be it a play, book, or General Electric newsletter. And since so many writing projects are "on spec," one of those projects had better pay. If you prioritize and schedule accurately, you'll never have to worry about having too much on the palette.

What do you do when there's a dearth of work? You can either fret or look. During dry periods, I make phone calls to magazine and newspaper editors. I talk up story ideas and then spend part of the day sending letters about the concepts. Once every two months I send a story idea—the single rose—with new story clips to editors who remain unaware of my abilities and eminent availability!

This way I have a backlog of . . . editors. I don't always have assignments, but since I keep a running log of ideas ranging from the ridiculous to the inspired to cull from, I know the editors are within calling or postage distance. (When I write or fax a letter, I spend part of a week pursuing it with follow-up calls.)

You could also use these periods to generate creative ideas for spec projects. I got started writing for television when I had no work, no prospects, and a great idea. My co-writer and I had two choices: no money for not working, or no money for something that would probably net cash later on.

Which leads me to the final, most valuable point of the story of a writing life: how Persistence pays off. Years ago, I sobbed on the phone to my father after my first steady freelance gig, *USA Today,* told me it was ceasing the use of outside writers. After that death sentence, I figured it was time to look for a full-time job. Yet, since my dad no longer considered my work habits crazy, he disagreed: "If you've been able to freelance for this long, you can probably do it forever."

I took that sage advice—and recall it frequently. I discovered that in this word business, every time a shoe drops, another piece of footwear is up for grabs. If you find an area has dried up, find a moister pasture elsewhere. During that slow career period, I realized quickly that "experts" on certain subjects were in demand. My years of being a New York reporter had made me well versed in "how to use New York City better." I began teaching courses and was soon speaking for private groups (and writing expert articles). In 1989, I wrote my first book on that subject.

If I'd taken my own advice and abandoned my writing career after getting the boot from *USA Today*, I would have felt stupid two months later when I returned home to this heartfelt request on my machine: "Richard, this is Tom from *USA*. Call us immediately—we need something now!"

That no one suspected I'd quit is something I cherished. Writers, they're so sentimental.

CHAPTER 9

The Art of Making Unagented, Unsolicited Submissions

JEFF HERMAN

Welcome to the jungle. Did you know that it may be more difficult for an unpublished writer to get an agent than it is to get a publisher? And did you know that many publishers, especially the larger houses, have an official policy of not considering unagented submissions? Do you think that leaves you up a creek without a paddle?

It sounds like a classic "Catch 22" situation. In reality, however, novice writers have a difficult but not hopeless road to travel. It's a matter of learning and effectively playing the game (having genuine talent is a given). What you need is a tactical strategy to win at a game in which the rules were not made for you. That's what this book is about!

Always remember this: Publishers need a steady stream of new books and people to write them. For every writer who gets published, there are many, many more who wish they could be. There are several tangible reasons other than lack of talent why only a relative handful gets published, while most others are left outside.

Question: What exactly does unagented/unsolicited (UNS) mean?

Answer: Exactly what it says. If you don't have an agent, you're unagented. And if the publisher didn't solicit you to make the submission, you're unsolicited.

Q: Why are publishers averse to receiving UNS submissions?

A: Because they annually receive thousands of trees' worth of manuscripts they never asked for. Most of this material is unsuitable for the publisher. Some of it, to be blunt, is garbage by anyone's definition. Editors are underpaid and overworked and they have little time or incentive to swim through what is generally referred to as the "slush pile." There are many encouraging stories about good books that were plucked out of the slush pile; but that's an aberration, not a tendency.

Agented submissions, on the other hand, are usually granted first-class access to editors. The editor knows that at least the material has been screened by the agent and perhaps even perfected, and that the agent is unlikely to submit material that isn't even remotely appropriate for the publisher.

Q: What if I don't have an agent and the publisher has a stated policy of not considering UNS submissions?

A: Now you have nothing to lose. Nobody ever went to jail for ignoring this policy. Here's what you can do to smash right through this iron curtain.

Don't write to an anonymous party (sir, madam, gentlemen). If you send it to nobody, it will go to nobody.

Don't send your material to one of the highest-placed officers (publisher, editor-in-chief, chairperson). Some of these people at the top of the organization may be purely administrative and have no real editing or acquisition responsibilities. Even if they do acquire books, they are the least favorable target for UNS writers.

Use the directory of publishers and editors in this book to target specific publishers and editors whose stated editorial interests are in sync with your work, and query them directly. Whatever the so-called house policy, most editors will receive and read mail that is addressed to them personally. If they are interested in what you're selling, you will hear from them.

Don't start by cold-sending your manuscripts or proposals to these people. They probably won't appreciate that. First, send them a brief well-written query letter and/or short synopsis with relevant background about yourself and invite them to request the actual material or a portion of it. Include a self-addressed, stamped envelope (SASE)—it's often appreciated and will never hurt.

If the editor doesn't respond to your query, you can safely assume that he isn't interested or at least not a good candidate for you. There's nothing to be gained by calling or requerying the same editor about the same project.

When making initial contact, don't cold-call the editor—only query her. Put the ball in her court; if she doesn't want to play, look for another partner.

It's okay to query more than one editor at a time, but be up front about it in your letter. If more than one editor requests your material, write to the others who are reviewing it to tell them that they're not alone. If you receive and accept an offer for your material, immediately notify all other editors who may be reviewing it that it's no longer available. Before you accept any offers, however, it would be wise to acquire an agent to get you the best deal possible.

Don't query more than one editor at a time at any given house. If several weeks go by with no word from a targeted editor, it's probably safe to target another editor at that house.

Finally, even though publishers' doors may often be closed and uninviting, the windows are always open for fresh air. Find the windows and fly through.

The Perfect Nonfiction Book Proposal

JEFF HERMAN

The nonfiction book proposal should be viewed as a sales brochure; it will invariably make the difference between success and failure.

Unlike fiction, agents and publishers don't require a complete manuscript to evaluate and buy nonfiction projects; a proposal alone can do the trick. This is what makes nonfiction writing a much less speculative and often more lucrative (relatively speaking) endeavor than fiction writing.

You may devote five years of long evenings to writing a 1,000-page fiction manuscript, only to receive a thick pile of computer-generated rejections. Clearly, writing nonfiction doesn't carry the same risks. Yet writing fiction is often an emotionally driven endeavor whose tangible rewards are in the actual doing, and not based on any rational or practical considerations. Furthermore, many successful nonfiction writers fantasize about being fiction writers.

Fiction writing, whether pulp or literary, is one of the most creative endeavors a person can accomplish. Millions of Americans still voraciously read fiction despite the preponderance of TV and other leisure opportunities. But as a writer, you should understand that writing nonfiction is the easier road to getting published.

There is substantial latitude regarding the structure, contents, and size of the proposal, and it's up to you to decide the best format for your purposes. Nevertheless, the following guidelines should serve as safe general parameters. In addition, an excellent model nonfiction proposal can be found in Appendix E.

TITLE PAGE

This should be the easiest part; and it also could be the most important, since, like your face, it's what will be seen first.

Try to conceive of a title that's attractive and effectively communicates your book's concept. Using a descriptive subtitle following a catchy title can help to achieve both goals. It's very important that your title and subtitle relate to the subject, or a prospective editor might make an inaccurate judgment about your book's subject and automatically dismiss it. For instance, if you're proposing a book about gardening, don't title it "The Greening of America."

Examples of titles that have worked very well are Dale Carnegie's *How to Win Friends and Influence People,* Napoleon Hill's *Think and Grow Rich,* and Dr. Benjamin Spock's, *Baby and Child Care.*

An example of an improbable title that went on to become a perennial success is *What Color Is Your Parachute?* by Richard Bolles.

A title should be stimulating and, when appropriate, upbeat and optimistic. If your subject is an important historic or current event, the title should be dramatic. If a biography, the title should capture something personal about the subject. Many good books have been handicapped by poorly conceived titles, and many poor books have been catapulted by favorable titles. Proctor & Gamble, for instance, spends thousands of manpower hours creating seductive names for its endless menu of soap-based products.

The title you choose is referred to as the working title. Most likely, the book will have a different title when published because (1) a more appropriate title may evolve with time, or

(2) the publisher has final contractual discretion over the title (as well as a lot of other things).

The title page should contain only the title; your name, address, and phone number; and your agent, if you have one. It should be neatly and evenly spaced. If available, jazzy computer graphics will contribute to its overall aesthetic appeal.

Miscellaneous Details

- Your proposal should be printed in black ink on clean letter-sized (8½" × 11") white paper.
- Avoid computer paper.
- Letter-quality printing is best. Make sure the ribbon is fresh and that all photocopies are dark enough to be read easily. Be wary of old manual typewriters; have the proposal retyped on good equipment, if necessary. Publishing is an image business and you will be judged, perhaps unconsciously, on the physical/aesthetic merits of your submission.
- Always double-space, or you risk reader antagonism—eyestrain makes people cranky.
- Make sure your proposal appears fresh and new and hasn't been dog-eared, marked-up, and abused by several previous readers. No editor will be favorably disposed if she thinks everyone else on the block has already sent you packing. You want editors to think you have lots of places to go, not nowhere else to go.
- Contrary to common practice in other industries, editors prefer not to get bound proposals. If an editor likes your proposal, he will want to photocopy it for his colleagues; and your binding will only be in the way. It's best to use paper clips and rubber bands.

Overview

The overview is a terse one- to three-page statement about your overall concept and mission. It sets the stage for what's to follow.

BIOGRAPHICAL SECTION

The information here helps you sell yourself. This section tells who you are and why you are the ideal person to write this book. You should highlight all relevant experience, media and public speaking engagements, and previous books and/or articles published. Self-flattery, if accurate, is appropriate.

MARKETING SECTION

This section justifies the book's existence from a commercial perspective. Who will buy it? For instance, if you're proposing a sales book, state the number of people who earn their living through sales; point out that thousands of large and small companies are sales-dependent and invest huge sums in sales training; and that all sales professionals are perpetually hungry for fresh, innovative sales books.

Don't just say, for instance, "My book is for adult women, and there are more than fifty million adult women in America." You must be much more demographically sophisticated when identifying your intended audience.

COMPETITION SECTION

To the uninitiated, this section may appear to be counterproductive. But if handled strategically, assuming you have a fresh concept, this section should win you points.

State other major published titles similar to your concept. If you're familiar with the subject, you'll probably know what those titles are off the top of your head; you have probably read most or all of them. If you're not certain, check *Books in Print*—in virtually every library—for all titles in print in every possible category. Don't list everything published on your subject—that could require a book in itself. Just describe the leading half-dozen titles or so and explain why yours will be different.

For example, there is no shortage of good sales books. But there's a reason for that: Sales books have a big market. If your subject is in a crowded area, turn that to your advantage by emphasizing what a substantial, insatiable demand there is for sales books, and how your book will offer a unique and innovative sales-success program. State that salespeople and companies dependent on sales are always looking for new ways to reinforce acquired sales skills (it's okay to reiterate key points).

PROMOTIONS SECTION

Here you will suggest possible ways to promote and market the book. Sometimes this section is unnecessary. It depends on your subject and what, if any, realistic promotional prospects exist.

If you're proposing a specialized academic book such as *The Mating Habits of Octopi,* the market is relatively finite, and elaborate promotions would be wasteful. But if you're proposing a highly popular consumer-oriented book such as *The Endless Orgasm in One Minute,* the promotional possibilities are endless. They would include most major electronic broadcast and print media, advertising agencies, and maybe even some weird contests. You want to help guide the publisher into seeing realistic ways to publicize your book.

CHAPTER OUTLINE

This is the meat of the proposal. Here's where you finally tell what the book includes. Each chapter should be tentatively titled and clearly abstracted. Some successful proposals have fewer than 100 words per abstracted chapter, while others have several hundred words per abstract. There are no hard-and-fast rules here; it's your choice. Sometimes less is more, and other times a too-brief outline is inadequate.

SAMPLE CHAPTERS

Sample chapters are optional. A strong well-developed proposal will often obviate the need for sample chapters. If you're a first-time writer, however, one or more sample chapters will give you an opportunity to show your stuff, and help dissolve an editor's concerns about your ability to actually write the book, thereby increasing the odds that you will receive an offer and, perhaps, enhancing the advance.

Again, the advisability of including sample chapters depends on the circumstances. Nonfiction writers are often wary of investing time in writing sample chapters, since they view the proposal as a means to avoid any speculative writing. This can be a shortsighted position, however, since a single sample chapter can make the difference between selling and not selling a marginal proposal. Occasionally, publishers will request that one or two sample chapters be written before they can make a decision about a particular project. If they seem to have a real interest, writing the sample material will be worth your time, and it can then be shown to additional prospects too.

Many editors say they look for reasons to reject books, and being undecided is a valid reason for rejection. Sometimes sample chapters may have tilted a nearly rejected proposal onto the playing field!

WHAT ELSE?

You may wish to attach a variety of materials to the proposal to further bolster your cause. These may include:

- Laudatory letters and comments about you
- Laudatory publicity about you
- A photo (not if you look like The Fly, unless you're proposing a humor or a nature book)
- Copies of your published articles
- Any and all information that builds you up in a relevant way

But be organized about it. Don't create a disheveled, unruly package.

LENGTH

The average proposal is probably between 15 and 30 double-spaced pages, and the typical sample chapter an additional 10 to 20 double-spaced pages. But sometimes they're 100 pages, and sometimes they're 5 pages. Extensive, long proposals are not a handicap.

Whatever it takes . . .

CHAPTER 11

How to Write the Perfect Query Letter

DEBORAH ADAMS

The query is a short letter of introduction to a publisher or agent enticing him or her to request to see your fiction manuscript or nonfiction book proposal. It is a vital tool that is often neglected by writers. If done correctly, it can help you avoid endless frustrations and wasted efforts. The query is the first hurdle of your individual marketing strategy. If you can leap over it successfully, you are well on your way to a sale.

The query letter is your calling card. For every book that makes it to the shelves, there are thousands of worthy manuscripts, proposals, and good ideas taken out of the running by poor presentation or marketing strategies. Do not forget that the book you want to sell is a product that must be packaged correctly to stand above the competition.

A query letter asks the prospective publisher or agent if she would like to see more about the proposed idea. If your book is fiction, you should indicate that a manuscript or sample chapters are available on request. If nonfiction, you should offer to send a proposal and, if available, sample chapters.

The query is your first contact with the prospective buyer of your book. Avoid common mistakes to ensure it is not your last. The letter should be concise and well written. You shouldn't try

Deborah Adams is an associate at The Jeff Herman Agency, Inc. She is also a licensed attorney.

to impress the reader with your mastery of all words over three syllables. Instead, concentrate on a clear and to-the-point presentation with no fluff. Think of the letter as an advertisement. You want to sell a product and you have limited space and time in which to accomplish that goal.

The letter should be one page, if possible. It will form the base of a query package that will include supporting materials. Do not waste words in the letter describing material that can be included separately. Your goal is to pique the interest of an editor who has very little time and probably very little patience. You want to entice her to keep reading and ask you for more.

The query package can include a short resumé, media clippings, or other favorable documents. Do not get carried away, or your package will quickly resemble junk mail. Include a self-addressed, stamped envelope (SASE) with enough postage to return the entire package. This will be particularly appreciated by smaller publishing houses and independent agents.

For fiction writers, a short, double-spaced synopsis (one to five pages) of the manuscript will be helpful and appropriate. Do not waste money and defeat the purpose of the query by sending an unsolicited manuscript. Agents and editors may be turned off by receiving a 1,000-page manuscript that was uninvited and not even remotely relevant to their field.

The query should follow a simple four-part format that can be reworked according to your individual preferences: (1) lead, (2) supporting material/persuasion, (3) biography, (4) conclusion/pitch.

LEAD

The lead can either catch the editor's attention or turn him off completely. Writers often misinterpret the concept of getting someone's attention in a short space as having to do something dramatic. Editors appreciate cleverness, but too much contrived writing can work against you. Instead, opt for clear conveyance of thoroughly developed ideas and get right to the point.

Of course, you don't want to be boring and stuffy in the interest of factual presentation. You will need to determine what is most important about the book you are trying to sell, and write your letter accordingly.

You can begin with a lead similar to one you would use to grab the reader in an article or a book chapter. You can use an anecdote, a statement of facts, a question, a comparison, or whatever you believe would be most powerful.

You may want to rely on the journalistic technique of an inverted pyramid where you begin with the strongest material and save the details for later in the letter. Do not start slowly and expect to pick up momentum as you proceed. It will be too late.

Do not begin a query letter like this: "I have sent this idea to 20 agents/publishers who said they do not think it will work. I just know you will be different, enlightened, and insightful and will give it full consideration." There is no room for negatives in a sales pitch. Focus only on positives unless you can turn negatives to your advantage.

Some writers make the mistake of writing about the book's potential in the first paragraph without ever stating its actual idea or theme. Remember, your letter may never be read beyond the lead; make it your hook.

Avoid bad jokes, clichés, unsubstantiated claims, or dictionary definitions. Don't be condescending; editors have egos, too, and have power over your destiny as a writer.

SUPPORTING MATERIAL/PERSUASION

If you are selling a nonfiction book, you may want to include a brief description of hard evidence gleaned from research that will support the merit of your idea. Here is where you convince the editor why your book should exist. Supporting material is more important for nonfiction than fiction, where the style and storytelling ability are paramount. Nonfiction writers must focus on selling their topic and their credentials.

You should include a few lines showing the editor what the publishing house will gain from the project. Publishers are not charitable institutions; they want to see how they can get the greatest return on their investment. If you have brilliant marketing ideas or know a specific market for your book that will guarantee sales, include this in place of other descriptive material.

In rereading your letter, make sure you have shown that you thoroughly understand your own idea. If it appears incomplete, editors are not going to want to invest time fleshing out your thoughts. Exude confidence so the editor can have faith in your ability to carry out the job.

In nonfiction queries, you can include a separate table of contents and brief chapter abstracts. Otherwise, these can wait for the book proposal.

BIOGRAPHY

In the biographical portion of your letter, brag about yourself, but in a carefully calculated, persuasive fashion. Listing that you won the third-grade writing competition and knew then you wanted to be a world-famous writer should be saved for the documentary done on your life after you have accomplished that goal.

In the query letter, you should include the most important and relevant credentials that will support the sale of your book and, as part of the package, a resumé or biography that will elaborate further.

The separate resumé should list all relevant and recent experiences that support your ability to write the book. Unless you are particularly young, start after high school in listing academic accomplishments. Don't overlook hobbies or non-job-related activities if they correspond to your book's story or topic. Often those experiences are more valuable than academic accomplishments.

Other items to include are any impressive print clippings about you; a list of your broadcast interviews and speaking appearances; and copies of articles and book reviews you may have written. This information can never hurt your chances and could make the difference in your favor.

There is no room for humility or modesty in the query letter and resumé. When corporations sell toothpaste, they list its best attributes and create excitement about the product. If you cannot find some way to make yourself compelling as an author, you had better rethink your career.

CONCLUSION/PITCH

In the close of your letter, ask for the sale. This requires a positive and confident conclusion with such phrases as: "I look forward to your speedy response." Such phrases as "I hope" and "I think you will like my book" sound too insecure. This is the part of the letter where you go for the kill. Be sure to thank the reader for his or her attention in your final sentence.

When finished, reread and edit your query letter. Cut out any extraneous information that dilutes the strength of your arguments. Make the letter as polished as possible so the editor will be impressed with you as well as with your idea. Don't ruin your chances by appearing careless; make certain your letter is not peppered with typos and misspellings. If you do not show pride in your work, the editor will take you no more seriously than you take yourself.

Aesthetics are important. If you were proposing a business deal to a corporation, you would want to present yourself in conservative dress with an image of professionalism. In the writing business, you may never have face-to-face contact with the people who will determine your future. Therefore your query package is your representative.

If an editor receives a query letter on yellowed paper that looks like it has been lying around for 20 years, he or she will wonder if the person sending the letter is a has-been or a never-was.

You should invest in a state-of-the-art letterhead with a logo to give you an appearance of pride, confidence, and professionalism. White, cream, or ivory paper are all acceptable, but you should use only black ink. Anything else looks amateurish.

Do not sabotage yourself by letting your need for instant approval get the best of you. Don't call the editor. You have invited him or her to respond, so be patient. Then prepare yourself for possible rejection. It takes many nos to get a yes. This is a tough business for anyone—but especially for newcomers.

C H A P T E R   1 2

Small Publishers Versus Large Publishers

JEFF HERMAN

Is it better to be published by a large or a small publisher? is one of the most commonly asked questions by book writers. The answer isn't simple, since each publisher, regardless of size, is a species unto itself.

First, it's necessary to know how to differentiate between a large and a small house. The corporate Fortune 500 monsters, such as Simon & Schuster, Macmillan, Random House, and a handful of others, are clearly large publishers. Each is a part of a much larger corporate structure that usually includes divisions whose activities are only remotely relevant to book publishing.

The corporate publishers tend to have a number of specialized imprints that publish books under company names that differ from the parent organization. An example is Simon & Schuster's Prentice Hall, Fireside, Summit, and Pocket divisions. Each of these has an autonomous tradition and editorial staff. S&S's sales and marketing force and contract policies cover all of the divisions equally. (Prentice Hall, however, still maintains an independent sales force.)

The publishing industry has taken on some of the appearances of the automotive industry. The big guns have absorbed several of their smaller competitors and have even swallowed each other (for example, Random House's recent acquisition of Crown). There has been a major consolidation at the top of the industry in recent years. This trend is likely to continue for the foresee-

63

able future, and the jury is still out about whether this is good or bad—it's probably both.

Just below the corporate houses are several medium-sized houses. They tend to be privately owned and only do one thing: book publishing; and they're less likely to have autonomous divisions within their structures. Some of the midsized houses are multimillion-dollar companies with dozens of employees. Examples are Contemporary Books, Workman Publishing, and Ten Speed Press.

And then there are the small houses. . . .

The book industry may eventually be dominated by a mere Big Three. But the industry's capitalization requirements are relatively small, and hundreds—perhaps even thousands—of small presses will continue to crowd and enrich the overall map. In addition, there are the dozens of excellent not-for-profit university and association publishers.

Some small houses may only publish one book a decade. Others may be just below the midsize range and publish several dozen titles a year with revenues in the low millions.

More than 100 public and private colleges maintain an autonomous publishing operation. A few of these universities, such as Yale, Harvard, and Columbia, employ several editors and publish a substantial number of excellent books each season. The smaller university presses only publish a few titles a year, and most of their books are of regional interest.

University presses are subsidized by a combination of endowments, contributions, and tuition. State university presses also receive subsidies from public coffers. The presses don't have the usual profit pressures and are expected to publish books of quality or that serve some purpose for the university——even if only a few hundred people are actually expected to buy the book.

The lack of bottom-line pressures enables the universities to publish many good books that might otherwise never get published. Many countries, particularly communist ones, heavily subsidize (and sometimes monopolize) their publishing industries with public money, thereby enabling nonmarketable books to get published. In the United States, this role is largely fulfilled by the university presses.

The university presses tend to publish nonfiction, noncommercial, academically oriented books with little popular appeal. Many of the books are extremely specialized and arcane, such as *The Evolution of Parrot Species in Peru*. Most university press books are sold to fellow academics for personal research or to be used as textbooks. Relatively few make it into bookstores, and they are not intended to. University press authors are usually college professors who need to publish to acquire tenure points.

These presses do occasional poetry and fiction, especially when there's a strong local angle. The best-selling novel, *And the Ladies of the Club,* which takes place in Ohio, was initially published by Ohio State University Press. It subsequently sold all the rights to a large commercial publisher.

Here are some potential advantages and disadvantages of being published by a big or small house.

Small houses may pay more attention to each title. A privately owned company has more to win or lose with each title it publishes. It can't afford to write off many commercial losers. On the other hand, corporate houses can afford to scatter several seeds and only worry about nurturing a relative few, while leaving the rest to fend for themselves in a hostile environment. The old cliché, "It's better to be a large fish in a small pond than a small fish in a large ocean," is appropriate here.

Depending on the publisher's size, the person who edits your book may also be the person who markets it, produces it, answers all the phones, and owns the company. You can't get more personal attention from the boss than that.

Writers like Norman Mailer will command all the attention and resources a large publisher can muster. But most of the other large publishers' writers will have to fight for their piece of the pie.

Large publishers have much better retail distribution. Most of the retail book trade is dominated by chains such as B. Dalton and Waldenbooks, and the chains favor the large publishers when it comes to ordering and maintaining inventory. Many small houses are effectively locked out of doing business with the chains, unless they can create a large consumer demand for individual titles. The chains find that they can get most of what they need from the large houses, and that it's much easier to streamline their ordering and billing procedures through the large houses. Doing business with small companies, whatever the industry, is much more quirky.

Many small houses, however, have effectively defeated this disadvantage by having all their distribution, sales, and marketing taken care of by a larger house. In fact, most of the larger houses, and many midsize and small houses, distribute for a number of small presses. This sometimes includes providing these presses with sales catalogs and marketing support equal to that of the large publisher's own titles. Other large houses may only fill orders and collect money for their distributees, and provide little or no marketing support. The type of support the small press receives from its distributor makes a big difference in the number of books sold.

The large houses receive a piece of the action against all orders they fulfill for their distributees, without having to make the up-front investment in the product beyond the catalog space or other support they may contribute.

Small presses may be better at marketing. Entrepreneurs are smarter. As the Soviet Union and China have grudgingly conceded, the stronger the link between personal effort and profit, the greater the output and overall level of innovation. Small businesspeople are the creators; the large companies eventually clone the good ideas and make them accessible to the widest possible market. Publishing is no exception. Many of the most original book-selling techniques and product concepts were developed by small houses. The large houses went on to refine and amplify these innovations.

Examples are the clever series of desktop calendars created by Workman; the undiminishing cult-like demand for Ten

Speed's *What Color Is Your Parachute?;* and the national success of the Zagat restaurant guides.

Small publishers may not have financial stability. The recent virtual bankruptcy of the venerable publisher Dodd, Mead left many innocent writers stranded. It's not the first time and it won't be the last. Hundreds of thousands of small businesses fail each year, and small publishers are no exception—especially when they try to grow too fast and run out of sources for cash.

Before committing yourself to a publisher about whom you know little, find out as much public information as possible: How long have they been in business? Do their authors complain about late or nonpayments? Are there any judgments pending against the company—either now or in the recent past? Do conditions seem to be going up or down? What's the mood and attitude of the employees you talk to?

When dealing with a small press, it's advisable to always have a contract clause stating that all your book's rights not licensed to third parties will automatically revert to you in the event of the firm's bankruptcy, liquidation, or cessation of business. This precaution is smart business and no one's entitled to take it personally.

It's more prestigious to be published by a house everyone has heard of. Ego and glamour are a legitimate part of the landscape. Nobody wants to hear,"You're published by whom!?" On the other hand, many highly distinguished writers and public figures have chosen to be published by publishers who were not household names. If everything else in the equation is right, the public will judge the book by its merits; the name of the company that publishes it will not be a big factor in the reader's mind.

Many books have failed to make any money at both large and small houses. The bottom line is: Success is guaranteed by neither, and failure no more likely with either. Each situation carries its own unique variables.

Smaller publishers tend to be more receptive to unagented writers. Smaller houses are more accustomed to working with unagented writers. In fact, many of them may have virtually no contact with agencies.

The primary reason is that small houses don't usually pay big advances. Since agents make a large part of their livings from their share of advances, they naturally favor large publishers— six- or seven-figure advances can only be afforded by a few. This reasoning is somewhat flawed, however, because even the largest publishers pay low advances (below $10,000) for many if not most of the books they acquire.

Another reason is one of simple organization. It requires substantial effort just to keep track of the major houses, and is difficult if not impossible for an agent to maintain an ongoing relationship with the literally hundreds of small presses that dot the map from Maine to Alaska. Small presses, therefore, need to maintain direct access to writers to ensure a healthy flow of fresh submissions.

CHAPTER 13

Proven Ways to Get Bigger Advances

Jeff Herman

There are three proven ways for unagented writers to get bigger advances. But first it's important to understand what the advance is and what it means for the writer and the publisher.

What Is an Advance?

An advance is the up-front money the publisher pays the writer against the writer's estimated future royalty and subsidiary rights income. For instance, if the writer receives a $10,000 advance, he will not receive any more money until the income due from the book recoups the entire advance.

What Does the Advance Mean?

As a rule of thumb, a publisher will usually be willing to pay upfront what it calculates the writer is likely to earn within the book's first year in print. The advance is also a rough indication of how much attention and support the book will receive from the publisher. Naturally, the publisher will be much more concerned about a book for which it has paid $100,000 than one for which it has paid $5,000.

There are, however, no hard-and-set rules in the advance game. Some publishers are universally known to be stingy across the board, and small presses and university houses often

69

don't have a lot of capital for speculation. Many books never come close to earning back their advances, while other books perform well beyond what anyone thought possible and earn back the advance several times.

THE WRITER'S ROAD
TO BIGGER ADVANCES

Determining the advance is one of the most arbitrary aspects of the book game and is completely subject to negotiation. It follows, therefore, that more savvy negotiators will tend to get bigger advances.

Like buyers in all industries, publishers are willing to pay a price that equals perceived value. It's the writer's job to effectively package herself and her material and to project as much potential value as possible. There are several tangible and subliminal ways to accomplish this. The most obvious is to have good materials and credentials. A less obvious way is to project a persona of confidence, professionalism, and an overall "winning image." Here are three concrete methods any writer can employ to enhance her power to get bigger advances.

Make a Multiple Submission

Don't just knock on one door! There are probably several appropriate publishers for your work. The ideal situation is to create a seller's market, which exists whenever more than one publisher wants to buy your work, as opposed to having only one publisher willing to buy your work, which creates a buyer's market.

When more than one publisher wants you, you can create a bidding situation and sell your work to the highest bidder or the one that offers the most attractive extras.

One way to implement a multiple submission is to choose from 5 to 20 publishers who you believe would be appropriate for your work, and then find out who the right editors would be to see your work at each house. The trick is to submit clean material in a professional manner, and personalize all correspondence—Dear Sir or Madam submissions often end up with no one. Be sure to state in each cover letter that you have made a multiple submission.

If and when you receive an offer, you should contact all the other houses by telephone and notify them that you have received an offer. You should then establish a deadline for additional offers to be submitted, which is usually from one to three weeks from the time the first offer is received, though there is a lot of flexibility here depending on circumstances. You're under no obligation at this stage to tell any of the publishers the precise offer you've received. It's better just to say it's less than X amount. But don't ever lie or say anything that's inaccurate, unless you're prepared to retire as an author.

What you can do is establish a floor—that is, to be in the game the publisher must offer at least X amount. If you become one of those lucky few who falls into a bidding situation between two or more publishers, then all bidders are entitled to know precisely what the current high bid is so that they can have a chance of beating it. Again, don't ever lie or mislead; it's too risky, it's unacceptable, and it may ruin you in the business.

Be advised that auctions are the exception, not the rule, and that you will do well by having at least one good publisher willing to buy your work. But it never hurts to have faith and aim high.

Don't Automatically Accept the First Offer: Negotiate

Don't sell yourself short! Don't think that you have to scream yes! immediately to the first offer you receive. You may have already decided this is the editor and publisher you want to work with, and that's fine. But that doesn't mean you can't negotiate with them for better terms. First offers are rarely the final offers. Publishers, like all buyers in all businesses, tend to offer what they think they can get away with. You have to show them what they can't get away with.

There are no set negotiating rules, and it's well beyond the reach of this article to teach the essential strategies in depth, but it can launch you in the right direction.

Let's say the publisher calls to say it wants to acquire your work and is prepared to pay you a $5,000 advance.

First, ask questions. Find out what format is intended (hardback, mass or quality paperback), whether royalties are paid against list price or net receipts, how large a first printing is planned, what the standard (very little is written in stone) royalty schedules are, what rights the publisher wants to keep, and what the percentages would be for each right. All these factors will influence your eventual royalties and should be taken into account when determining a fair advance. Be advised, however, that the publisher may not yet have definitive answers to all these questions.

Second, say as little as possible. Otherwise you run the risk of binding yourself to an unfair situation, one the publisher would have been willing to negotiate. Buy a few days to educate yourself and then come back once you understand the game.

Find out everything you can from experienced friends and colleagues, but beware: Well-meaning but inexperienced or unknowledgeable people may lead you astray. Try to talk to other people who write for the same publisher. See if their terms match yours. Before you even begin the submission process, you should buy and read *How to Understand and Negotiate a Book Contract* (Writer's Digest Books) and *Author Law and Strategies* (Nolo Press). Both books (deductible against your writing income) will walk you through the typical book contract, though no two publishers have identical contracts.

It's important for every writer to recognize that every contract has "soft" and "hard" areas; that is, there are aspects the publisher expects to give-and-take on, and aspects that can rarely be hedged by anyone.

In addition to the advance, the areas with the most negotiating latitude include royalty schedules, ownership of subsidiary rights and the way such income is split (foreign; first and second serial; product licensing; audio, TV, and movie adaptations; reprint editions), author discounts and resale rights, options, revisions, and competing works. You must learn about these things or you'll be seriously disadvantaged.

Let's return to that $5,000 advance that's still on the table. You have discovered that the publisher tends to pay considerably more, perhaps $15,000, for books much like yours. So, once you're confident and ready to play, call the publisher back and request $20,000 or more and the game just begins. Always be courteous, professional, and flexible. And remember, the publisher may not want to pay more than $5,000 for your book, period.

Get Noteworthy People to Promise Endorsements or a Foreword

How often do you pick up a book in a store and are impressed by the laudatory endorsements crowding the jacket from well-placed people? In fact, those endorsements may be the most important factor in helping you decide whether or not to buy the book.

The right endorsements add significant value to a book's commercial prospects, and will therefore be reflected in the advance. If you can assure the publisher that Iacocca is prepared to write a foreword for your business book and that Perot is ready to contribute a great blurb, you're cooking with gas, as they say. Of course, it doesn't only have to be household names who back you up; writs from people with the right credentials, even if they're not famous, will also be effective.

There are many ways to get endorsements. It's important to only focus on people or organizations that are relevant to your material. For instance, Iacocca would not be the most appropriate endorsement for a cookbook, but the White House chef would be. Whom do you know? Whom do your friends know? And whom do their friends know? Don't be bashful; seek out all possibilities.

Many noteworthy people are happy to endorse books they believe in. In many cases, it may provide valuable publicity for them. The hard part is reaching these candidates and getting them to notice your work. It may, like most endeavors in writing and publishing, require tenacious work, but it will often prove to be well worth the exertion.

If possible, conspicuously show the publisher all the flattering comments you've gotten when you make the initial submission. This will establish at the outset that significant people know you and are willing to vouch for your work. This will make a favorable first impression and is likely to win you serious consideration from the publisher and enhance your work's perceived value from day one.

The Dos and Don'ts of Writing Humor

P. S. MUELLER

Many people are capable of writing very funny stories and articles, but few produce humor that will make its way into print. Humor is a personal matter to the writer, editor, and reader. Yet before a reader laughs, an editor must smile.

What does this have to do with the dos and don'ts of writing humor? Everything and nothing. You see, I can't really provide a formula for writing humor, but I may be able to set down a few guidelines for getting humor into print.

You need those things all successful writers must have: talent, discipline, and research. If you have the talent, much of what you discover through your research will automatically affect the quality of your writing. Discipline will take care of the finer points. That said, let's get on with a few suggestions that may be helpful to a writer wishing to publish humor.

Know your strengths. Write from experience. Use your background. Using this approach will help you find your niche. In other words, you will discover the humor you write best.

There are few things more formidable than a blank sheet of paper. You sit down to the typewriter and say to yourself, "Okay, it's time to write a funny piece." Then what? Sometimes nothing. Most writers have a subject in mind when they begin,

Pete Mueller's cartoons are syndicated in more than 35 newspapers and magazines. He has authored two cartoon books, including *Playing Fast & Loose with Time & Space*, from Meadowbrook.

but quite often their initial approach to the subject changes as the writing progresses. I find that as I write, my ideas about what makes the subject funny may change radically. Many factors will stimulate creativity. Something on the radio perhaps. Or a newspaper article. Anything. Always keep an open mind when confronted with a blank sheet of paper.

For example, the other day I was sitting here at the keyboard. I was distracted and uninspired. Then, from the neighbor's garage, I heard a loud, high-pitched grinding sound. He was sanding a vintage car. I got up and looked out. He never drives the car, but works on it constantly. Then I noticed the two cars in his driveway. Both are in bad shape, and one rarely starts. Before I knew it, I was back at the keyboard working out a piece about a guy who works all the time on a car he never drives, except to jumpstart the cars he uses every day. In this case, a little distraction and an open mind helped to get the wheels turning. There are many ways to do this, and no one technique will work for everyone, but I find that sometimes simply paging through the dictionary can be more of a stimulus than merely pacing around and worrying about trying to be funny.

You may have written the funniest story in the world, but unless you can find a reader, you will have nothing more than words on paper. Perhaps that piece of satire you've written makes frequent use of literary reference. It's polished and ready to go . . . but where? This leads me to a further suggestion.

Know your readers. If you have just written the greatest piece of political satire since *Gulliver's Travels,* you need to know who wants to read it. At this point, you should ask yourself where you would go to find such an article; and, just as you're doing so, you remember your favorite political quarterly. There's your start. You're lucky. Many talented writers never get into print because they don't give their readers much thought. They just write.

Now that you have that quarterly in hand, you should study it thoroughly. Get a feel for the total editorial style, and, if necessary, emulate that style when rewriting your piece.

How far do you go? Taste, like humor, is personal, but for a writer it's always a matter of knowing the reader. What may delight one reader will offend another. I've found this to be true nearly all the time, especially with satire. To know where the line is drawn and when to cross it calls for a sort of silent collaboration, a mental conversation among yourself, your readers, and your editor.

Once I simply didn't go far enough. My own sense of taste actually prevented me from selling the piece. I had neglected to remember that the editor is the distilled critical essence of his readers, and that guidelines, tasteless or otherwise, are guidelines. This brings me to a final suggestion.

Know your editor. As a writer and cartoonist, I believe that a good editor is a gift from god. A talented editor will help you to focus more clearly on the subject at hand. This is especially true and important with humor. If you're unfamiliar with your subject, a good editor will spot it right away. A good editor is looking for a piece precisely tailored to the requirements of her readers, and, in the last analysis, no one other than your editor can possibly explain the dos and don'ts of writing humor.

The Pen Is Mightier Than the Sword:
How What You Write Can Make a Difference

JAN BARRY

Throughout most of my life, books have been my lifeline. Whether getting through a winter in bed with pneumonia as a small child, enduring the endlessness of adolescence, or surviving the battle with boredom waiting for action in the Army, I could count on the escape hatch found in books. Within their pages, hidden between colorful cardboard covers, I could be transported instantly to other lands, other situations, the absorbing adventures of other lives.

Novels, plays, poetry, short stories, autobiographies, biographies, history, science fiction, fables, mysteries, philosophy, religion—the diverse topics addressed in a good story, and the variety of ways of telling it, have fascinated people since the advent of storytelling. As millions of rapt readers have discovered, and hopefully will continue to discover, books are a passport around the world and across the ages.

Later in my life, trying to make sense as a soldier of the inscrutable Vietnam War, I discovered that books are also in-

Jan Barry is a journalist. He edited *Winning Hearts and Minds: War Poems by Vietnam Veterans*. His own poetry has been widely published. A Vietnam veteran, he was a founder of the Vietnam Veterans Against the War movement.

79

valuable tools of self-discovery, of revelation of realities that amplify one's own experience, and of intense communication between oneself and others. To convey a vivid vision of war and its aftermath, I became a poet, a compiler of anthologies of poetry about the Vietnam War, and an editor and publisher of books.

Along the way, I learned that behind the magic of literature is a mundane world of hard work. Creating a book—writing, editing, typesetting, proofreading, page layout, printing, binding—is a series of steps not much different from manufacturing a car engine or a television set, where sweat and long hours of repetitive work count for as much as inspiration and clever planning.

Writing day after day, week upon week, can at times turn to agony for authors. Editing is often a thankless job of clearing a path through someone else's beloved thicket of thoughts. Piecing together a book from the typesetting stage to binding is like any factory job: running the parts of the product as fast as possible through the impersonal precision of machines. Yet, a finished book is far more than the sum of its parts. Ink and paper, sweat and inspiration have created something alive in the hands of a reader drawn to the story or wealth of information found in its pages.

The pen has been compared to the power of the sword. Indeed, writers have kept alive tales of wars and warriors and the clashing clans and cultures they lived in, otherwise buried by the sands of time. "The glory that was Greece, and the grandeur that was Rome" owes as much to Edgar Allan Poe, who penned such memorable lines, as to the silent swords of long-buried Spartans and Roman legions.

The great edifices of religions rest on ancient books by ancient authors, whose works have long outlived the swords of their time. In our own time, authors wrestle with the cosmic darkness, writing books to remind us and our children of the horrors of the Holocaust and nuclear war, to warn us that our future explanation of the frontiers of Space is bound inseparably to our birth amid Earth's dust.

Besides the Great Issues, authors also focus on how to improve our little corner of Earth: how to eat well, exercise, and live a more healthful life, among other things. For those who have wrestled with the dark powers of illness, these works are often welcome sources of inspiration—just as a slim volume of poetry can relight a snuffed candle of the soul.

These are some of the rich rewards for readers, but what of the rewards for authors? Those who wrote the Bible died in obscurity. Famous authors of classic literature died in poverty. A survey of U.S. authors a few years ago found that the majority earned less than $5,000 a year from their writings.

For every author who strikes it rich, hundreds of others pan sand instead of gold. Those sobered souls whose books are not transmuted into million-dollar movie deals, which is the overwhelming lot of most authors, must be content with just seeing one's work in print, hoping it reaches enough readers to have been worth the effort . . . and makes a little income.

To make ends meet, most authors earn their livings as journalists, teachers, editors, business executives, taxicab drivers, anything that buys time to write that special project, a book. Chances are you may not get rich as a writer, but there are other rewards.

A doctor in a small town in New Jersey jotted down poems published in a modest collection called *Paterson* that trailblazed the direction of modern American poetry. William Carlos Williams's poetry inspired many other writers and won a devoted following of readers far beyond his circle of patients along the Passaic River in the vicinity of mill-town Paterson.

A Mississippi River boat pilot, hard-lick miner, and itinerant journalist set down some tall tales in a series of books that have delighted readers for a hundred years. Mark Twain's cross-continent misadventures in learning how to be a self-sufficient author fill up much of his autobiography. It is clear from that widely admired, posthumous collection how much Samuel Clemens enjoyed telling tales, even on himself.

A biologist with an obscure government agency virtually launched the modern environmental movement with a slim book published in 1962 called *Silent Spring*. Rachel Carson's exposé of the lethal effects of pesticides on the balance of life on Earth set in motion a train of action by concerned citizens that led to the creation of state and federal environmental protection agencies; citizen watchdog groups monitoring watersheds, rivers, and seacoasts across the nation; and an environmental-protection consciousness among people and governments worldwide. Rachel Carson died in 1964, too soon to see the harvest of her work.

The value of a book often lives on long after the author dies. Over 80 years after his death, Walt Whitman's poems once helped keep me alive. The author of *Leaves of Grass* couldn't possibly have known how a reader in the next century would draw strength from his zest for life. Yet, rereading Whitman's powerful poems while fighting a jaw infection, I was sustained between hourly rounds of gargling hot salt water, and greatly comforted through a long night by the spirit of these poems— giving me the courage that I would survive what modern medicine could not cure. Now I look, as an author, for what I might leave future souls to see them safely through some dark night.

Tax Tips for the Self-Employed:
How Long to Keep Tax Records

JULIAN BLOCK, ESQ.

You need no reminder to hold onto your tax records in case your returns are questioned by the Internal Revenue Service. But just how long do you need to save those old records that clutter up your closets and desk drawers? Unfortunately, there is no flat cutoff date. According to the IRS, the answer depends on what is in those records and the transaction involved.

The IRS does not even require you to keep copies of your tax forms. Nevertheless, the agency warns that supporting records must be kept for "as long as they are important for any Internal Revenue law." Translation: Hang onto receipts, canceled checks, and whatever else might help support income, deductions, exemptions, credits, exclusions, deferrals, and other items on your return, at least until the statute of limitations runs out for an IRS audit or for you to file a refund claim, should you find an error after filing.

THREE-YEAR RULE

Generally, the IRS has three years from the filing deadline to

Julian Block is an attorney and a leading tax authority. He is the author of *Julian Block's Year-Round Tax Strategies for the $40,000-Plus Household* from Prima Publishing.

83

take a crack at your return. For example, a return for 1990, with a filing deadline of April 15, 1991, the due date for most persons, remains subject to an audit until April 1994.

It matters not if you are an early filer. The law treats a return filed before its due date as having been filed on its due date. In the case of a return for 1990 that is filed in January 1991, the three-year period does not elapse until April 1994. Conversely, should you obtain a filing extension, the three years are calculated from the date on which you file your original return.

EXCEPTIONS TO THE THREE-YEAR RULE

After three years have passed, you could dispose of copies of returns and supporting records. But be aware that this general rule is subject to important exceptions. In some situations, you need to keep tax papers much longer than three years.

For starters, the tax code gives the IRS six years from the filing deadline to begin an examination if you omitted from your return an amount that was more than 25 percent of your reported income. Worse yet, there is no time limit on when the IRS can begin an audit if you fail to file a return or if you file one that is considered fraudulent. The tax for that year can be assessed "at any time."

AMENDING A FRAUDULENT RETURN

Like most other tax deadlines, the ones for audits are spelled out precisely. Real-life situations, however, do not always fall conveniently into place.

Consider these circumstances. A taxpayer files a fraudulent return, but later files a nonfraudulent amended return. Does the later submission of a corrected return (that alerts the IRS to the wrongdoing) purge the initial fraud and begin the three-year period, or does the statute of limitations remain open indefinitely? The answer, says a pro-IRS decision by the Supreme Court, is that the amended return has no effect; therefore, the feds have an unlimited time to assess the tax and exact a fraud penalty. It makes no difference that more than three years have elapsed since the filing of the amended return.

But the IRS does not always have its way. A different rule applies when a taxpayer originally files no return at all and then files a delinquent, nonfraudulent return. The later submission triggers the three-year period, even though the taxpayer's failure to file a timely return was fraudulent. This does not "elevate one form of tax fraud over another," the Supreme Court concluded, as Congress intended that different limitations should apply in this situation.

THREE-YEAR DEADLINE EXTENDED BY THIRD-PARTY RECORDS DISPUTE

The law authorizes the IRS to obtain records from third parties, such as banks and brokerage firms, that do business with taxpayers whose returns are being audited. But the three-year statute of limitations continues to run even when disputes arise between the tax collectors and third parties over access to those records. The problem is that the statute of limitations could, and often does, expire before there is a final determination by a court on whether the IRS is entitled to the records at issue, though the statute is suspended when the taxpayer intervenes in such a dispute.

To sidestep this problem, the IRS persuaded Congress to change the law. Buried in the Tax Reform Act of 1986 is a provision that authorizes a suspension whether or not the taxpayer intervenes. The result is that when the IRS issues a summons to a third party to turn certain records over to the IRS and six months elapse with an IRS-versus-third-party dispute still unresolved, the statute is suspended until the dispute is resolved.

Some other legislative fine print may require a third-party recordkeeper to provide notification of the statute suspension to the taxpayer targeted for audit. The third party becomes obligated to perform that chore when the IRS issues what is known as a John Doe summons—that is, a summons that demands certain records, but does not identify the taxpayer by name. Note, though, that the third party's failure to notify the taxpayer does not stop a statute suspension.

COPIES OF RETURNS

You should retain copies of returns indefinitely. They take up little space and are always helpful as guides for future returns or amending previously filed returns. Also, copies of tax forms may prove helpful in case the IRS claims you failed to file them.

Do you want to really nail things down at filing time? You can hand deliver a return to your local IRS office, which will stamp the receipt date on both the filed copy and the copy you keep. That way, there should be no question that your return was filed.

If you failed to copy your returns and now need them, get IRS Form 4506, Request for Copy of Tax Form. To obtain Form 4506, call 1-800-424-3656 (allow ten working days for mailing) or drop by the IRS office serving your local area to obtain one immediately.

If you have moved since filing the returns, send Form 4506 to the IRS service center where the returns were filed, not to the service center for your current address.

If your returns were filled out by a paid preparer, check first to see if you can get them from the preparer. This may save you both time and money, as the IRS imposes a charge for a copy of a tax form.

Incidentally, the IRS does not keep returns as long as you should. It usually destroys the originals six years after the filing date.

CHECKS TO THE IRS: HANDLE WITH CARE

It's wise to keep all canceled checks for tax payments. Before you mail any check to the IRS, make sure to note the following on it:

1. The reason for the payment, the form number, and the year of the return for which the check is being sent (for instance, "balance due on Form 1090 for 1990").

2. Your social security number or, if you operate a business, your employer identification number.

Also, the IRS asks that you use separate checks and note the necessary information on each one when you pay two different taxes at once, such as past-due income taxes and interest for an earlier year and an estimated tax payment for the current year. Separate checks make it much easier for the IRS to identify and credit the payment if your check is prematurely separated from the accompanying correspondence or return.

Overlooking this simple step may confuse the computers and, at a minimum, direct attention to your return and require otherwise avoidable correspondence. Even worse, it may cause those relentless computers to erroneously charge you with a penalty for failing to make a timely payment.

Yet another problem may occur if you are casual about what you write on the pay-to-the-order-of line of your check to the IRS. If you merely make the check payable to IRS, instead of Internal Revenue Service and it winds up in the wrong hands, that IRS can easily be altered to MRS followed by a name, or altered to a name combining the initials I. R. with a last name, for instance, I. R. Smith. And some obliging taxpayers even send checks without filling in the payee line.

Also, make sure that mailings to the IRS bear the proper amount of postage and show a full return address. Otherwise, you run the risk of being assessed a nondeductible late-filing penalty. Mail without stamps—including tax returns—goes undelivered and is returned to the sender by the postal service. Worst of all, mail without stamps and without a return address goes to the Dead Letter Office.

Win Some, Lose Some

In the ongoing tussle between taxpayers and the IRS, many persons have learned the hard way that they should have saved copies of their returns and canceled checks for tax payments. For instance, the IRS charged that returns had not been filed by

Clem Block, a Michigan attorney (no kin to the author). Clem contended he had filed, but was unable to produce copies of the returns, canceled checks, or any other records to back up his claims. The tax court refused to believe him; he was penalized with additional taxes, interest, and late-filing penalties.

On the other hand, a federal district court held that just because the IRS failed to find any records of a particular return didn't necessarily mean the taxpayer had failed to file. The court found that Aaron Harzvi had been a regular filer before and after and refused to impose any penalties. Moreover, the judge noted that the IRS's "faith in the perfection of its system is commendable, but the court is not persuaded that IRS index records are the only man-made records free from error."

PROPERTY RECORDS

Besides copies of returns, which should be kept for at least three years, other records should be kept until they can no longer affect future returns, which may be much longer than three years. For example, you need to retain records of property costs, as well as payments for stocks and other investments. These records are vital, not only because you may need them for an IRS audit, but because you need them to figure your profits or losses on sales that may not take place until many years later.

Increase Your Profits with Worldwide Sales

MICHAEL H. SEDGE

I consider myself an international marketer, though I am actually a writer.

Last Monday, for example, Bob Campbell, English editor of *Editions Berlitz* called from Switzerland to accept my offer to update their pocket guide to Florence. That same afternoon, a telefax came from R&R in Germany. Editor Marji Hess was confirming an assignment.

On Wednesday, a letter arrived from Arthur Hullett, editor of *Silver Kris* in Singapore. He wanted a piece on Noah's Ark that I had already sold in West Germany and the United States.

On Thursday, Nicky Holford of Sunrise contacted me from London regarding a feature on the oceans that had been published in North America and Australia. She was interested in buying the Arabic language rights, since the magazine she edits is distributed to passengers aboard Kuwait Airways.

On Friday, a letter came from Joseph Yogerst, managing editor at Emphasis Publishing Company in Hong Kong. He'd taken a soccer story I had originally written and sold in Italy. He also accepted a feature on swimming the English Channel.

This would be the third time that the soccer article had sold. To round out the week, John Treaorgy of the *Robb Report* called

Michael H. Sedge lives and writes in Naples, Italy, where he sells and resells articles throughout the world. He is the author of *How to Double Your Income Through Foreign & Reprint Sales*, available from Strawberry Media.

to accept an article that has sold eight times, in several languages, during the past three years.

The week's total was $2,750; so being an international marketer/writer has its advantages.

It is not always easy; waiting periods are longer than usual, postage rates are high, payments are often slow. For those who can overcome these obstacles and learn to market internationally, however, the rewards are great and the satisfaction overwhelming.

The best way to begin selling abroad is to consider overseas publications as secondary markets. Don't waste time thinking up new ideas for foreign publications. These may come later. Right now, what you do is pinpoint those magazines and newspapers that use the type of material you are now selling.

To give you a better idea of what I mean, let me explain how I began selling internationally. I had published an article on scuba diving in oceans. Shortly thereafter, I read that *Off-Duty Europe* was looking for articles similar to the one I had done. Because it only asked for rights for military market publications, I sent it to the editor. Bingo! An additional $170. A week later a friend sent me the name and address of the editor of Philippine Airlines' inflight magazine, *Mabuhay*. I packaged the diving story and sent it out again. I waited a month before receiving a letter stating, "We like your article and will pay you $250 for exclusive inflight magazine rights." Soon I was sending the same article to editors around the world—and reaping the rewards.

When selling abroad, authors become self-syndicators of their articles. The world—not merely the United States or Canada— becomes their marketplace. As a result, what once was a one-time article becomes a valuable product to be sold, resold, and sold again. To date, my diving article has sold three times in the United States, twice in Asia, once each in Germany, Italy, Sweden, India, England, and Australia. Over a five-year period it has brought in nearly $5,000—and it is still making the rounds.

Unlike reprint sales, what you are selling to foreign editors are language or country rights. Suppose, for example, you have sold a piece to *Travel-Holiday*. It purchased first North American serial rights. Now you've found an editor in Italy who wants to use the same article. You offer him exclusive Italian-language rights. This leaves you free to sell the article in Germany, France, Hong Kong, Singapore, Australia, and many other places. If a magazine is published in English—and many foreign publications are—you can sell exclusive English-language rights in a given geographical area. This could be a single country, such as New Zealand, or a continent such as Asia or Europe. And you still are open to sell foreign-language rights in these same areas.

Like other American writers, much of my time is spent sending out queries to editors in New York, Los Angeles, and other U.S. cities. Once I land an assignment, though, I begin to think internationally. During the research and writing of an article, I begin a list of possible clients abroad. By the time I've finished writing, I normally have several potential markets in mind.

At this point, one must make a choice: Submit a query or the completed manuscript. In 12 years of foreign marketing, I've learned that the latter works best for several reasons. First, foreign editors do not know you and, even if you sent a query, they would want to see the finished piece before accepting it. Second, you'll save money on postage by sending the manuscript the first time, rather than sending a letter and then having to send the article. Third, international mail is often slow. The average transit time for an airmail letter to Europe, for instance, is 3 to 16 days. A submission might sit on an editor's desk for a week; then another two weeks may go by before a reply reaches you. Had you sent the manuscript, you might already be holding an acceptance letter. If you had sent a query, you would probably have to wait another 40 days before knowing the final decision.

Another reason for sending the entire article is that it is complete. The idea behind a query is to sell a piece before it's been written. Once written, it makes sense to copy and send the manuscript, telling editors if they are not interested to simply discard the copy and send you a note saying as much.

I have dealt with hundreds of foreign editors and, using this system, only twice have I been asked to provide return postage. An editor in Germany, in fact, told me that the SASE and return postage is an "American fixation that, fortunately, has not traversed the oceans."

Most often the same subjects that sell well in North America sell well around the world. Modern communications have shrunk the globe, and everyone watches the United States closely. Foreign news broadcasts regularly cover Washington and U.S. affairs. As a result, U.S. business and politics are hot topics for many foreign weeklies and daily newspapers.

Most of the popular U.S. television series are aired in foreign countries one year later. Thus, celebrity articles are extremely popular, as are *National Enquirer*–type features. Anyone who is in the U.S. spotlight will sell abroad.

Several years ago I visited the Frankfurt Book Fair and noticed several countries were releasing translated versions of works by the author Stephen King. Since I had recently written a feature on King for a U.S. magazine, I began circulating the article abroad. To date it has appeared in Germany, Italy, Sweden, Spain, India, and Hong Kong.

Many foreign travel magazines cover American destinations. Inflight magazines are as lucrative a market elsewhere as they are in North America. I've sold general-interest pieces covering topics ranging from jellyfish to macrophotography in this market.

Sports, medicine, military affairs, fashions, makeup, cooking—anything that is popular at home can also find a market abroad, if the piece is not too Americanized.

The United States is the only country in the world that does not use the metric system. Therefore, when you send an article with measurements, they should be in metric units. When researching, look for sources outside North America. Quote experts from various nations, get the European viewpoint as well as that of Asia. And know the background of the country in which you are trying to sell. Don't, for example, try to sell a piece on world tobacco products in Sweden—law prohibits such articles there—or Western religions in Moslem countries. Such submissions merely alert an editor that you do not know the readership.

Once you have an article ready for world circulation, where do you find your markets? There are a number of excellent references available. Most, however, are extremely expensive annuals produced for library use. These include the six-volume *International Media Guides, World Press Encyclopedia, Willing's Press Guide, Bacon's International Publicity Checker, Europa Yearbook,* and *Ulrich's International Periodicals Directory.* A good sourcebook that the average writer can afford is the *International Writers' & Artists' Yearbook,* published in England by A&C Black and sold in the United States by Strawberry Media, 2460 Lexington Drive, Owosso, MI 48867. For $16.45 (postage included), this title lists newspapers, magazines, and book publishers in Africa, Australia, Canada, Hong Kong, India, Ireland, New Zealand, the United Kingdom, and many other countries.

Markets Abroad, my own quarterly newsletter, offers information on publications around the world that buy articles in the English language for direct use or translation. Subscription is $25 a year from Strawberry Media.

Once you've sold an article to a foreign market, what can you expect to be paid? As I mentioned, I've had several good sales overseas. I have a rule, however: If someone offers $1,000, I take it. If someone offers $25, I take that, too. This is particularly true when selling articles originally written and paid for in North America. The reason I accept even low pay is for long-term results. A few years back a magazine in Italy bought a piece—it had already sold in the United States for $425. Today the same magazine pays $120 and purchases two to four articles plus five photos at $35 each per month. As the editor told me, "You were one of the few that would work with us during our early years; now we're happy to repay you."

Most of the foreign weeklies are excellent payers, ranging from $1,000 up. On the average, though, you can expect to earn $300 for a good 1,500- to 2,000-word article. A recent survey of the readers of *Markets Abroad* revealed the best overseas buyers/payers are currently Sweden, Norway, Finland, Denmark, the United Kingdom, Iceland, Belgium, France, Germany, and Italy. Following these came Spain, Switzerland, Australia, Japan, South Korea, Singapore, India, and Hong Kong.

Most foreign publishers can pay in U.S. dollars, if you request it. It is sometimes easier for both parties to have payments transferred directly into your bank account. This often saves time and keeps you from paying high fees for foreign check cashing.

Authors can also sell books abroad, though this requires greater patience and more business skill. Some literary agents thrive on foreign book sales, as do some publishers. A good example of this was the foreign sales, a few years ago, of Trevanian's novel *The Summer of Katya;* in Britain it was purchased for $85,000, in Germany $1,000, in Spain $30,000, in France $15,000. The Dutch paid $10,000 for Dutch-language rights, and the Finnish paid the equivalent of $750. All of this purchasing action occurred four months before the book even appeared in U.S. bookstores. As is obvious from this and the thousands of other overseas book transactions that take place every month, foreign publishers are eager to find talented writers on the opposite side of the Pacific or Atlantic. Would-be authors should, therefore, seriously consider these markets in their book-selling strategy.

Peter Straub, author of such best-selling titles as *Floating Dragons, Ghost Story,* and *Shadowland,* found a home for his first novel in London, after numerous unsuccessful attempts to be published in New York, as have several other American authors.

In addition to the personal and financial satisfaction an author receives from placing a book manuscript with a foreign publisher, he or she also has the advantage of a completed—edited, typeset, and bound—work to offer U.S. publishing houses.

Many authors find that doors open much wider—even after previous rejection—for a book that has already been released abroad.

A newcomer to the book-selling game should probably stick with English-language countries when submitting manuscripts. This will make the business aspects easier. Like articles, you must keep your rights. If a publisher in London wants your book, sell U.K. rights only. A good lawyer can help with book contracts and negotiations.

There are several ways to locate acquisition editors at foreign publishing houses. Perhaps the best is the *International Literary Market Place,* published by R. R. Bowker. The *International Writers' & Artists' Yearbook* also lists such information. The third option is to patronize some of the better-known international book fairs (Frankfurt Book Fair, London International Book Fair, ABA Book Fair). If you are truly serious about selling your books to foreign publishers, you'll find it helps greatly to belong to such organizations as Publishers Marketing Association, 2401 Pacific Coast Highway, Suite 206, Hermosa Beach, CA 90254. They can provide advice, support, and offer cooperative market and display at many book fairs and trade shows.

If you do not want to do all the work yourself, you can send your book manuscripts to foreign agents listed in *International Literary Market Place* and *International Writers' & Artists' Yearbook.*

As I said, selling overseas is not always easy. You must become a marketer as well as a writer. Marketing, I feel, is the name of the game. As individuals we might consider ourselves unique. But let's face it, there are many writers out there as good or better than you or I. Few, however, know how to market their works successfully worldwide.

Selling what you have already sold is what foreign marketing is all about. Once you start, you'll discover, as I have, that you can decrease your workload and increase your profits. Selling abroad opens your eyes to new ideas and techniques in the writing business.

Publicity Sells Books

KAREN ROMER

Now that your book is published, you face yet another challenge—getting it into the hands of the audience you wrote it for.

Publicity helps sell books. Bear in mind that nonfiction books are generally promotable, whereas fiction is not promotable unless the author is a celebrity or the book has a large popular following.

Your audience needs to know your book exists, and how and why it will benefit them to read it. The way to reach your audience is through electronic and print exposure (TV, radio, and print). It is often left to you the author to make sure your book is given the exposure it deserves, since publishers are notoriously negligent in this regard. (Sometimes the author's promotion and sales experience and potential is a prime reason the publishing package is bought.)

Knowing what you are getting from your publisher in advance will help you plan your course of action. Publishers can be depended upon to handle the distribution of review copies, but unless you are one of the chosen few you can't expect a whole lot more. Publishing houses devote very little of their budget to marketing and publicity, and the salaries paid their marketing staffs are very low compared to the Fortune 500 standards.

Karen Romer is founder and president of Romer Communications, a New York–based public relations firm specializing in author publicity.

To guide you in what to ask for in a publicity campaign, I have outlined the following basic four suggestions from my experience as a book publicist:

1. Begin the publicity campaign three to six months prior to the publication date (pub date) of your book. Galleys of the book should be sent to the appropriate editors of trade and national magazines that reach the audience for which the book has been written. These publications have minimum lead times of three months.

2. Plan the national media circuit four to five weeks prior to the date the books will be in the stores. This prior planning allows the publisher's sales force to use the media placement information to place more books in the bookstores. Ideally a tour of 10 to 20 cities will provide the exposure necessary to sell the book. These cities should include the top four media markets: New York, Los Angeles, San Francisco, and Chicago. The additional cities should be determined based upon the concentration in each city of the audience you are trying to reach. The tour should be scheduled to begin on the pub date, provided the book is available in bookstores. Please be warned that publicity does not benefit anyone if the book is not available to the public.

3. Target publicity to reach the most interested audience. Media placements should reach the audience for which the book is written. For example, the author of a book about negotiating a raise would not benefit from an appearance on a daytime talk show where the majority of the audience is homemakers. The author of such a book would want to be on shows aired before 9 a.m. and after 5 p.m. and viewed by people who have a normal workday and watch TV in their off hours. The best print publicity is in publications this audience commonly reads, such as the local paper's business section; business magazines like *Success, INC.*, and *Forbes;* and the leisure publications a businessperson would read, such as business periodicals and news weeklies.

4. Arrange appearances on national shows to occur prior to the halfway mark of the tour. After that, the producers of such

shows may feel that the author has been overexposed by the time he or she is on their show. Author appearances on *Donahue* and *Oprah* can make a book into a best-seller. Both shows have been known to sell several thousand books subsequent to an appearance by the author. If one of these shows calls, drop everything and run. It is not unusual for these shows to want to schedule an author on very short notice.

If your publisher has arranged for this amount of coverage and is following through—terrific. Your book is being given the opportunity it deserves. If that is not the case, you had better start moving right away. A book has only three months to make itself known before it is pulled from the bookstore shelves. If a book has not sold after three months, booksellers will begin to return it to the publisher. That is why it is important to act quickly. A publicist needs at least three weeks' lead time to set up a publicity tour. The tour schedule itself can help delay the return of books and will entice bookstores to keep the book in stock so they are able to respond to the demand created for it by a local publicity appearance.

How to Find a Publicist

If you decide either to supplement or completely control your book's publicity, you will need to retain a publicist. You will want a publicist who has a good track record for books in the same category as yours. If you have written a book on nutrition, you will want a publicist who has a history of working with books on health. By doing so, you are assured that the publicist has the media contacts with the appropriate shows and publications. You also want a publicist who shows enthusiasm for your material. If the publicist cannot convince you that your book is of value to him, then it is very unlikely that he will be able to convince anyone else of its value.

Publicity companies have two modes of operation. They work either on a retainer basis or on a per-placement basis. The average monthly retainer for a book publicist is between $2,000 and $4,000 per month. These publicists also offer a flat rate for city-by-city tours. If you are sufficiently convinced that they will place you on the shows and in the publications that you would benefit most from, they would be a good choice. Just keep in mind that they only guarantee they will *try* to place you. The alternative is an agency that works on a per-placement basis. This is a performance-oriented agreement. This agency will charge you a one-time start-up fee for preparing a press kit, coaching you for interviews, discussing production ideas, and the like. The fee will range from $750 to $1,500, and there are no other charges until a media placement has been made. There is a minimum guarantee of several hundred dollars in city-by-city tours as well. Under such an agreement, a publicity company probably won't take your account unless it believes it can place you. You should check the company's references to determine if it has the contacts you need.

Once you have a publicist, you must work with her. I always tell my authors, "The more information you give me, the more I have to work with." If you have a contact at a particular media outlet, let your publicist know in advance. If you wish to approach the media contact yourself, do so. If you wish your publicist to do so, tell her before she proceeds along her usual route. Once she has approached one contact at a show, she cannot approach a different one at the same show. Supply your publicist with a list of any and all media on which you have appeared in the past, along with the dates. Press clippings and videotapes are especially effective in a press kit, which includes clippings of you, your company, your book, and so forth. Also, supply your publicist with your availability for the next two months, so she can schedule interviews for you.

You should expect your publicist to notify you well in advance of any publicity placements. She should supply you with an updated itinerary, arrange local escorts in each city you visit, and coach you on interview techniques.

Choosing a publicist is like choosing a doctor or a dentist; thumbing through the yellow pages just won't do. Referral is the best method for finding a publicist. Talk to your writer friends. Find out what publicists they have worked with and whether or not they were pleased with the results. It is also an excellent idea to contact an author whose book is selling well and is in the same category as your book. Usually authors who have had an excellent experience with a publicist are happy to refer your business to them.

Another way to continue your search is to flip through booksellers' publications, such as the American Booksellers Association *Newswire*. These publications list author tours and the publicity company sponsoring them. Watch some of the shows you believe your book would be appropriate material for. See what authors appear on these shows. By calling the show or the publisher of the show, you will be able to find out who the publicist is.

MAXIMIZING YOUR PUBLICITY EFFORT

There are a number of ways an author can maximize the effect of publicity expenditure—in effort as well as dollars. Here are some points to keep in mind to both cut publicity costs and take the most advantage of publicity opportunities.

Have your publicist pursue an armchair tour for you: a telephone publicity campaign. Both radio and print interviews can be arranged throughout the country by telephone. It is wise to specify that the radio interviews be only with stations that are 5,000 watts or more, and in cities that fall into the markets where your book is available.

Approach your publisher to match you dollar-for-dollar in publicity costs, reminding him that the company, too, will benefit from the time, energy, and money you are investing to sell the book.

Combine business and pleasure trips with publicity by adding an extra day to your trip for your publicist to arrange media interviews for you. If you are speaking or consulting in a particular city, the local tie-in will be helpful in arranging interviews.

Don't spend time, energy, and money on publicity in a city where your book isn't available.

If you lack proper distribution, investigate the 800-number fulfillment services so people can order your book directly by telephone.

If you can include a plug for your publishing house, approach it to help finance your publicity, since it may be interested in the exposure.

If you have time between interviews, stop by the local bookstore and see if the manager will allow you to do a spontaneous book signing. This usually accomplishes two things: It moves the book to the front of the store where most booksellers display a rack of autographed books, and it prevents the bookseller from being able to return the books to the publisher.

Keep your publisher well informed of your media placements at all times.

List your tour in booksellers' trade publications like the ABA's *Newswire*. This helps get the word out to sellers, reminding them to reorder books prior to your media blitz of their city.

Never, never turn down a national show. National shows will call you when they are doing a show on the subject area in which you are an expert. If you say no, they will easily find someone else to fill your shoes. They are definitely worth rescheduling your life to attend.

And my final tip to the touring author is: Be nice to everyone. The old saying that today's secretaries are tomorrow's producers is true. No matter how small the events, treat each one as if it is the most important interview of your tour.

U.S. Publishers and Editors

Before sending a query, call the publisher to verify that the editor you have in mind is still employed there

ABINGDON PRESS

(division of United Methodist Publishing House)
201 Eighth Avenue South
Nashville, TN 37202
615-749-6000

Abingdon, which celebrated its bicentennial in 1989, is the publishing division of the United Methodist Church. In addition to religious and inspirational books for the lay reader, Abingdon publishes titles on church leadership and organization, as well as academic works on Biblical study. The list includes *Raising PG Kids in an X-Rated World* by Tipper Gore, and *Mixed Blessings* by Barbara and William Christopher.

Acquisitions contacts and areas of interest

Mary C. Dean, Editor, trade books
Nonfiction books "that help families and individuals live Christian lives"; contemporary social themes of Christian relevance.

Gregory Michael, Editor, Professional Books
Methodist doctrine and church practices for clergy and laity.

David Perkins, Editor, Academic/Reference Books
Books for Sunday and parochial schools and seminaries; dictionaries and general reference guides relevant to Methodist history and policy.

Ronald P. Patterson, Vice President and Editorial Director
Nonbook, church resource products: calendars, class work-
books, activity sheets, academic guideline books.

HARRY N. ABRAMS, INC.
(subsidiary of the Times-Mirror Corporation)
100 Fifth Avenue
New York, NY 10011
212-206-7715

Abrams, a subsidiary of Times-Mirror Corporation,
was established in 1950. It publishes some of the most beautiful
"coffee table" books on the market. Its high-quality art books
on painting, the decorative arts, and photography include *De-
gas, The History of Beads,* and *Avedon in the American West.*
Abrams also publishes *The Audubon Society Book of Wild Birds*
and illustrated regional studies, such as *The Armenians,* and
photographic books on Hawaii and Alaska. Abrams's list includes a few paperbacks and some books that are more text-
oriented than their art and photographic books.

All queries should go to Ms. Leta Bostelman, Managing Editor.

ACROPOLIS BOOKS, LTD.
2400 Seventeenth Street NW
Washington, DC 20009
202-387-6805

Acropolis has been publishing informational and how-
to books since 1960, but added a fiction title to its list in the
fall of 1989. Past titles include *Sell Like a Pro* and the best-
selling *Color Me Beautiful.* Noted for its excellent book production facilities, Acropolis has worked collaboratively with organizations such as USA Today and the Smithsonian. In addition
to handling its own domestic and foreign distribution, the com-

pany has launched Acropolis Publishing Services, which provides editorial and publicity services to smaller houses.

Acquisitions contacts and areas of interest

Submissions can be made to any of the following:

Alphons J. Hackl, President

Kathleen Hughes, Publisher

Ms. Sandy Trupp, Vice President

BOB ADAMS, INC.

840 Summer Street
Boston, MA 02127
617-268-9570

Bob Adams, perhaps best known for its city-by-city job-bank series, was founded in 1980 as a publisher of business and career titles. Although primarily trade paper nonfiction, its list includes some popular psychology such as *Why Love Is Not Enough,* nutritional guides, and even a how-to magic book titled *The Magic World of the Amazing Randy.* Bob Adams handles its own distribution.

Submissions can be made to any of the following:

Acquisitions contacts and areas of interest

Robert L. Adams, President

Victor Gulotta, Vice President, Marketing

Brandon Toropov, Vice President, Reference and Trade Publications

---

ADDISON-WESLEY PUBLISHING CO., INC.

General Books Division
Jacob Way
Reading, MA 01867
617-944-3700

Addison-Wesley, a major textbook publisher, has a flourishing trade division that specializes in health care, child development, management, general business, and computer books. *Magic's Touch*, coauthored by "Magic" Johnson and the Boston Celtics, shows that Addison-Wesley has a lighter side. The acquisition of Aris Books in 1988 added a series of gourmet cookbooks to the list. Merloyd Lawrence, who has her own imprint with Addison-Wesley, brings the Radcliffe Biography series, including *Balm in Gilead* and *The Alchemy of Survival*, to its list, as well as quality child development titles.

Acquisitions contacts and areas of interest

John Bell, Assistant Editor
Fun books, kids' activity books, some politics

Ms. Chris Carduff, Assistant Editor
Literary biographies, literary criticism/essays, tax guides.

Ms. Merloyd Lawrence, President, Merloyd Lawrence Books
(own imprint)
102 Chestnut Street
Boston, MA 02108
617-523-5895
Child care, women's health, female-oriented biography.

William Patrick, Senior Editor
Health, science, sports, some business.

Julie Stillman, Editor
Computer books.

New York office:
105 Madison Avenue
New York, NY 10003
212-463-8440

Acquisitions contacts and areas of interest

John Harris, Publisher

Nancy Miller, Senior Editor
Gardening, popular culture, psychology, general how-to.

Martha Moutray, Senior Editor
Politics, government, current events, essay collections.

ALGONQUIN BOOKS OF CHAPEL HILL
Box 2225
Chapel Hill, NC 27515
919-933-2113

Algonquin, a division of Workman, published in the fall of 1989 the first volume in its new Major Battles and Campaigns series: *The Defeat of Imperial Germany: 1917–1918.* Its literary fiction, with a focus on work by Southern writers, includes novels by Kaye Gibbons, Jill McCorkle, and Clyde Edgerton, as well as the annual anthology *New Stories from the South.* In addition to military history, the nonfiction list comprises memoirs, baseball histories, and nature books.

Acquisitions contacts and areas of interest
Susan Ketchin, Associate Editor
or

Louis J. Rubin, Jr., President
American and military history, baseball, nature, short stories, serious literary fiction with strong Southern setting.

Ms. Shannon Ravenel, Senior Editor
6315 Pershing Avenue
St. Louis, MO 63130
Serious fiction with Southern orientation.

AMACOM BOOKS
(division of the American Management Association)
135 West 50th Street
New York, NY 10020
212-586-8100

AMACOM, the publishing division of the American Management Association, produces business books on management and marketing for general trade and professional audiences. *Toughminded Leadership* and *Romancing the Brand: The Power of Advertising and How to Use It* are among the trade titles; *The Complete Book of Product Productivity* and *The AMA Guide for Media and Event Planners* are titles directed at industry professionals.

Acquisitions contacts and areas of interest

Adrienne Hickey, Senior Editor
General management, human resources, marketing, advertising.

Andrea Pedolsky, Editor
Career development, personal growth, general business, consulting.

Myles Thompson, Editor
Manufacturing, information systems, technology, computers, finance.

ANDREWS & MCMEEL
(division of Universal Press Syndicate)
4900 Main Street
Kansas City, MO 64112
816-932-6700

With Universal Press Syndicate as its parent company, Andrews & McMeel has a family relationship with a number of popular cartoonists and advice columnists; Gary Larson's *The Far Side* collections, Gary Trudeau's *Doonesbury* books, and Abigail Van Buren's *The Best of Dear Abby* are among its most popular titles. Some "reference" books, such as *The Stephen King Companion* and *Roger Ebert's Movie Home Companion* and discount shopping guides round out the list.

Submissions should be directed to:

Donna Martin, Vice President and Editorial Director.

ARCADE PUBLISHING
141 Fifth Avenue
New York, NY 10010
212-475-2633

Arcade is a new house founded by Dick and Jeannette Seaver, publishing veterans who most recently had their own imprint at Henry Holt. Arcade's books include fiction, nonfiction, paperback reprints, and children's titles. Recent titles include *Voices in the Evening* by Natalia Ginzburg, *The Nature Notes of an Edwardian Lady* by Edith Holden, and *The Disinformer: Two Novellas* by Peter Ustinov. Arcade's titles are distributed by Little, Brown.

Acquisitions contacts and areas of interest
Dick Seaver, Editor-in-Chief
or
Jeannette Seaver, Executive Editor
Quality trade fiction and nonfiction, current events, politics, history, biography, cookbooks.

Julie Amper, Editorial Director, Children's Books
Preschool through young adult.

ARIS BOOKS
(division of Addison-Wesley)
1621 Fifth Street
Berkeley, CA 94710
415-527-5171

Greg Caplan, Assistant Editor
Gourmet/literary cookbooks.

ATHENEUM PUBLISHERS
(division of Macmillan)
866 Third Avenue
New York, NY 10022
212-702-2000

A member of the Macmillan Publishing Group, Atheneum has experienced frequent editorial changes in recent years, as well as a decrease in the size of its staff and list. Atheneum, however, maintains a reputation as a publisher of quality fiction and nonfiction books, including *Man in His Time: The Best Science Fiction Stories of Brian W. Aldiss* and Tim Page's *Page After Page: Memoirs of a War-Torn Photographer.*

Acquisitions contacts and areas of interest

Cynthia Merman, Senior Editor
Primary nonfiction, history, biography, popular science, current events.

Evan Oppenheimer, Editor
Literary and commercial fiction in hardcover, history, biography, politics, current events.

THE ATLANTIC MONTHLY PRESS
19 Union Square West
New York, NY 10003
212-645-4462

The Atlantic Monthly Press, created in 1917 as an outlet for the writers of *Atlantic Monthly* magazine, is known for literary fiction by such writers as Raymond Carver, Joy Williams, J. P. Donleavy, and Richard Ford, and for its nonfiction books on current events and issues. Its Traveler's series, rather than being made up of standard tour guides, comprises personal narratives and memoirs describing experiences in unusual locales. Purchased in 1985 by Carl Navarre, the publisher's pre-1985 list is owned by Little, Brown, who continues to handle AMP's distribution.

Acquisitions contacts and areas of interest

John Barstow, Editor
Sports, gardening, cookbooks.

Gary Fisketjon, Editorial Director
Literary fiction, travel essays, some poetry.

Ann Godoff, Senior Editor
Nonfiction: politics, current events, contemporary issues, true crime. Some fiction. Vietnam-related poetry.

AUGSBERG-FORTRESS PUBLISHING
426 South Fifth Street
Minneapolis, MN 55440
612-330-3300

Augsberg-Fortress, the third largest Protestant-owned publishing house in the United States, is the official publisher of the Evangelical Lutheran Church. It specializes in inspirational and self-help books such as *Bringing Out the Best in People* and *Stress/Unstress,* as well as Sunday school and vacation Bible school materials. With sales offices throughout the country, Augsberg-Fortress has powerful distribution capabilities.

The acquisitions contact is
Robert Moluf, Senior Editor.

AVERY PUBLISHING GROUP
120 Old Broadway
Garden City Park, NY 11040
516-741-2155

Avery's trade division publishes alternative health, self-help, natural cooking, child care, and children's books, such as *The Macrobiotic Community Cookbook* and *Taking Care of Your New Baby.* Avery produces the new Paper Tiger line of fantasy art books, as well as the West Point Military History series. Its list is complemented by the new age titles of Prism Press and Ashgrove Press. Avery's distribution network includes health food stores, university presses, and other small-press distributors, most notably Publishers Group West in California.

The acquisitions contact is

Rudy Shur, Managing Editor.

AVON BOOKS
(division of the Hearst Corporation)
105 Madison Avenue
New York, NY 10016
212-481-5600

Avon Books, a division of the Hearst Corporation communications conglomerate, has been a mass market paperback reprint house since 1941; it added a quality paperback line in 1990. Avon's list covers the spectrum of mass market categories in fiction: romance, Westerns, mysteries, science fiction, fantasy, horror, etc. It also does trade Latin American literature and a few poetry titles. Nonfiction areas include business, health and fitness, food and drink, current issues, history, and popular psychology.

Acquisitions contacts and areas of interest

Michael Bradley, Editor
Fiction: horror, thrillers, men's adventure, military, Westerns.

John Douglas, Senior Editor
Fiction: science fiction, war stories, mass market originals and reprints.

Ellen Krieger, Editorial Director
Early childhood through young adult.

Judith Riven, Executive Editor
General nonfiction (quality paperback and mass market): health, business, child care, general how-to and self-help.

Nancy Yost, Associate Editor
Women's fiction, historical novels, romance.

BAEN PUBLISHING

260 Fifth Avenue
New York, NY 10001
212-532-4111

Although Baen occasionally publishes nonfiction computer and futuristic titles, most of its books are mass market science fiction and fantasy titles. According to the publisher, one in four of its current titles has been recommended by *Locus*, the science fiction trade magazine. Baen's list is distributed by Simon & Schuster.

Queries may be submitted to James P. Baen, President and Publisher; Josepha Sherman, Consulting Editor; or Ms. Toni Weiskopf, Editor.

BALLANTINE/DEL REY/FAWCETT/ IVY BOOKS

(division of Random House)
201 East 50th Street
New York, NY 10022
212-751-2600

Together these four enterprises form one full division of Random House. Although all four publish commercial nonfiction and fiction, each has its specialties. Del Rey handles science fiction and fantasy books; Fawcett is known for its popular fiction, romance, mystery, young adult, and popular nonfiction; Ivy is the mass market paperback imprint; and Ballantine is the most upscale, with its Available Press producing original literary fiction in trade paper. Ballantine/Epiphany publishes inspirational fiction and nonfiction.

Acquisitions contacts and areas of interest

Nancy Alderman, Editor, Fawcett Books
General commercial fiction and nonfiction, self-help, how-to, beauty, health.

Joe Blades, Senior Editor, Ballantine
Mainstream original fiction, mass market originals, trade paperback and hardcover. Likes mysteries, espionage, and male adventure.

Veronica Chapman, Senior Editor
Fantasy for the Del Rey imprint.

Christopher Cox, Senior Editor, Ballantine
Fiction: mysteries, crime, suspense.

Mary Ann Eckles, Editor, Ballantine
Westerns, adventure, suspense.

Dorothy Harris, Editor-in-Chief, House of Collectibles
Consumers' and collectors' art guidebooks, antiques, hobbies and crafts.

Owen Lock, Editor-in-Chief, Del Rey Books
Science fiction and fantasy.

Elizabeth Rapoport, Senior Editor, Ballantine
Fiction: historical themes and contemporary female-oriented plots. Nonfiction: health, medical, popular psychology. Not interested in diet or humor.

Stephen Sterns, Associate Editor
Science fiction for the Del Rey imprint.

Cheryl Woodruff, Editor, Ballantine
New age subjects: astrology; metaphysics, spirituality.

Daniel Zitin, Executive Editor, Fawcett Books
Mysteries, spy thrillers, true crime, horror, adventure.

BALLINGER PUBLISHING COMPANY
(division of Harper & Row)
10 East 53rd Street
New York, NY 10022
212-207-7000

Ballinger, a division of Harper & Row, is best known for its business books, which are primarily geared for the professional market. Ballinger has a strong direct-response sales program, and Harper & Row handles its trade distribution.

Acquisitions contacts and areas of interest

Mark Greenberg, Publisher
Oversees entire publishing program, with special interest in large business reference directories.

Martha Jewett, Editor
Finance, investment industry, accounting.

Virginia Smith, Editor
Marketing, management, banking, human resources, sales.

BANTAM BOOKS
(division of Bantam/Doubleday/Dell)
666 Fifth Avenue
New York, NY 10103
212-765-6500

Bantam is a part of the giant Bertelsmann Publishing Group, a West German firm whose other American divisions include Doubleday and Dell. For years a mass market reprinter, Bantam has expanded its list to include hardcover and paperback originals in all genres of fiction and nonfiction. Its New Fiction trade paperback line with titles by Ann Hood, and hardcover detective fiction with authors Loren Estleman and Robert Crais, have been quite successful. Some of Bantam's best-selling authors are Louis L'Amour, Shirley MacLaine, Lee Iacocca, and Chuck Yeager. Self-help books, cookbooks, travel guides, young reader/young adult books, and computer titles fill out its list.

Acquisitions contacts and areas of interest

Diana Ajjan, Associate Editor
Young adult fiction for the Starfire line.

Barbara Alpert, Senior Editor

General-interest fiction and nonfiction.

Thomas Dyja, Associate Editor
Sports, true crime, environmental issues.

Deborah Futter, Senior Editor
Fiction: quality, upscale trade and paperback originals. Also acquires for Bantam New Fiction line, which introduces first-time contemporary writers in quality paper format.

Ann Harris, Senior Consulting Editor
Hardcover serious and commercial fiction. Nonfiction, except self-help, health, medicine, science, psychology.

Maria Mack, Associate Editor
Nonfiction: health, nutrition, beauty, popular psychology. General commercial fiction. No romance or science fiction.

Kate Miciak, Senior Editor
Mysteries, thrillers, true crime: hardcover and mass market originals.

Colleen O'Shea, Executive Editor
Cookbooks, illustrated books.

Susanna Porter, Editor
General commercial fiction. Nonfiction: current events, biography, all history, women's issues. No how-to or self-help books.

Michelle Rapkin, Senior Editor
Religion, inspiration, spirituality, psychological self-help.

Nessa Rapoport, Senior Editor
Autobiographies and biographies of well-known contemporary people.

Richard T. Scott, Publisher, Bantam Travel Books
Edits Bantam's travel guidebooks (developed mostly in-house).

Jenny Kuntz Frost, Director, Bantam Audio Division
Audio adaptations for recently published fiction and nonfiction books (mostly Bantam/Doubleday/Dell books).

Linda Lowenthal, Associate Editor
Health-related books, popular psychology.

Leslie Meredith, Senior Editor
Bantam New Age book line: astrology; extraterrestrials; reincarnation; metaphysics and general new age subjects, mostly in mass market original format.

Greg Tobin, Senior Editor
Fiction: Westerns, historical novels, espionage thrillers, war stories. Nonfiction: military history.

BANTAM COMPUTER BOOKS
(division of Bantam Books)

Acquisitions contacts and areas of interest

Steve Guty, Editor
Software languages, operating systems, data bases.

Mr. Jono Hardjo, Editor
Software languages, operating systems, data bases.

Mike Rony, Editor
Desktop publishing, system communications.

BARRON'S EDUCATIONAL SERIES, INC.
250 Wireless Boulevard
Hauppauge, NY 11788
516-434-3311

Barron's, which is well known for its standardized test preparation books, has broadened its scope to encompass other popular fields. It has had success with children's titles, cookbooks, and business handbooks. In addition to titles such as *The Joy of Cheesecake* and *The Finance and Investment Handbook,* Barron's has a series of breed-specific pet care manuals and training guides for dogs and cats.

The acquisitions contact is

Grace Freedson, Acquisition Manager.

BASIC BOOKS, INC.
(subsidiary of Harper & Row)
10 East 53rd Street
New York, NY 10022
212-207-7057

Basic Books, a subsidiary of Harper & Row, is known for its distinguished line of nonfiction books on history, the social sciences, and, most recently, women's studies and science. In the 1980s several of its titles were awarded Pulitzer prizes: *Goedel, Escher, Bach; Social Transformation of American Medicine;* and *Heavens and the Earth: A Political History of the Space Age.* New Republic Books, a Basic imprint sponsored by *The New Republic* magazine, publishes works concerned with contemporary social and political issues.

Acquisitions contacts and areas of interest

Susan Arellano, Senior Editor
Scholarly trade books in the behavioral and social sciences.

Steven Fraser, Senior Editor
American history, politics, current affairs, business, economics, Judaica.

Richard Leibman-Smith, Senior Editor
Consumer-oriented science.

Jo Anne Miller, Senior Editor
Technical nontrade for practicing mental health professionals.

Bill Newlin, Editor, New Republic Books
Economic policy, politics, public policy, foreign relations.

BEACON PRESS
25 Beacon Street
Boston, MA 02108
617-742-2110

Beacon Press has established a reputation as a publisher of serious nonfiction titles in religious studies, gender and women's studies, philosophy, history, and anthropology. Additionally, Beacon is committed to publishing African-American studies books, as well as other ethnic and area studies. Its adult fiction consists, for the most part, of reprints. Each year the Barnard New Women Poets series publishes a collection of original poems by the winnner of the Barnard competition. Night Lights, a children's line, was added in 1988. Beacon's books are distributed by Harper & Row.

Acquisitions contacts and areas of interest

Deb Chasman, Assistant Editor
Judaica, African studies, black American studies.

Deborah J. Johnson, Senior Editor
Religion, philosophy.

Johanne Wychoff, Executive Editor
Women's studies, current affairs, black women, psychology, sociology, anthropology, history, politics, Asian studies.

BEAR & COMPANY, INC.
506 Agua Fria Street
Santa Fe, NM 87501
505-983-5968

Known primarily for its Native American spirituality books, such as the commercially successful *The Mayan Factor,* Bear is a small publisher of highly respected new age books. It handles its own distribution.
The Acquisitions contact is Barbara Clow, Vice President.

BERKLEY PUBLISHING GROUP
(subsidiary of Putnam-Berkley Group)
200 Madison Avenue
New York, NY 10016
212-951-8800

Berkley, the mass market division of the Putnam-Berkley Group, publishes best-seller reprints and all types of mass market fiction and nonfiction: mystery, horror, romance, Westerns, health, self-help, true crime, biography, and new age. Jove Books and Charter, whose ranges are similar, were added to the group; the acquisition of Ace in 1982 introduced science fiction and fantasy to Berkley's list.

Acquisitions contacts and areas of interest

Susan Allison, Editor-in-Chief
Science fiction.

Ginger Buchanan, Editor
Medical thrillers, science fiction.

Hilary Cige, Editor
Mass market romances and mysteries.

Tom Colgan, Editor
Westerns.

Beth Fleisher, Editor
Science fiction.

Melinda Metz, Assistant Editor
Fiction: romance, men's adventure, mysteries.

Jim Morris, Editor
Mass market male-oriented action, adventure, and combat.

Natalie Rosenstein, Senior Editor
Spy thrillers.

Ms. Damaris Rowland, Executive Editor
Women's fiction, historical romance, women-in-jeopardy stories, romantic suspense, occult, and murder mysteries.

John Talbot, Editor
Men's mass market fiction. Nonfiction: mass market originals, popular business, sports, parenting, and health.

Trish Todd, Editor
General adult, mass market, original nonfiction; self-help, how-to, humor, business, travel.

Ms. Mercier Warriner, Editor
Historical fiction, and women's adventure.

Ellen Zucker, Assistant Editor
Fiction: romance, suspense, espionage, medical mysteries, horror, science fiction, fantasy.

BETHANY HOUSE PUBLISHERS
6820 Auto Club Road
Minneapolis, MN 55438
612-944-2121

Bethany publishes evangelical Christian fiction and nonfiction books. Its publications range from devotional titles to Christian books on relationships and family and Biblical reference books. Bethany's most popular fiction authors are Jeannette Oak and Bodie Thoene. Distribution for Bethany House is handled by Genesis Marketing.

The acquisitions contact is

Sharon Madison, Acquisitions Manager.

BIRCH LANE PRESS
(division of Carol Communications)
600 Madison Avenue
New York, NY 10022
212-486-6800

Birch Lane, created in 1989 as the newest imprint of the Carol Publishing Group, joins Citadel Press, Lyle Stuart, and University Books. Its first catalog featured an unauthorized biography of Diana Ross and a debut novel by Camilla Carr entitled *Topsy Dingo Wild Dog.* The Birch Lane Press/Irma Heldman Mystery and Suspense Novels series was developed by Heldman, who is a well-known mystery editor.

Acquisitions contacts and areas of interest

Hillel Black, Editor-in-Chief
Serious fiction, current events, biography, politics, sports, history; all nonfiction titles.

Dan Levy, Editor
Popular culture, media, music industry.

Bruce Shostak, Associate Editor
Nonfiction: investigative journalism and exposés, controversial subjects, popular culture, mysticism, general commercial how-to and self-help.

Liza Wachter, Associate Editor
Literary fiction, mysteries. General-interest nonfiction.

BONUS BOOKS
160 East Illinois Street
Chicago, IL 60611
312-467-0580

Founded in 1985, Bonus is best known for its sports titles, such as the successful Mike Ditka autobiography, but it also publishes a wide assortment of nonfiction books. Two recent titles, *Official Frequent Flyers Guide* and *Sex Tips for Modern Liberals,* show the range of its list. Bonus has a special interest in books by Chicagoans or with Midwestern themes.

The acquisitions contacts are

Aaron Cohodes, President,
or
Ellen Slezak, Editor.

BRADBURY PRESS
(division of Macmillan)
866 Third Avenue
New York, NY 10022
212-702-9809

Bradbury, established in 1968 and acquired by Macmillan in 1982, publishes fiction and nonfiction children's books for preschoolers through young adults. Titles include *When I See My Doctor* and the award-winning *The News About Dinosaurs*.

The acquisitions contact is

Barbara Lalicki, Editor-in-Chief.

GEORGE BRAZILLER, INC.
60 Madison Avenue
New York, NY 10010
212-889-0909

Braziller is best known for its art and architecture books, such as the Library of Far Eastern Art series and the New Directions in Architecture series. Although much of Braziller's fiction is foreign literature in translation, it does publish literary novels and nonfiction in literature and the arts. Braziller also has a fine list of contemporary poetry.

The acquisitions contact is

George Braziller, Publisher.

BROADMAN PRESS
(division of Southern Baptist Convention)
127 Ninth Avenue North
North Nashville, TN 37234
615-251-2533

Broadman, the publishing division of the Southern Baptist Convention, has a strong Baptist orientation. Its list is primarily an assortment of inspirational titles, Christian textbooks, and Baptist history books. Broadman also publishes cookbooks, juvenile fiction, and some general self-help books.

The acquisitions contact is

Harold Smith, Manager, Book Section.
All submissions should go through Mr. Smith.

CAMBRIDGE UNIVERSITY PRESS
32 East 57th Street
New York, NY 10022
212-688-8885

Cambridge University Press has had the same publishing philosophy for hundreds of years: It is an academic press committed to quality scholarly books. Its list includes titles in literature and the arts, social science, and science. The U.S. office remains editorially independent of the British home office.

Acquisitions contacts and areas of interest

Michael Agnes, Editor
Academic reference books.

Emily Loose, Executive Editor
Politics, government, public policy.

Mr. Terry Moore, Executive Editor
Philosophy, humanities.

Beatrice Rehl, Editor
Fine arts.

Frank Smith, Executive Editor
U.S. history.

CARROLL & GRAF PUBLISHERS
260 Fifth Avenue
New York, NY 10001
212-889-8772

Carroll & Graf, founded in 1983, is a small publisher with a wide array of titles: from *Russia at War* to *The Secret*

Language of Success. Nonfiction includes history, business, and self-help; in fiction, tales of the supernatural, fantasy, science fiction, and mysteries make up the bulk of the list. In addition to publishing original fiction in trade paper and hardcover, Carroll & Graf reprints American classics and foreign literature in translation. Publishers Group West distributes its books.

The acquisitions contact is

Kent Carroll, Publisher and Executive Editor.

CELESTIAL ARTS
(subsidiary of Ten Speed Press)
P.O. Box 7327
Berkeley, CA 94707
415-524-1801

Celestial Arts, acquired by Ten Speed Press in 1983, is known as a publisher of new age books. The titles on its list deal with relationships, intuition, pregnancy, and parenting, as well as self-help and health. A small but expanding book program on gay issues and AIDS has recently resulted in *The New Loving Someone Gay.* Celestial Arts also publishes single-subject cookbooks, of which *The Garlic Lover's Cookbook* is an example.

The acquisitions contact is
Paul Reed, Editor.

CHRONICLE BOOKS
275 Fifth Street
San Francisco, CA 94103
415-777-7240

Best known for its well-illustrated, single-theme cookbooks, Chronicle has added a children's line, fiction titles, and poetry books. Its list of travel titles, such as *Historic Hotels* and *Places to Go with Children,* has also been expanded. Chronicle has a special interest in books relevant to San Francisco and the Bay Area.

Acquisitions contacts and areas of interest

Mr. Nion MacEvoy, Executive Editor
Cookbooks, food, travel, regional-interest picture books, nature, art.

Victoria Rock, Editor
Illustrated children's books.

CITY LIGHTS BOOKS, INC.
261 Columbus Avenue
San Francisco, CA 94133
415-362-8193

City Lights, founded in the 1950s by the Beat poet Lawrence Ferlinghetti, is a San Francisco institution. It started with the Pocket Poets series, introducing Ginsberg, Kerouac, Corso, and other Beats to a wider audience. In addition to poetry, City Lights now publishes literary first novels, essays and criticism, biography, and traditional and esoteric philosphy. Each fall it issues the *City Lights Annual Journal of Literature and Politics,* with original poetry, essays, and fiction.

City Lights is distributed by the Subterranean Company.

The acquisitions contact is

Lawrence Ferlinghetti, President and Editor.

CLARION BOOKS
(division of Houghton Mifflin)
52 Vanderbilt Avenue
New York, NY 10017
212-972-1190

Clarion, an imprint of Houghton Mifflin, produces high-quality juvenile books. Its list for toddlers and young readers includes picture books, such as *Ghost's Hour* and *Patrick's Dinosaur*, plus newly illustrated folk tales, fairy tales, and fables. For middle-grade students and young adults, Clarion offers fiction, poetry, history, biography, social studies, and language arts. Clarion's fiction focuses on complex emotional and social issues, from divorce to death.

Acquisitions contacts and areas of interest

James C. Giblin, Publisher
Picture books; all fiction.

Ann Troy, Senior Editor
All nonfiction.

COLUMBIA UNIVERSITY PRESS
562 West 113th Street
New York, NY 10025
212-316-7100

Columbia University Press, well known for its encyclopedias and reference works, publishes a range of academic and professional titles, as well as some books for the general reader. In addition to titles in the social sciences, history, literature, and science, Columbia has a women's studies series, and a new line of books on gay and lesbian studies.

Acquisitions contacts and areas of interest

Jennifer Crewe, Executive Editor
Humanities, literary criticism, journalism, media, film, Asian literature.

Edward E. Lugenbeel, Executive Editor
Science.

Laurie Waller, Executive Editor
Sociology, anthropology, psychology, psychiatry, philosophy.

Kate Wittenberg, Executive Editor
Political science, international affairs, modern studies, history.

COMPCARE PUBLISHERS
2415 Annapolis Lane
Minneapolis, MN 55441
1-800-328-3330

CompCare Publishers is a division of the Comprehensive Care Corporation, which runs crisis centers for the treatment of substance abuse and behavioral addictions. It was one of the early publishers of books associated with the twelve-step approach to self-help for addictive behaviors. *A Day at a Time* is one of CompCare's best-known titles; others include *A Gentle Path Through the Twelve Steps* and *Do I Have to Give up Me to Be Loved by You?*
Do not send resumés; send only concrete proposal or manuscript. CompCare does not like multiple submissions.

The acquisitions contact is

Bonnie Hess, Managing Editor.

COMPUTE BOOKS
324 West Wendover Avenue, #200
Greensboro, NC 27408
919-275-9809

Compute is owned by Capital Cities/ABC. It is a mid-sized publisher of computer, high technology, and general business titles.

The acquisitions contact is

Stephen Levy, Editor-in-Chief.

CONSUMER REPORTS BOOKS
(division of Consumers Union)
51 East 42nd Street, #800
New York, NY 10017
212-983-8250

Consumer Reports Books, the book division of the widely respected Consumers Union, publishes books that help consumers make informed purchasing decisions.

The acquisitions contact is
Sarah Uman, Executive Editor.

CONTEMPORARY BOOKS
180 North Michigan Avenue
Chicago, IL 60601
312-782-9181

An ambitious midsized publisher. At this writing, three-quarters of the novels under contract are first novels. Contemporary's nonfiction list, which was once dominated by sports titles, now encompasses biography, health, self-help, cookbooks, and crafts. Recent titles include *Cold Fusion: The Discovery That Has Astounded the Scientific World and Will Change Our Lives Forever* and Antonia Fraser's *Love Letters: An Illustrated Anthology.*

Acquisitions contacts and areas of interest

Ms. Jodi Block, Assistant Editor
Pop culture, biographies of music-entertainment personalities.

Sue Buntrock, Editor
Specialty sports (biking, boating, etc.); parenting.

Nancy Crossman, Publisher, Editorial Director
Cookbooks, gardening, British royal family, sports.

Acquisitions contacts and areas of interest

Nancy Coffey, Vice President, Executive Editorial Director
Serious and commercial hardcover fiction.

Ms. Stacy Prince, Editor
Women's interests, family, psychology, sports, gimmick books; some fiction.

Bernard Shir-Cliff, Editor-in-Chief
General-interest nonfiction, especially how-to, self-help titles.

THE CONTINUUM/CROSSROAD PUBLISHING GROUP

370 Lexington Avenue
New York, NY 10017
212-532-3650

Continuum and Crossroad have been affiliated since 1980, but retain their distinct identities. Crossroad, with its Herder & Herder imprint, produces scholarly and general titles in spirituality and theology. Continuum's broader focus incorporates literature and criticism, psychology and counseling, and social issues, exemplified by Paulo Freire's classic *Pedagogy of the Oppressed*. Continuum's Frederick Ungar imprint specializes in literature, film, and the performing arts. Continuum/Crossroad books are distributed by Harper & Row.

Acquisitions contacts and areas of interest

Robert T. Heller, President, Associate Publisher, Crossroad
Religion, philosophy/ecumenical.

Michael Leach, President, Associate Publisher, Continuum
Current affairs, history, education, psychology, scholarly subjects.

DAVID C. COOK PUBLISHING COMPANY

850 North Grove Avenue
Elgin, IL 60120
312-741-0800

David C. Cook is an interdenominational, Bible-based, Christian publisher. Its Life Journey Books imprint produces inspirational books for the general reader, church curricula, and Christian parenting books. Chariot Books is Cook's children's imprint, which features the Parables for Kids series.

Acquisitions contacts and areas of interest

Cathy Davis, Editor, Chariot Books
Religion-oriented fiction; nonfiction for preschool through middle years.

Paul Mouw, Editor, Life Journey Books
Religious inspirational and reference books.

CORNELL UNIVERSITY PRESS
Box 250
124 Roberts Place
Ithaca, NY 14851
607-257-7000

Cornell University Press, the oldest university press in the United States, publishes all types of academic and scholarly titles. It is strong in literary criticism, women's studies, moral and political philosophy, and U.S. history; other categories include classics, medieval studies, history, and nature books.

The press distributes its own books, as well as books for a number of other university presses.

Acquisitions contacts and areas of interest

John G. Ackerman, Editor-in-Chief
Philosophy, Russian studies, European studies, history of science.

Peter A. Agee, Editor
U.S. history, law, agriculture, social sciences.

Holly M. Bailey, Editor

Political science.

Bernard Kendler, Editor

Literary criticism.

Rob Reavill, Editor

Science.

CRAIN BOOKS

(division of National Textbook Company)
4255 West Touhy Avenue
Lincolnwood, IL 60646
312-679-5500

Formerly part of the Crain family publishing empire, Crain was recently acquired by the National Textbook Company. Business how-to, advertising, and marketing make up Crain's list. Recent titles include *Successful Telemarketing* and *The Advertising Agency Business.*

Acquisitions contact and areas of interest

Harry Briggs, Business Books Manager
Professional books and directories in advertising, public relations, marketing, and sales promotions. Also publishes excellent career titles.

CROWN PUBLISHERS INC.

(division of Random House)
201 East 50th Street
New York, NY 10022
212-254-1600

Crown, a division of Random House since 1988, publishes a wide variety of fiction and nonfiction. In addition to commercial novels by Judith Krantz, Dominick Dunne, and Pat Booth, Crown also publishes first novels such as Lindsey Davis's *Silver Pigs* and 19-year-old Holly Uyemoto's *Rebel Without a Clue.* In nonfiction, Crown does everything from art monographs, film guides, and flower arranging books to self-help titles and a selection of poems by Jimmy Stewart. The Orion imprint handles military, aviation, automobile, and nautical books; Clarkson N. Potter and Harmony Books are two other Crown imprints.

Acquisitions contacts and areas of interest

Brandt Aymar, Senior Editor
All nonfiction; especially, interesting illustrated books.

Andrea Cascardi, Executive Editor
Preschool through young adult fiction and nonfiction.

David Groff, Editor
Open to general nonfiction ideas, with how-to or self-help orientation; is not strong in business. Likes commercial fiction, except science fiction.

Barbara Grossman, Senior Editor
Literary quality fiction, history, popular psychology.

Lisa Healey, Senior Editor
Fiction: historical themes, contemporary themes, suspense. Nonfiction: serious upscale subjects, illustrated books.

Erica Marcus, Assistant Editor
Coffee-table books, cookbooks. Some serious fiction.

Jane von Mehren, Assistant Editor
Literary fiction; books about cats.

Stephen Topping, Editor, Orion Books imprint
Nonfiction: aviation, military affairs, military history.

James Wade, Executive Editor
Fiction: male adventure, espionage, psychological thrillers, some serious literary fiction. Nonfiction: serious subjects such as science, history, biography; some business.

CLARKSON N. POTTER
(Crown Publishing Group imprint)

Acquisitions contacts and areas of interest

Pamela Krauss, Editor
Cookbooks; crafts, such as sewing and quilting.

Isolde Motley, Editor
Only the Martha Stewart series.

Martha Schueneman, Assistant Editor
Cookbooks, crafts, shopping guides.

Lauren Shakely, Editor
Decorating books, how-to style books, coffee-table books.

Shirley Wohl, Editor
Travel and entertainment guides, literary and historical biography, serious fiction, picture books for preschoolers.

HARMONY BOOKS
(division of Crown)

Acquisitions contacts and areas of interest

Kathy Belden, Assistant Editor
Literary hardcover fiction, musicians and musical culture, women's studies, humor and cartoons.

Harriet Bell, Executive Editor
Cookbooks; women's self-help; beauty and design, such as the Laura Ashley series.

Margaret Garigan, Associate Editor
New age books: metaphysics, practical new age books regarding ecology, a healthy earth, and vegetarian cooking; progressive self-help books, such as *Love and Sex for the Handicapped*; parenting. No commercial fiction or true crime.

Mary Ellen O'Neil, Assistant Editor
Serious hardcover fiction; fun-oriented nonfiction, such as game books and activity guides.

Michael Pietsch, Senior Editor
Literary hardcover fiction, rock-and-roll, biographies about contemporary figures.

THE DARTNELL CORP.
4660 N. Ravenswood Avenue
Chicago, IL 60640
312-561-4000

This privately owned publisher produces various media tools for business: books, bulletins, newsletters, and audio- and videocassettes. In addition to guidelines for streamlining businesses, Dartnell publishes *The Direct Mail and Mail Order Handbook, The Sales Manager's Handbook,* and *The Marketing Manager's Handbook.* Dartnell handles its own distribution, primarily through direct response.

Acquisitions contacts and areas of interest

Keith Keller, Editor
Business-oriented audio and videocassette packages.

Scott B. Pemberton, Editorial Director
Full range of business books and training manuals for professionals and small-businesspeople, many in binder format.

DELACORTE PRESS
(division of Bantam/Doubleday/Dell Publishing Group)
666 Fifth Avenue
New York, NY 10103
212-765-6500

Delacorte, an imprint of Dell Publishing and a division of Bantam/Doubleday/Dell Publishing Group, publishes fiction and popular nonfiction in hardcover and under the Delta Books imprint in trade paper. Danielle Steele, J. C. Pollock, Maeve Binchy, and Sarah Caudwell are Delacorte novelists. Pediatrician T. Berry Brazelton's *Toddlers and Parents* and Tony Randall's show biz memoir *Which Reminds Me* give an idea of the range of nonfiction titles. The Delacorte Books for Young Readers imprint is part of Dell's extensive juvenile book line.

Acquisitions contacts and areas of interest

Olga Litowinsky, Executive Editor
Quality paperbacks and hardcovers for preschool through the 12th grade (mostly fiction).

Emily Reichert, Editor
Hardcover general nonfiction, including relationships, self-help, how-to, business, cooking.

Jane Rosenman, Editor
Quality hardcover fiction, true crime.

Patricia Soliman, Editor
Primarily women's hardcover fiction; some celebrity biography.

DELL PUBLISHING COMPANY
(division of Bantam/Doubleday/Dell Publishing Group)
666 Fifth Avenue
New York, NY 10103
212-765-6500

Dell, a division of Bantam/Doubleday/Dell Publishing Group, is a general publisher with enormous mass market and trade divisions. In mass market fiction, Dell publishes romance, Westerns, men's adventure, and historical novels. Nonfiction categories include business, cooking, humor, sports, and true crime. Many of Dell's books are paperback reprints of hardcovers published elsewhere. Its Intrepid Linguist imprint handles books about language, style, and grammar; *Get Thee to a Punnery* is one of its titles. Dell Yearling and Young Yearling are the company's juvenile lines.

Acquisitions contacts and areas of interest

Chuck Adams, Editor
Fiction: Hollywood or celebrity themes, celebrity biographies. Nonfiction: films.

Jacqueline Cantor, Editor
Fiction: women's and men's adventure, historical romance.

Sheila Curry, Associate Editor
General nonfiction mass market originals.

Brian Defiore, Editor
Mass market men's adventure, mystery, military fiction, psychothrillers, reprints and originals.

Tina Diaz, Assistant Editor
Fiction: women's fiction, contemporary romance, historical themes.

Maggie Lichota, Editor
Primarily mass market historical and contemporary romances, originals and reprints.

Michelle Poploff, Executive Editor
Mass market originals for children through young adult; mostly fiction.

Ms. Jody Rein, Editor
General nonfiction, quality paperbacks, general self-help, business, health, cookbooks.

Kevin Smith, Editor
Crossword/puzzle books, sports, health, popular business.

Cynthia White, Editor
Fiction and nonfiction mass market reprints.

Marilyn Wright, Editor
New age, astrology, spirituality, inspiration.

DEMBNER BOOKS
80 Eighth Avenue, #1803
New York, NY 10011
212-924-2525

Founded in 1975 by the former president and founder of Newsweek Books, Dembner has a small eclectic list. Dembner has a special interest in quality fiction and also publishes mysteries, history, and serious medical self-help, such as *Coping with High Blood Pressure*. Dembner Books are distributed by W. W. Norton.

The acquisitions contact is

S. Arthur Dembner, President and Editor-in-Chief.

DIAL BOOKS FOR YOUNG READERS
(division of NAL Penguin, Inc.)
2 Park Avenue
New York, NY 10016
212-725-1818

Dial Books for Young Readers, owned by E. P. Dutton, is a publisher of distinguished and award-winning children's titles. Its books are known for their sensitivity to social issues; one of Dial's authors, Julius Lester, was the first African-American author to win a Newberry Award for *To Be a Slave*. Its list is made up of picture, board, pop-up, and easy-to-read books; and stories for older children.

The acquisitions contact is

Janet D. Chenery, Executive Editor.

DOUBLEDAY & CO.
(division of Bantam/Doubleday/Dell Publishing Group)
666 Fifth Avenue
New York, NY 10103
212-765-6500

Doubleday publishes a wide array of fiction and nonfiction in hardcover and paper. In fiction, the Anchor Press imprint handles literary titles, as well as poetry and academic books. Science fiction is under the Foundation imprint, and the

Loveswept, Crime Club, and Double D Westerns series manage their respective categories. N. Scott Momaday, Howard Frank Moser, Arkady Lvov, and A. G. Mojitbai are recent Doubleday fiction authors. Nonfiction ranges from a book of child care advice by Captain Kangaroo to Phyllis Rose's *Jazz Cleopatra,* an excellent biography of Josephine Baker. Other categories include cooking, self-help, sports, history, and contemporary politics. Juvenile books are handled by Doubleday Books for Young Readers.

Acquisitions contacts and areas of interest

Ms. Shaye Areheart, Editor
Fiction: serious and commercial. Nonfiction: serious biographies, celebrity biographies, popular psychology.

Sally J. Arteseros, Senior Editor
Fiction: serious and commercial hardcover. Nonfiction: literary biographies, popular psychology.

Wendy Barish, Publisher, Books for Young Readers Division
Fiction and nonfiction, preschool through middle years.

Loretta A. Barrett, Vice President and Executive Editor
Nonfiction: scholarly subjects, politics, science, philosophy, biographies, women's studies. Fiction: books by and about women.

James Bell, Director of Religious Publishing
Evangelical, ecumenically oriented books.

Teresa D'Orsogna, Editor, Religious Publishing Division
Scholarly academic nonfiction: Biblical studies, research, archeology, the Holy Land. Some Judaica.

John Duff, Director, Special Interests Publishing Division
All nonfiction in quality paper and hardcover; some reprints. Open to wide range of practical how-to guides.

Patrick Filley, Vice President and Executive Editor
Fiction: thrillers, stories regarding business or social issues. Nonfiction: social history, politics.

Joel Fishman, Associate Editor

Medical self-help, sports, travel, business, equestrian, popular science.

Ms. Casey Fuetch, Associate Editor
Nonfiction: public policy, contemporary culture.

David Gernert, Associate Publisher and Senior Editor
Fiction: quality literary. Nonfiction: sports; serious, not overly commercial subjects.

Lucy Herring, Associate Editor
Nonfiction: Likes "unusual" topics; fun/humor books; some new age; general how-to/self-help books.

Judith Kern, Senior Editor, Special Interests Division
Cookbooks; health-related how-to books.

Patricia Kossman, Senior Editor, Religious Publishing Division
Catholic, ecumenically oriented books on theological and social issues; some with new age crossover appeal.

Sallye Levinthal, Editor, Anchor Books Division
Fiction: poetry and quality. Nonfiction: upscale, academically oriented books regarding human behavior, biography, history, and contemporary issues. Reprints.

Patrick LoBrutto, Senior Editor
Science fiction, Westerns.

Ms. Jackie Onassis, Editor
Celebrity biographies.

Barbara Plumb, Senior Editor
Nonfiction: lifestyle, gardening, decorating, home repair, how to entertain, movie star biographies and autobiographies, history of film.

Harriet Rubin, Executive Editor
Nonfiction: business, economic issues, public policy.

Michelle Tempesta, Crime Club Editor
Fiction: suspenseful crime stories, who-done-its.

Steve Wasserman, Executive Editor
History, biography, politics, current affairs.

DOW JONES–IRWIN BOOKS

1818 Ridge Road
Homewood, IL 60430
312-798-6000

Dow Jones–Irwin, now part of the Times-Mirror Company, produces books for the professional business and finance communities. These are mainly how-to books written by professionals in personnel, marketing, management, technology, and communications. Sample titles include *Service America: Marketing to the Affluent, Bringing Home the Gold,* and *The Money Market.* Dow Jones–Irwin will soon be changing its name as part of its affiliation with Times-Mirror.

Acquisitions contacts and areas of interest

Amy Hollands, Editor
Finance and individual investors.

Ralph Rieves, Editor
Finance and investment strategies, large-business reference books.

New York office:
11 Penn Plaza
New York, NY 10001
212-216-8120

Jim Childs, Editor
Technically oriented professional books on general management, banking, and manufacturing.

Jeff Krames, Editor
Popular-oriented, how-to business books; business biographies.

DUTTON CHILDREN'S BOOKS

(division of E. P. Dutton)
2 Park Avenue
New York, NY 10016
212-725-1818

Acquisitions contacts and areas of interest

Donna Brooks, Senior Editor
Middle-level and young adult fiction (mostly illustrated).

Jo Ann Daley, Editorial Director, Cobble Hill Books
Fiction and nonfiction: preschool through junior high.

Lucia Monfried, Editor-in-Chief
Preschool and early-readers (mostly picture books).

WILLIAM B. EERDMANS PUBLISHING CO.
255 Jefferson Avenue SE
Grand Rapids, MI 49503
616-459-4591

Eerdmans, a self-described "theological religious publisher," is a scholarly press whose list is directed at "professors, ministers, and serious Bible students." Eerdmans publishes titles in Old and New Testament studies, theology, ethics and philosophy, and religion and literature. Its list includes reference works, such as Bible commentaries and theological dictionaries.

The acquisitions contact is

Jon Pott, Editor-in-Chief.

M. EVANS AND CO., INC.
216 East 49th Street
New York, NY 10017
212-688-2810

M. Evans, the original publisher of Kenneth Cooper's *Aerobics,* specializes in popular psychology and health. Recent titles include *Men Who Can't Love* and *What Really Happens in Bed.* In addition to an assortment of cookbooks, Evans publishes a romance line launched in the fall of 1989. Under the M. Evans Novels of the West imprint are titles such as Edward Gorman's

Blood Game as well as children's and young adult fiction. Its list is distributed by Little, Brown.

Acquisitions contacts and areas of interest

George C. De Kay, President
or
Ms. Ferris Mack, Senior Consulting Editor
Popular psychology, health, cookbooks, romance.

Sara Ann Freed, Editor
Hardcover Westerns.

FACTS ON FILE
460 Park Avenue South
New York, NY 10016
212-683-2244

Facts on File, which has been producing reference titles since 1940, publishes a broad range of nonfiction categories. Titles run the gamut from *Dictionary of Archeology* to *The Dixon Baseball Encyclopedia*, in addition to reference books on mammals, aquatics, insects, and other natural history topics. Facts on File, in its own words is an "information publisher." Facts on File handles its own distribution.

Acquisitions contacts and areas of interest

Deb Brodie, Project Editor
Reference books on entertainment, leisure, travel, sports, health.

Helen Flynn, Assistant Editor
Young adult nonfiction (ages 10–14) and biographies.

Kate Kelly, Senior Editor
Business-oriented reference books that can generate significant library, institutional, professional, and consumer sales.

Deirdre Millane, Editor

Reference books on natural history, archeology, science, cultural history, Biblical/religious studies, architecture.

James Warren, Senior Editor
Reference books on military history, Americana, sports, music; nonfiction young adult reference books.

FARRAR, STRAUS & GIROUX, INC.

19 Union Square West
New York, NY 10003
212-741-6900

A publisher of distinguished literary fiction and essays, Farrar, Straus & Giroux counts Philip Roth, Tom Wolfe, and Susan Sontag among its authors. Its list comprises literary biography, memoirs, short stories, poetry, and fiction in translation. FS&G's nonfiction, which is literary rather than commercial, includes a social history of the Catskills, *Borscht Belt* and Roger Simon's *Road Show,* an account of the 1988 presidential campaign. Among the authors on the children's list are William Steig, Maurice Sendak, and Madeleine L'Engle. Paperbacks are handled by the Noonday Press imprint for adult titles and Sunburst Books for young readers. FS&G's books are distributed by Harper & Row, but FS&G also distributes books for several small, quality houses, such as North Point Press and Soho Press.

Acquisitions contacts and areas of interest

Jane Bobko, Senior Editor
Fiction: serious literary fiction; favors Asian, British, Eastern European, and Russian translations. Nonfiction: historical and literary biographies and autobiographies.

Elizabeth Dyssegaard, Editor
Fiction: serious literary fiction, especially German and Scandinavian translations. Nonfiction: cookbooks, current events; open to many nonfiction ideas.

Paul Golub, Associate Editor, Hill & Wang

Primarily nonfiction: history, political science, foreign relations, Asian studies, historical biographies, memoirs.

Linda Healey, Executive Editor
Primarily nonfiction: current events, politics, investigative books by journalists.

Ms. Lee Ann Martin, Associate Editor
Preschool and middle readers (3–10 years); fiction and nonfiction; illustrated books.

Roslyn Schloss, Senior Editor
Quality literary fiction.

DONALD I. FINE, INC.
19 West 21st Street
Suite 402
New York, NY 10010
212-727-3270

This publisher of general hardcover adult fiction and nonfiction was created in 1983 by the founder and former publisher of Arbor House. Fine's fiction includes three Dale Brown best-sellers—*Flight of the Old Dog, Silver Tower,* and *Day of the Cheetah*—as well as mysteries, technothrillers, suspense novels, and science fiction. Its nonfiction includes Myrna Loy's *On Being and Becoming,* and Garson Kanin's *Tracy and Hepburn* and other biographies and memoirs. Its Primus imprint offers original paperbacks as well as reprints.

Acquisitions contacts and areas of interest

Donald I. Fine, President and Publisher
Acquires broad range of adult trade fiction and nonfiction.

David Gibbons, Associate Editor
Male-oriented nonfiction: military history, aviation; true crime. Male-oriented fiction.

Susan Schwartz, Senior Editor

Female-oriented nonfiction: relationships, biography, new age subjects. Fiction: general-interest, especially medical, thrillers.

FOUR WALLS EIGHT WINDOWS
P.O. Box 548, Village Station
New York, NY 10014
212-463-0316

Founded in 1987, Four Walls Eight Windows is a small house with a limited, discriminating list and a commitment to social and political issues. Mainly nonfiction, its list includes a history of World War II entitled *A Child's War* and *No One Was Killed,* a book about the 1968 Democratic National Convention. *The Best of Health* is a bibliography of the best health books on the market. Four Walls Eight Windows also publishes the avant-garde novels of Michael Brodsky.

Submissions should go to John Oakes, copublisher, or Dan Simon, copublisher.

THE FREE PRESS
(imprint of Macmillan)

Acquisitions contacts and areas of interest

Adam Bellows, Senior Editor
Literary essays, memoirs, literary and historical biographies.

Peter J. Dougherty, Senior Editor
Economics, finance, political science, philosophy.

Susan Milmoe, Senior Editor
Behavioral science, primarily for professionals, students, and academia.

Ms. Joyce Seltzer, Senior Editor
Politics, history, current affairs, women's studies; wide range of academic and scholarly subjects.

Robert Wallace, Senior Editor

Business and economics from an academic perspective. No popular, how-to subjects.

THE GLOBE PEQUOT PRESS INC.
(subsidiary of Affiliated Publications)
138 West Main Street
Chester, CT 06412
203-526-9571

Globe Pequot, a subsidiary of Affiliated Publications, is a nonfiction publisher specializing in travel guides, among them the Country Inn Guides, Cadogan Guides for the sophisticated traveler abroad, and the U.S. Off-the-Beaten-Path series. Other areas of interest are exemplified by some recent titles: *Ski Mountaineering, Family Camping Made Simple,* and *The Handbook for Beach Strollers from Maine to Cape Hatteras.* Globe Pequot also publishes cookbooks and gardening, woodworking, and needlecraft books.

The acquisitions contact is

Betsy Amster, Senior Editor.

DAVID R. GODINE, PUBLISHER, INC.
Horticultural Hall
300 Massachusetts Avenue
Boston, MA 02115
617-536-0761

Godine has been publishing beautifully designed books for over 20 years. Literary fiction authors include William Maxwell, Stanley Elkin, and the late Georges Perec, whose *Life: A User's Manual* was quite successful. In general nonfiction, Godine has a strong gardening collection, titles in design and typography, and some fine art and photography books as well as poetry and quality children's books.

Acquisitions contacts and areas of interest

Audrey Bryant, Editor
Juvenile and preschool books especially foreign translations; poetry for all ages.

David Godine, President
Photography and art, New England interests, poetry, literary fiction, foreign translations.

THE STEPHEN GREENE PRESS
(subsidiary of Penguin USA)
15 Muzzey Street
Lexington, MA 02173
617-861-0170

A subsidiary of Penguin USA, Stephen Greene publishes nonfiction in hardcover and paperback. Greene is best known for sports books that range from titles on popular team sports to the more unusual *The Handbook of Jumping Essentials.* Travel books, outdoor guides, fitness and health, and cookbooks round out the list.

The acquisitions contact is

Tom Begner, President and Publisher.

GROVE-WEIDENFELD
841 Broadway, 4th floor
New York, NY 10003
212-614-7860

Grove, which merged with Weidenfeld & Nicolson in 1988, has a distinguished reputation for the quality of its titles. Grove-Weidenfeld is a relatively recent entrant onto the scene. The company, which produces a mix of fiction and nonfiction, is still forging an identity for itself.

Acquisitions contacts and areas of interest

Walter Bode, Editor
Mainstream fiction, literary biographies, politics and current issues, popular science.

William Strachan, Senior Editor
U.S. history, current events, natural history, biographies.

HAMMOND, INC.
515 Valley Street
Maplewood, NJ 07040
201-763-6000

After a brief venture into book publishing, Hammond is returning to the role of cartographic publisher for which it is well known. Hammond has begun to produce travel guides— *Passport Travel Mate and World Atlas* and *Passport Travel Mate and U.S. Atlas*—but these contain very little text.

The acquisitions contact is

Martin A. Bacheller, Vice President and Editor-in-Chief.

HARCOURT BRACE JOVANOVICH, INC.
111 Fifth Avenue
New York, NY 10003
212-614-3000

Harcourt Brace Jovanovich's trade division publishes fiction ranging from Alice Walker's *The Temple of My Familiar* to Umberto Eco's *Foucault's Pendulum,* as well as mysteries, thrillers, science fiction, popular novels, and literary fiction. The nonfiction list is also broad and encompasses politics, history, popular psychology, science, cooking, and travel. Biography and memoirs are represented by titles such as *The Lost Childhood* by Yehuda Nir and *Cary Grant: The Lonely Heart.* Harvest/HBJ is the paperback imprint, and Gulliver Books and

Voyager Paperbacks handle the juvenile and young adult titles. Study and professional reference guides and test preparation materials fall under the HBJ Books for Professionals imprint.

Acquisitions contacts and areas of interest

Ms. Drenka Willen, Editor
Serious fiction: literary, especially foreign translations; some poetry.

Ms. Daphne Merkin, Editor
Commercial hardcover fiction. Nonfiction: celebrity and contemporary biographies, some poetry.

San Diego office:
1250 Sixth Avenue
San Diego, CA 92101
619-231-6616

Acquisitions contacts and areas of interest

Mary Larkin, Editor, Miller Accounting Division
Professional books for the accounting industry.

Gary Peipenbrink, Senior Editor
Humor, sports biographies, parenting, cookbooks, current affairs. No fiction or self-help.

Willa Perlman, Director, Children's Books Division
Fiction and nonfiction: preschool through age 17, picture books;

John Radzeiwicz, Senior Editor
Harvest paperback line: fiction reprints; some travel and humor. No self-help or how-to. Hardcover serious literary fiction.

HARMONY BOOKS
(division of Crown)
201 East 50th Street
New York, NY 10022
212-254-1600

HARPER & ROW, PUBLISHERS, INC.

10 East 53rd Street
New York, NY 10022
212-207-7000

Harper & Row has been fully owned by Rupert Murdoch since 1988. Its adult trade division publishes popular fiction of authors such as Russell Banks, John Ehle, Michael Gilbert, and first-time novelist Paula Sharp. Nonfiction titles include *The 8-Week Cholesterol Cure, Love, Medicine, and Miracles, The Writing Life* by Annie Dillard, *Making Sense of Adoption,* and an array of titles on current events, travel, and gardening. Other divisions are the new mass market Harper Paperback line, the Perennial Library, and Harper & Row San Francisco, which specializes in religious and new age books. Harper's Junior Books Group, with its Charlotte Zolotow Books and Trophy subdivisions, handles titles for young readers.

Acquisitions contacts and areas of interest

Larry Ashmead, Exective Editor
Fiction: mysteries, thrillers. Nonfiction: biographies and autobiographies, gardening, general self-help.

Kathy Banks, Associate Editor
Fiction: literary detective and suspense stories. Nonfiction: current events, women's health.

Cornelia Bessie, Copublisher, Bessie Books
Quality fiction. Nonfiction: foreign current events; science; theater, music, and the arts; animals.

Simon Michael Bessie, Vice President, Bessie Books
History, current events, economics, politics, theater.

Daniel Bial, Editor
Quality literary fiction. Nonfiction: history, current events, humor, sports, popular reference.

Edward Burlingame, Publisher, Edward Burlingame Books

Nonfiction: history, current events, biographies, and autobiographies.

Mr. Cass Canfield, Jr., Senior Editor
Nonfiction: history; social and intellectual issues; gardening; foods, wine, and cookery; art, design, and architecture. Fiction: Latin American translations.

Gladys Justin Carr, Vice President and Associate Publisher
Literary and commercial fiction. Nonfiction: biographies and memiors, military and general history, nutrition, medicine, celebrity stories, popular culture, true crime, sports, current events, business.

Carol Cohen, Associate Publisher, Director of Reference Publishing
General reference titles, word books, atlases, travel, health, education, child care, and family.

D. Graham Combs, Associate Editor
U.S. history, business, politics, minority/immigrant experience, literary and historical biography, popular music.

Susan Friedland, Senior Editor
Food, cookbooks, literary history.

Janet Goldstein, Senior Editor
Women's and feminist issues; relationships and popular psychology; social trends, parenting, and family issues.

Ms. Terry Karten, Senior Editor
Quality literary fiction. Nonfiction: biographies and autobiographies, history, current issues, women's issues.

Richard P. Kot, Senior Editor
Quality literary fiction. Nonfiction: music and film, humor, history, biography.

John Michael, Associate Editor
Mainstream fiction. Nonfiction: science, natural history, politics, current events, consumer affairs, gardening.

Lisa Miles, Associate Editor
Quality literary fiction. Nonfiction: memoirs, women's issues, social/cultural history.

Thomas W. Miller, Senior Editor
Nonfiction: biography, true crime, health and medicine, current affairs, politics, business, popular culture, military history, music.

Craig Nelson, Senior Editor
Commercial fiction. Nonfiction: film, theater, and music; true crime; science.

Susan Randol, Associate Editor
Informational and reference books, word books, science and health.

Christine Schillig, Vice President and Editorial Director
Commercial fiction. Nonfiction: popular culture, true crime; investigative journalism; current affairs; women's issues; health/popular psychology; nature.

Hugh Van Dusen, Executive Editor, Perennial Library
History, biography, child care, business. Fiction and nonfiction reprints into quality paperbacks.

Margaret Wimberger, Associate Editor
Fiction: mysteries. Nonfiction: holistic health and nutrition, psychology, film, current affairs.

Buz Wyeth, Executive Editor
Commercial and literary fiction. Nonfiction: biography, history, inspiration, human interest, popular reference, nature and outdoor activities, military affairs.

HARPER & ROW, PUBLISHERS, INC.
(Caedom Audio Division)
10 East 53rd Street
New York, NY 10022
212-207-7000

Caedom recently acquired the entire McGraw-Hill/TDM audio backlist of primarily nonfiction, business-oriented, how-to titles. It also acquires fiction and nonfiction audio rights.

The acquisitions contact is

Anne Gaudiner, Acquisition Editor.

HARPER & ROW JUNIOR BOOKS GROUP

H & R's Junior Books Group publishes picture books for preschoolers, titles for early childhood through adolescence.

HARPER & ROW SAN FRANCISCO
(Winston-Seabury Press)
Icehouse One, Suite 401
151 Union Street
San Francisco, CA 94111
415-477-4400

Acquisitions, contacts, and areas of interest

Thomas Grady, Editor
Wellness, recovery, new age, Catholic issues.

Ms. Lonnie Hull, Editor
Evangelical Christian books.

Yvonne Keller, Editor
Feminist-oriented books.

Ronald Klug, Editor
Christian books; general theology; religious books for professional and library use.

Roland Sebolt, Editor
Christian books; general theology; religious books for professional and library use.

Michael Toms, Senior Editor
New age and personal growth.

HARVARD BUSINESS SCHOOL PRESS
Morgan 41, Soldiers Field Road
Boston, MA 02163
617-495-6700

The Harvard Business School Press was established in 1984 to handle the increasing volume of business titles published by Harvard University Press. Subjects include accounting and control, joint ventures, leadership styles, and defense and procurement. Some representive titles are *Future Competition in Telecommunications* and *Ethics in Practice: Managing the Moral Corporation.*

The acquisitions contact is

Richard Luecke, Acquisition Editor.

HARVARD UNIVERSITY PRESS
79 Garden Street
Cambridge, MA 02138
617-495-2600

Harvard University Press, established in 1913, produces a balanced list of scholarly titles and an increasing number of general-interest books for an educated readership—for example, Marcus Greil's *Lipstick Traces,* Andrew Greeley's *Religious Change in America,* and Jane Goodall's *Chimpanzees of Gombe.*

Acquisitions contacts and areas of interest

Michael A. Aronson, Editor
Economics, business.

Howard D. Boyer, Editor
Hard sciences, medicine.

Ms. Ida Donald, Editor
History, social sciences.

Margaretta Fulton, Editor
Humanities, Judaic studies.

Angela von der Lippe, Editor
Behavioral sciences.

Mr. Lindsey Waters, Editor

Literary criticism.

HAZELDEN PUBLISHING
P.O. Box 176
Center City, MN 55012
612-257-4010

A division of the Hazelden Foundation, which runs well-known drug and alcohol treatment centers, this press publishes books for professionals and the general public on substance abuse, eating disorders, and AIDS. *Co-Dependent No More* and *Each Day a New Beginning* center on people in recovery, and a children's line focuses on prevention. Hazelden Books are sold through its own catalog as well as distributed to the trade market by Harper & Row.

The acquisition contact is Linda Peterson, Executive Editor.

HIPPOCRENE BOOKS, INC.
171 Madison Avenue
New York, NY 10016
212-685-4371

Initially known as a publisher of Judaic and military books, Hippocrene has developed a strong domestic and foreign travel collection, including the first guidebook for Vietnam. Its travel series include *Where to Go in . . .*, Michael Haag's off-the-beaten-track guides, and miscellaneous titles such as *Travel Safety* and *Tropical Traveller*. Hippocrene is also known for its books on Polish culture and history and for World War II histories.

The acquisitions contact is

George Blagowidow, President and Editorial Director.

HOLIDAY HOUSE, INC.
18 East 53rd Street
New York, NY 10022
212-688-0085

Holiday House, an independent publisher of children's books, specializes in books for the very young, with a limited number of books for young adults. Picture books include original stories, retelling of folk and fairy tales, and nonfiction titles such as *Prehistoric Animals*. For older children, Holiday House offers novels such as *Yours Truly, Shirley* for middle-grade students, *Fire in the Heart* for young adults, and some nonfiction titles. Holiday House is not interested in "problem novels" for its young adult division. It handles its own distribution.

The acquisitions contacts are

Margery S. Cuyler, Editor-in-Chief,
and
Shannon Maughan, Assistant Editor.

Send manuscripts with SASE. Because of the volume, unsolicited manuscripts have a turnaround time of 8 to 10 weeks. Do not send original artwork—send only photos or photocopies. Holiday does not accept certified, registered, or insured mail.

HENRY HOLT & CO.
115 West 18th Street
New York, NY 10011
212-886-9200

When Harcourt Brace Jovanovich acquired Holt Rinehart & Winston's textbook division in 1987, Henry Holt retained its autonomy as a trade publisher of fiction and nonfiction. In fiction, Holt has published Louise Erdrich's three novels; Michael Dorris's *Yellow Raft in Blue Water;* books by

Edward Abbey; and mysteries by Joseph Hansen, Sue Grafton, and Patricia Moyes. A biography of Richard Nixon, the true-crime title *The Woodchipper Murder*, and *Rating Your Psychotherapist* give an idea of the range of nonfiction on its list, which also includes gardening, craft, and home improvement books, as well as cookbooks and humor titles. Holt has published a number of poetry books, from *The Poetry of Robert Frost* to volumes by contemporary poets. Holt's children's division has added the Redfeather Books line for 7- to 9-year-olds.

Acquisitions contacts and areas of interest

Ms. Tracy Bernstein, Associate Editor
Fiction: popular mysteries. Nonfiction: how-to/self-help categories, careers, popular health, some history and entertainment books. No diet or cookbooks.

Brenda Bowen, Juvenile Books Editor
Especially interested in nonfiction picture books, and fiction for ages 7 through 9 and 9 through 12.

Teresa Burns, Editor
Nonfiction: original quality paperbacks in a wide range of how-to and self-help areas.

Elizabeth Crossman, Editor-at-Large
Cookbooks.

Joann Haun, Associate Editor
Word books, general reference books.

Amy Hertz, Assistant Editor
Nonfiction: popular sciences, new age, metaphysics and inspiration, Asian history, Asian events. Fiction: Spanish translations; anything imaginative.

Donald Hutter (own imprint, Donald Hutter Books)
Primarily nonfiction: current affairs, biographies, medical/health, sports. No get-rich-quick, beauty, or diet books.

Cynthia Vartan, Editor-at-Large
Nonfiction: how-to practical books with strong backlist potentials; especially health, child care, popular business. No biographies.

Marion Wood, Executive Editor
Nonfiction: history, Americana, biography, travel essays, nature, military history, Judaica, biological sciences. No self-help/how-to, inspiration, or popular psychology.

HOUGHTON MIFFLIN CO.

1 Beacon Street
Boston, MA 02108
617-725-5000

Houghton Mifflin's trade and reference division publishes adult trade hardcover and paper in nonfiction and fiction. Nonfiction categories vary in scope from investigative journalism to the Birnbaum Travel Guides and the Peterson Field Guides. Its fiction, which includes the Seymour Lawrence imprint, tends to be literary. Peter Davison Books is its poetry imprint. Its Ticknor & Fields imprint produces serious literary fiction, literary biographies, and other upmarket nonfiction titles. The children's line includes the successful *The Way Things Work,* as well as books by Clarion, the juvenile imprint (see Clarion Books).

Acquisitions contacts and areas of interest

Michael Janeway, Executive Editor
Nonfiction: politics, current events, biographies of political or historical figures, political history, investigative journalism. Fiction: stories with political themes.

Matilda Welter, Senior Juvenile Editor
All juvenile books, preschool through teenager, fiction and nonfiction.

New York office:
215 Park Avenue South
New York, NY 10003
212-420-5850

Acquisitions contacts and areas of interest

Peter Davison (own imprint, Peter Davison Books)
Poetry.

Henry Ferris, Senior Editor
American history and biography, current events.

Ms. Frances Kiernan, Senior Editor
Nonfiction: literary essays, travel. Fiction: short stories, literary novels.

Seymour Lawrence (own imprint, Seymour Lawrence Books)
Serious literary hardcover original fiction.

John Sterling, Senior Editor
Fiction: commercial, mysteries, thrillers. Nonfiction: current affairs, politics, history. No self-help, how-to, or popular material.

Caroline Sutton, Assistant Editor
Literary biographies, history (no specific preferences). No how-to, cookbooks, or anything overly popular. Fiction: serious literary hardcover original fiction.

INDIANA UNIVERSITY PRESS
Tenth & Morton Streets
Bloomington, IN 47405
812-335-4203

A publisher of trade as well as scholarly books, Indiana University Press offers titles in regional studies, women's studies, film, semiotics, philosophy, literary criticism, gay and gender studies, and Jewish history. It also publishes the *Middle East Journal, Discourse,* and several journals in feminist studies. (Indiana University Press is committed to gender-neutral language and recommends *The Handbook of Nonsexist Writing for Writers* to its authors.)

Acquisitions contacts and areas of interest

Laura Bryant, Sponsoring Editor
Religious and Judaic studies.

Joan Catapano, Senior Sponsoring Editor
Women's studies, film, folklore, black studies, literary theory, regional studies, cultural history and theory.

John Gallman, Director
All areas.

Janet Rabinowich, Senior Sponsoring Editor
Russian and East European studies, African studies, Middle Eastern studies, philosophy, art.

Robert Sloan, Sponsoring Editor
Science, business, medical ethics, history.

Natalie Wrubel, Editor and Music Sponsor
Music studies.

THE JEWISH PUBLICATION SOCIETY

1930 Chestnut Street
Philadelphia, PA 19103
215-564-5925

The Jewish Publication Society, which celebrated its centenary in 1988, functions both as a publisher and a book club, distributing its own and other publishers' Judaic titles. JPS publishes histories such as *Jews in the Renaissance,* books on the Holocaust and Zionism, philosophy, holiday anthologies, and literary studies, as well as poetry and fiction. JPS also produces preschool to young adult children's books.

The acquisitions contacts are
Sheila F. Segal, Consulting Editor,
and
David Adler, Juvenile Acquisitions Editor.

MICHAEL KESEND PUBLISHING, LTD.

1025 Fifth Avenue
New York, NY 10028
212-249-5150

A small press, Michael Kesend specializes in nature, animal, sports, health, and travel books. It is the publisher of such handbooks as *Walker's Guide: Serendipitous Outings near New York City Including a Section for Birders* and the Signs series: *Winter Signs in the Snow, Spring Signs,* and *Mountain Signs.* Health titles include *Hysterectomy: Learning the Facts, Coping with the Feelings, Facing the Future* and *Understanding Pacemakers.* Kesend also publishes literary fiction, including first novels. Michael Kesend books are distributed by the Talman Company.

The acquisitions contact is
Michael Kesend, Publisher.

ALFRED A. KNOPF
(division of Random House)
201 East 50th Street
New York, NY 10022
212-751-2600

Knopf, a subsidiary of the Random House empire, has a strong line of quality popular fiction by authors such as Alice Adams, Anne Tyler, Julian Barnes, John Updike, and a number of first-time novelists. Its excellent biographies include A. Scott Berg on Samuel Goldwyn, Martin Duberman on Paul Robeson, and Barry Paris on Louise Brooks. Knopf also does memoirs, poetry, cultural history, quality cookbooks, and fine arts and photography. With picture books through young adult titles, the children's line, which has absorbed that of Pantheon, another Random House subsidiary—is more upscale than Random House's juvenile line.

Acquisitions contacts and areas of interest
Barbara Bristol, Editor
Fiction: serious fiction by well known writers. Nonfiction: historical and literary biography, natural and social history.

Anne Close, Editor
Fiction: original contemporary themes by new young writers; likes books with a Southern or Western slant. Nonfiction: art, cookbooks.

Harry Ford, Editor
Poetry.

Ms. Frances Foster, Juvenile Editor
Preschool through young adult, nonfiction, picture books.

Jane Garrett, Senior Editor
Nonfiction: American history (all periods), U.S. cultural history, some European and Middle Eastern history, antiques, home repairs, architectural guides, gardening, crafts.

Judith Jones, Senior Editor
Fiction: espionage, mysteries, thrillers. Nonfiction: Judaica.

Susan Ralston, Editor
Mostly nonfiction: biography, cultural history, visual arts, music, dance, current issues and contemporary history.

Jonathan B. Segal, Senior Editor
Twentieth-century history, contemporary issues and events from a journalistic perspective, personalities; biographies relevant to above subjects and periods.

LEXINGTON BOOKS
(division of D. C. Heath)
125 Spring Street
Lexington, MA 02173
617-862-6650

Lexington Books, a division of D. C. Heath, publishes a variety of trade nonfiction, although its specialties are economics, business, international relations, and the behavioral sciences. A number of its titles deal with current social issues: *Mothers Without Custody, Home-Alone Kids,* and *Secret Lovers: Affairs Happen—How to Cope.* Lexington also publishes professional, scholarly, and college-level textbooks and is concertedly pursuing professionally oriented business works. Lexington handles its own distribution.

Acquisitions contacts and areas of interest

Robert Bovenschulte, Editor-in-Chief
Wide range of professional business books, including contemporary management; marketing; finance.

Paul E. O'Connell, Editor
Foreign relations, international business.

Margaret Zusky, Senior Editor
Human behavior, family relationships, dealing with terminal illness, drugs and addiction, serious health books, sports therapy.

LITTLE, BROWN & COMPANY, INC.
(subsidiary of Time, Inc.)
34 Beacon Street
Boston, MA 02108
617-227-0730

A subsidiary of Time, Inc., Little, Brown publishes quality popular fiction and nonfiction. Among its fiction authors are Thomas Berger, Ellen Gilchrist, Edward Abbey, and Martha Grimes. Thomas Pynchon's *Vineland,* his first novel in 17 years, is a recent Little, Brown book. Nonfiction categories include biography, history, nature, gardening, cooking, and health. Jill Krementz's *How It Feels to Fight for Your Life* and Roy Strong's *Creating Formal Gardens* are representative titles. The Bullfinch Press imprint handles art, photography, and design.

Acquisitions contacts and areas of interest

Jennifer Josephy, Senior Editor
Primarily nonfiction: history, open to all periods and regions; women's issues; psychology; Judaica; some business.

Ms. Kit Ward, Associate Editor

Fiction: literary noncommercial serious fiction. Nonfiction: natural history; some business, especially if it is socially oriented; medical discoveries; literary and historical biographies; some practical how-to books.

New York office:
205 Lexington Avenue
New York, NY 10016
212-683-0660

Acquisitions contacts and areas of interest

Patricia Mulcahy, Senior Editor
Fiction: frontlist, commercial, and serious literary fiction. Nonfiction: politics, current events, women's issues, funny books (not cartoons). Does very few how-to/self-help books.

Ray Roberts, Senior Editor
Fiction: general hardcover, frontlist fiction; mysteries. Nonfiction: heavily illustrated books, U.S. history, historical and literary biography, fine arts, TV and movie tie-ins.

LODESTAR BOOKS
(imprint of E. P. Dutton)
2 Park Avenue
New York, NY 10016
212-725-1818

Lodestar, E.P. Dutton's juvenile imprint, offers books for young readers from the second grade through high school. In nonfiction, Lodestar publishes the Time Detective series on archeology and history, the Mysteries of the Universe science series, and the Jewish biography series, in addition to books on politics and government. Lodestar also publishes quality contemporary fiction and the popular Encyclopedia Brown books.

All submissions should go to
Ms. Virginia Buckley, Editorial Director.

LONGMAN FINANCIAL SERVICES PUBLISHING
520 North Dearborn Street
Chicago, IL 60610
312-836-0466

Longman, a division of the Longman Financial Services Institute, began in 1982 as a professional and textbook publisher in real estate and insurance. It has since developed materials for financial planners and securities brokers. Longman is beginning to publish books with such titles as *The 100 Best Stocks to Own in America* and *Crash: Ten Days in October—Will It Strike Again?* for consumers and investors. Longman continues to produce prelicense tests and postlicense course and professional books in real estate, insurance, and securities. It handles its own distribution.

Acquisitions contacts and areas of interest

Wendy Lochner, Editor
Real estate books for professionals.

Kathy Welton, Executive Editor
Financial investments, insurance, banking, financial planning, general investments.

LOTHROP, LEE & SHEPARD BOOKS
(division of William Morrow & Co.)
105 Madison Avenue
New York, NY 10016
212-889-3050

This division of William Morrow & Co. publishes an assortment of books for young children, plus nonfiction for older children. Although many of its titles are imported from England, Lothrop also publishes U.S. authors.

All submissions should go to

Dinah Stevenson, Executive Editor.
Her areas of interest are picture books and fiction and nonfiction for preschoolers and juveniles.

MCGRAW-HILL, INC.
(Professional and Reference Division)
11 West 19th Street
New York, NY 10011
212-512-2000

The adult trade division of McGraw-Hill has discontinued all acquisitions, and its entire list, both current and backlist, is for sale. The computer and business book divisions are not affected by this change and continue to thrive.
Submissions may go to any of the following:

Elisa Adams, Senior Editor,

Jim Bessent, Sponsoring Editor,
or

William Sabin, Publisher.
General business and management books for professionals, includes marketing, entrepreneurial studies, quality control, manufacturing, banking, finance. Also publishes large directory and reference books.

MACMILLAN PUBLISHING CO.
866 Third Avenue
New York, NY 10022
212-702-2000

The Macmillan Publishing Group is a huge conglomerate made up of, among others, Macmillan, which is primarily a nonfiction publisher; Atheneum and Charles Scribner's Sons, acquired in 1984, which handle most of the fiction and literary nonfiction; The Free Press, specializing in social sciences and current affairs; and the Jossey-Bass business imprint. Macmillan's nonfiction categories include sports, military history, religion, art, biography, cooking, and reference (see Rawson Associates). Macmillan also publishes children's books, including Margaret K. McElderry Books.

Acquisitions contacts and areas of interest

Pamela Hoenig, Senior Editor
Cooking, gardening, pregnancy, child care, serious self-help, addiction problems. No popular psychology or diet books.

Elisa Petrini, Editor
Popular culture and popular reference books, illustrated books, cartoon humor books, travel series.

Philip Turner, Editor
Popular reference books, Judaica, reprint mystery and suspense novels, humor and cartoon books, word and linguistics books, literary and historical biography, U.S. Civil War, World War II, sports.

Rick Wolf, Senior Editor and Director of Sports Books
Children's Books Division
Each of the following imprints publishes from preschool through young adult fiction and nonfiction.

Cindy Kane, Editor-in-Chief, Four Winds Press

Barbara Lalicki, Editor-in-Chief, Bradbury Press

Margaret K. McElderry, Editor-in-Chief, Margaret K. McElderry Books

Ms.Whitney Malone, Editor-in-Chief, Aladdin/Collier Books
All submissions should be made to

Clare Costello, Director, Macmillan Children's Books.

MICROSOFT PRESS
16011 N.E. 36 Way
Redmond, WA 98073
206-882-8080

Microsoft Press, a division of the Microsoft Corporation, publishes sophisticated books on computer software. These books—which are generally about, but not limited to, Microsoft products—are not manuals, but rather books for high-end users: *Running MS-DOS, Supercharging MS-DOS,* and *Desktop Publishing by Design.* Tempus Books, a general trade imprint founded in 1987, publishes reprints and some original titles in science, technology, and economics. Most Microsoft and Tempus books are softcover.

Acquisitions contacts

Min S. Yee, Publisher and General Manager
Dean Holmes, Acquisition Editor
Marjorie Schlaikjer, Acquisition Editor

WILLIAM MORROW & COMPANY, INC.
(subsidiary of Hearst Corporation)
105 Madison Avenue
New York, NY 10016
212-889-3050

Morrow, a subsidiary of the Hearst Corporation, is a conglomerate with a dozen imprints. Among its best-selling fiction authors are Ken Follett, Ed McBain, Kinky Friedman, Piers Anthony, John Irving, and debut novelist Jonathan Ames. Recent nonfiction titles include *The Don Juan Dilemma: Should Women Stay with Men Who Stray, Courtroom Crusaders,* and *Swim with the Sharks.* Cooking, health, history, film, biography, and autobiography are just some of the nonfiction categories they publish. The Greenwillow Books and Mulberry Books imprints handle some of Morrow's children's titles. (See also Morrow Junior Books and Lothrop, Lee & Shepard Books.)

Acquisitions contacts and areas of interest

Liza Dawson, Senior Editor
Women's contemporary fiction, mysteries. Nonfiction: child care, how-to business books, superior self-help books.

Lisa Drew, Senior Editor
True crime, sports (especially football), celebrity biographies and autobiographies.

Harvey Ginsberg, Senior Editor
Most fiction and nonfiction: all topics, except medical; popular self-help/how-to; popular psychology; diet.

Maria Guarnaschelli, Senior Editor
Popular science, cookbooks, literary biographies.

David Hartwell, Senior Editor
Hardcover science fiction.

Ms. Randy Ladeheim, Senior Editor
Edits Fielding's travel book series (produced in-house).

Bruce Lee, Senior Editor
Business, public affairs, government and politics.

Susan Leon, Senior Editor
Upscale serious fiction. In nonfiction, likes serious, hard subjects.

Constance Roosevelt, Senior Editor, Hearst Marine Books
Nonfiction: boating, marinas.

Douglas Stumpf, Senior Editor
General fiction and nonfiction. Doesn't like pop titles, such as feel-good psychology books.

Margaret Talcott, Editor
Female-oriented frontlist fiction. Nonfiction: popular science, space, theology.

Jennifer Williams, Editor, Silver Arrow Books
Nonfiction: popular psychology, contemporary cultural events, Hollywood biographies.

MORROW JUNIOR BOOKS DIVISION
105 Madison Avenue
New York, NY 10016
212-889-3050

Morrow Junior Books, one of William Morrow's juvenile imprints, handles fiction, nonfiction, and picture books for children in the middle grades. In addition to fiction by Beverly Cleary, the list includes animal books such as *A Fish's Body;* Seymour Simon's *Mars, Jupiter,* and *Stars;* and Joanna Cole's *The New Baby at Your House* and *Asking About Sex and Growing Up.*

All submissions should go to Meredith Charpentier, Executive Editor.

JOHN MUIR PUBLICATIONS
P.O. Box 613
Santa Fe, NM 87504
505-982-4078

Muir, which started out in 1969 with *How to Keep Your Volkswagon Alive,* publishes general nonfiction in the areas of ski equipment and repair; travel guides, including the Kidding Around series for young travelers; and women's health.

The acquisitions contact is

Ken Luboff, President.

MUSTANG PUBLISHING COMPANY
PO Box 9327
New Haven, CT 06533
203-624-5485

Mustang's books are nonfiction trade paper geared to an audience of 18- to 35-year-olds. It publishes travel guides, guides for people applying to college and graduate school, and *The Complete Book of Beer Drinking Games.*

The acquisitions contact is

Rollin Riggs, President and Publisher.

MYSTERIOUS PRESS
129 West 56th Street
New York, NY 10019
212-765-0923

Specializing in mystery fiction and mystery-related nonfiction, Mysterious's fiction authors include Ross Thams, Ted Allbeury, and Donald Westlake. In nonfiction, the press offers *History of Mystery* by Robin Winks, *The Columbo File,* and *Murder on the Air.* The Penzler Books imprint handles non-mystery fiction by well-known mystery authors. Mysterious Press has a copublishing agreement with Warner Books, and its books are distributed by Ballantine.

The acquisitions contact is

Sara Ann Freed, Editor.

THE NAVAL INSTITUTE PRESS
Annapolis, MD 21402
301-268-6110

Naval Institute Press, the official university press of the U.S. Naval Academy, publishes a wide array of hardcover books for Navy and Marine officers, as well as for a general audience. Titles include *Seamanship: Fundamentals for the Deck Officer, U.S. Coast Guard Cutters and Craft of World War II,* and *The American Flying Boat: An Illustrated History.* Its history books range in subject from ancient Rome to the twentieth century, with a special emphasis on World War II topics. In fiction, *The Hunt for Red October* by Tom Clancy was a mega best-seller. The Naval Institute Press handles its own distribution.

The acquisitions contact is

Deborah Estes, Manager of Acquisitions.

THOMAS NELSON, INC.
Nelson Place at Elm Hill Pike
Nashville, TN 37214
615-889-9000

Thomas Nelson, one of the largest Bible publishers in the United States, publishes Christian trade books in health, self-help and parenting, and some children's titles. The books are primarily hardcover, with titles such as *Gifts of Love, Straight Answers in the New Age, Creative Dating,* and *Relief for Hurting Parents;* and Robert Schuller's best-selling *Believe in the God Who Believes in You.*

The acquisitions contact is

Bill Watkins, Managing Editor.

NEW AMERICAN LIBRARY
(division of Penguin USA)
1633 Broadway
New York, NY 10019
212-397-8000

New American Library, a division of Penguin, is known as a mass market publisher of historical romances, horror, science fiction and fantasy, true crime, and Westerns. It also publishes a significant number of hardcover and trade paper fiction, in addition to reprints of classics and recent quality titles, such as the novels of Toni Morrison and Alice Munro. Recent nonfiction hardcovers include *Brando: The Unauthorized Biography, Unstable at the Top: Inside the Neurotic Organization,* and *Women Who Date Too Much.* NAL also produces a variety of cookbooks, among them the Weight Watcher's line.

Acquisitions contacts and areas of interest

Molly Allen, Senior Editor
Cookbooks.

Linett Attai, Editor
Female-oriented fiction, romances.

Laura Bernstein, Editor
Wide range of fiction and nonfiction, hard and soft originals and reprints.

Arnold Dolin Editor in Chief
Business, political and social issues, theater.

Rachel Klayman, Editor
Nonfiction: women's issues, mental health, Judaica, current events. Literary fiction.

Alexia Dorszynski, Senior Editor
Parenting and child care, health and fitness, education.

Ms. Michaela Hamilton, Executive Editor
Nonfiction: true crime, relationships, diets. Fiction: female-oriented stories.

Gary Luke, Executive Editor
Fiction: stories with gay/lesbian themes. Nonfiction: commercial quality paper and hardcover books, humor, general how-to and self-help, some popular business, celebrity and rock-and-roll autobiographies and biographies.

Kevin Mulroy, Executive Editor
Popular how-to business books, sports. Fiction: male adventure, thrillers.

Hugh Rawson, Editor
Military History, reference.

Susan Rogers, Editor
Fiction: women's/feminist-oriented stories. Nonfiction: books for the academic and library markets in women's studies; African-American studies; U.S. history; humanities.

Hilary Ross, Associate Executive Editor
Fiction: hardcover originals, women's stories, suspense, medical thrillers.

Matthew Sartwell, Editor
Fiction: westerns, suspense, thrillers, hardcover and mass market originals. Nonfiction: new age topics; metaphysical subjects,

astrology, etc., mostly in mass market original; true crime; humor.

Christopher Schilling, Associate Editor
Science fiction, fantasy, offbeat horror, general contemporary fiction.

John Silbersack, Executive Editor
Hardcover frontlist technothrillers and science fiction.

NEWMARKET PRESS
18 East 48th Street
New York, NY 10017
212-832-3575

Newmarket's quality, mainly hardcover nonfiction books include the What's Happening to my Body series and *The Female Stress Syndrome.* In addition to child care, psychology, and health, Newmarket publishes biography, business, and media titles. Newmarket also published *Words of Martin Luther King, Jr.,* which is part of the Words of . . . series. Its books are distributed by Harper & Row.

All submissions should be made to Esther Margolis, President and Highlight Publisher.

NOLO PRESS
950 Parker Street
Berkeley, CA 94710
415-549-1976

Nolo Press, whose first book in 1971 was *How to Do Your Own Divorce in California,* is the leading publisher of self-help law books. A number of its titles are specifically geared to California residents, but many are for the national market. In addition to guides such as *How to File for Bankruptcy,* Nolo publishes legal software and a quarterly self-help law newsletter, *Nolo News—Access to Law.* Publisher's Group West and Book-people distribute its books to the trade, while Nolo handles its own direct-mail sales.

Most Nolo books are done in-house by staff people, but outside manuscripts are acquired.

The acquisitions contact is

Barbara Repa, Acquisitions Director.

NORTH POINT PRESS

850 Talbot Avenue
Berkeley, CA 94706
415-527-6260

Established in 1980, North Point is a prestigious literary press. It is noted for producing beautiful books on acid-free paper. It publishes fiction, poetry, essays, biography, and unusual books about food, such as M.F.K. Fisher's *The Gastronomical Me*. Among its best-sellers is *West with the Night*. North Point Press books are distributed by Farrar, Straus & Giroux.

All submissions should be sent to the attention of Jack Shoemaker, Editor-in-Chief.

W. W. NORTON & COMPANY, INC.

500 Fifth Avenue
New York, NY 10110
212-354-5500

Norton publishes literary fiction, first novels, poetry, and short story collections, as well as college, professional, and medical texts. Among its authors are Rick DeMarinis, Rita Dove, Rick Bass, and May Sarton. Norton has a broad assortment of nonfiction titles, including history, criticism, biography, psychology, natural history, and science. It has scored great success with *The Rotation Diet*. Norton also has a sailing line and distributes the Blue Guide travel books.

Acquisitions contacts and areas of interest

Jill Bialosky, Associate Editor
Serious literary fiction. Nonfiction: biographies, narrative/memoirs, books by journalists, poetry. No politics or sports.

Mary E. Cunnane, Editor
Primarily nonfiction: biography, science, parenting, open to most other subjects that are compatible with Norton's overall approach.

Mr. Hilary Hinzman, Editor
Nonfiction: government, current events, U.S. history, minority issues, sports, historical and literary biographies. Fiction: serious literary hardcover.

Gerald Howard, Senior Editor
Literary fiction. Nonfiction: business stories, political issues from a liberal point of view.

Mr. Starling R. Lawrence, Vice President and Editor
No specific preferences; open to all fiction and nonfiction submissions that are appropriate for Norton.

Ms. Carol Houch Smith, Editor
Nonfiction: biographies; animal and human behavior; popular science; personal experiences, such as travel memoirs; anthologies; nature. Literary fiction. Does not like politics or economics; prefers emotional subjects.

OSBORNE MCGRAW-HILL
2600 Tenth Street
Berkeley, CA 94710
415-548-2805

Acquisitions contact and areas of interest

Cynthia Hudson, Vice President, Editorial Services
Computers, communications information.

THE OVERLOOK PRESS
12 West 21st Street
New York, NY 10010
212-337-5200

Primarily a publisher of hardcover and trade paper nonfiction, Overlook also produces a limited selection of original literary fiction and poetry. Overlook's nonfiction titles range from *Graphic Design* to *Full Tilt: From Ireland to India with a Bicycle;* other categories include illustrated architecture and martial arts history and instruction. Penguin USA distributes its books.

The acquisitions contact is

Jessika Hegewisch, Editorial Manager.

OXFORD UNIVERSITY PRESS, INC.
200 Madison Avenue
New York, NY 10016
212-679-7300

In addition to *The Oxford English Dictionary* and *The Oxford Dictionary of the American Language,* this university press publishes trade, scholarly, and professional books in the sciences, social sciences, arts, and humanities. Oxford is well known for its books on jazz, such as Kathy Ogren's *The Jazz Revolution.* Oxford is strong in both ancient and modern world history and in U.S. history. It also produces the Past Masters series of books about outstanding intellectual figures and a series of anecdote books, such as *Baseball Anecdotes* and *The Oxford Book of Royal Anecdotes.* The New York division is editorially independent of the British home office.

Acquisitions contacts and areas of interest

Herbert Addison, Executive Editor
Business and economics from academic and theoretical viewpoints.

Valerie Aubrey, Editor
Political science, law, current affairs.

Joyce Berry, Senior Editor
Medicine and science.

Donald Kraus, Editor
Bibles.

Nancy Lane, Editor
Non-European history.

Sheldon Meyer, Editor
U.S. history.

William Sisler, Executive Editor
Humanities, sociology, anthropology.

PANTHEON/SCHOCKEN BOOKS, INC.
(division of Random House)
201 East 50th Street
New York, NY 10022
212-751-2600

Pantheon/Schocken, a division of Random House since 1987, publishes fiction, much of it in translation, and nonfiction. Pantheon publishes history, biography, memoirs, current affairs, political science, photography, and cartoons. Schocken publishes many of the same nonfiction categories, with an emphasis on Judaica and the history of the Holocaust. In fiction, Pantheon has published *The Men Who Loved Evelyn Cotten* by first novelist Frank Ronan, *Skeleton in Waiting* by Peter Dickinson, and *Archipelago* by Michel Rio. Schocken publishes, in translation, the works of Gershom Scholem, Primo Levi, and S. Y. Agnon and the Kafka library series.

Acquisitions contacts and areas of interest

Tom Engelhardt, Senior Editor
Nonfiction: public policy and current events. Fiction: foreign translations.

Bonnie Fetterman, Editor, Schocken Books
Judaica for the Schocken imprint.

Helena Franklin, Editor
Fiction: mysteries by British writers. Nonfiction: literary and historical biographies, cultural histories, art books.

Susan Rabiner, Senior Editor
Nonfiction: books for and about women, history (no military history), relationships, medical/health books.

David Sternback, Editor
Nonfiction: popular culture, politics, civil rights era books.

PARAGON HOUSE PUBLISHERS
90 Fifth Avenue
New York, NY 10011
212-620-2820

Paragon House, founded in 1982 by the Unification Church (the "Moonies"), is a publisher of quality nonfiction and college text and reference books. Areas of interest include biography such as *O'Neill: Son and Playwright,* political science and history, new age, philosophy, military history, and religion. Paragon House doesn't publish fiction. To date, it is editorially independent of Reverend Moon's Unification Church and handles its own distribution.

Acquisitions contacts and areas of interest

Ken Stewart, Editor-in-Chief
Literary scholarly nonfiction, biographies, poetry, the United States during the 1950s and early 1960s.

Ms. P. J. Dempsey, Editor
Biographies, general history, reference books.

Evelyn Fazio, Executive Editor
College- and graduate-level course books: political science, international relations, foreign studies, philosophy.

Don Fehr, Editor

Nonfiction: trade- and college-oriented anthropology, sociology, philosophy, religion.

Juanita Lieberman, Editor
Wide range of scholarly books for quality paperback reprints.

THE PAULIST PRESS
997 Macarthur Boulevard
Mahwah, NJ 07430
201-825-7300

Paulist, a Roman Catholic press, publishes religious studies geared for undergraduates and professionals, such as *Reading the Old Testament.* Its list, which has become more ecumenical in recent years, includes titles in religion and public affairs for the general reader; church history; spirituality; and general psychology and self-help, with or without a spiritual bent. Among its best-selling titles is *Hope for the Flowers.* The Paulist Press does not publish fiction or poetry.

All of the following are acquisitions editors; their interests and specialties overlap: Don Brophy, Lawrence Boadt, Georgia Christo, Douglas Fisher, Robert Hamma.

PELICAN PUBLISHING CO.
1101 Monroe Street
Gretna, LA 70053
504-368-1175

Pelican, primarily a nonfiction publisher, specializes in travel, photography, cooking, and children's books—often, although not always, with a Southern slant. It also publishes Southern regional books and is interested in Southern fiction. It has scored great success with Zig Ziglar's *See You at the Top.* Pelican distributes its own books.

Send submissions to James L. Calloun, Executive Editor.

VIKING PENGUIN, INC.
(See Penguin USA)

PENGUIN USA
40 West 23rd Street
New York, NY 10010
212-337-5200

Viking Penguin—Penguin USA as of January 1989—consists of the imprints Viking, Penguin, New American Library, Dutton, and the subsidiary Stephen Greene Press. (See NAL, Dutton, and Greene.) Viking publishes trade hardcover fiction and nonfiction of all varieties, including children's books. Among its fiction authors are Garrison Keillor, Salman Rushdie, and T. C. Boyle. Its nonfiction categories run the gamut from history to biology. Penguin, its paperback imprint, is equally broad scoped, excluding only romances and Westerns. It produces the Contemporary Fiction series and King Penguin, the international fiction series.

Acquisitions contacts and areas of interest

Kathryn Court, Senior Executive Editor.
Kathryn is interested in literary and commercial fiction, including third world and European fiction, humor, travel and writing, biography, current affairs, business, nature, women's issues, and true crime. Her assistant is Caroline White.

Pamela Dorman, Senior Editor.
Pam is interested in commercial fiction, especially women's fiction, as well as literary fiction and popular fiction from the UK. Non-fiction interests include true crime and other investigative stories, human interest stories, self-help, popular science, personal finance, parenting, consumer issues, social history and biography. Her assistant is Emily Barker.

Michael Fragnito, President and Editorial Director, Studio Books
Large, illustrated, high-priced coffee-table books on decorating, cooking, design, entertaining, and gardening. Also lower-priced, quality paperbacks on same subjects, with high production values.

Dan Frank, Executive Editor.
Dan is interested in contemporary, regional American fiction as well as serious areas of non-fiction—history, science, nature, economics, politics, biography and environment. His assistant is Roger Devine.

Nan Graham, Senior Editor.
Nan's interests include American fiction, fiction about clashing cultures—third world and european; contemporary social and political issues, historical and literary biography, biographies of artists. Oversess *Granta* for Penguin.

Lisa Kaufman, Editor.
Lisa is interested in popular culture; history; mysteries, thrillers and true crime; commercial/historical and contemporary literary fiction self-help and addiction recovery; and especially quirky, personal narrative non-fiction. Her assistant is Leslie Herzik.

Lori Lipsky, Associate Editor.
Lori's interests include health and social issues, self-help, child care and parenting, nature, popular culture and personal stories as well as contemporary and historical commercial fiction.

Michael Millman, Associate Editor.
Michael is interested in literary fiction, history (political, social, labor), biography, politics, travel and literary criticism. He oversees the Penguin American Classics series.

Al Silverman, Contributing Editor.
Al is interested in contemporary fiction as well as mysteries and thrillers. American history—political, literary, social; 20th century biography, business, sports, jazz, dance, wine, poker.

Dawn Seferian, Senior Editor.
Dawn's interests include literary fiction, 20th century political, social and health issues, literary biography, popular culture, the-

atre, art, literary criticism, and eastern European writers. She oversees the King Penguin series. Her assistant is Leslie Herzik.

David Stanford, Editor.

David's interests include American history, current events, biography and autobiography, cartoons and humor, science and environment, literary fiction, and unusual projects. He has a special interest in working with writers from the western US—history, sense of place, and issues of perpectives particular to the West. His assistant is Roger Devine.

Amanda Vaill, Executive Editor.

Amanda is interested in serious literary fiction, current affairs, business, history, science, nature, art, theatre, dance and biography. Her assistant is Scott Anderson.

Mindy Werner, Senior Editor.

Mindy is interested in both literary and commercial fiction, women's issues, Judaism, some history, contemporary issues, health pop psychology, cookbooks, true crime and humor. She oversees the Virago Modern Classics series. Her assistant is Janine Steel.

CHILDREN'S BOOKS DIVISION

Acquisitions contact and areas of interest

Nancy Paulsen, Executive Editor.

Fiction and nonfiction: preschool through early adolescence.

PERSEA BOOKS, INC.

60 Madison Avenue
New York, NY 10012
212-779-7668

An independently owned small literary press, Persea shares space with and is distributed by George Braziller. It publishes contemporary fiction by such writers as William Goyen and Elizabeth Jolley, and poetry by Randy Blasing and Les A. Murray. Essays, literary criticism, and women's studies are among its nonfiction categories.

The acquisitions contact is
Karen Braziller, Editorial Director.

POCKET BOOKS
(division of Simon & Schuster)
1230 Avenue of the Americas
New York, NY 10020
212-698-7000

Pocket, the mass market division of Simon & Schuster, publishes a wide range of pulp genre fiction. In recent years it has begun publishing original hardcovers and trade paperbacks in general fiction and nonfiction. Recent trade fiction titles include Robert Campbell's *Nibbled to Death by Ducks,* Mary McGarry Morris's *Vanished,* and D. M. Thomas's *Summit.* Cookbooks, self-help and psychology, true crime, health, sports, and business make up its recent nonfiction list.

Acquisitions contacts and areas of interest
Kathy Bradley, Editor
Fiction: female-oriented books, romance. Nonfiction: popular how-to, health-related books.

Jane Chelius, Senior Editor
Fiction: mysteries, suspense.

Dana Edwin Isaacson, Assistant Editor
Mysteries.

Anne Greenberg, Senior Editor
Does no acquiring. Edits the Nancy Drew and other young adult fiction series.

Linda Marrow, Senior Editor
Fiction: romance and historical romance.

Paul McCarthy, Senior Editor
Fiction: men's adventure. Nonfiction: business, general interest.

Sally Peters, Associate Editor
Fiction: horror; generally open to all popular fiction. Nonfiction: movie tie-ins, health and fitness, child care, relationships.

Elaine Pfefferbilt, Senior Editor
Offbeat nonfiction and humor (such as *Catmopolitan* and "Vanity Fur"). Also does true crime. No fiction.

Stacy Shiff, Senior Editor
Fiction: serious literary books for the Washington Square Press imprint. Nonfiction: current events and cultural affairs, popular how-to business.

Ms. Leslie Wells, Senior Editor
Hardcover and mass market originals. Nonfiction: general how-to/self-help, relationships, celebrity biographies and autobiographies, current affairs, popular business.

Claire Zion, Associate Executive Editor
Fiction: female-oriented books. Nonfiction: new age and metaphysics.

POSEIDON PRESS
(division of Simon & Schuster)
1230 Avenue of the Americas
New York, NY 10020
212-698-7000

Poseidon is one of the smaller Simon & Schuster imprints. They publish a limited list of high quality fiction and non-fiction titles.

Acquisitions contact and areas of interest

Kathleen Anderson, Senior Editor
Fiction: serious literary hardcover fiction. Nonfiction: history, especially Vietnam-related; books by journalists; media books;

biographies of literary and historical figures; popular culture and politics.

PRENTICE-HALL PRESS
(division of Simon & Schuster)
15 Columbus Circle
New York, NY 10023
212-373-7500

Prentice-Hall is a division of Simon & Schuster. Its trade division publishes hardcover and paperback books that run the gamut of popular nonfiction categories, with a significant number of new age, psychology, and self-help titles; cookbooks, travel, and military history are also strong on its list.

Acquisitions contacts and areas of interest

Marilyn J. Abraham, Vice President and Editor-in-Chief
Psychology, self-help, enlightenment.

Paul Aron, Senior Editor
Nonfiction: business, how-to and histories; sports; current events; politics.

Linda Raglan Cunningham, Editor-at-Large
New age and spirituality.

Burton Gabriel, Executive Editor, Brady Books
Computers and high-technology; software-user guides.

Charles Levine, Associate Publisher, J. K. Lasser Books
Income-tax guides, finance and investment reference books.

Mary Hall Mayer, Executive Editor, Prentice-Hall Editions
Illustrated books.

Ms. Toula Polygalakos, Editor
Nonfiction: practical but interesting-to-read cookbooks, how-to gardening and crafts, biographies, literary essays.

Ms. Toni Sciarra, Senior Editor

Nonfiction: general commercial self-help/how-to; popular psychology and health; women's issues; parenting; relationships; light, popular business; new age and inspirational.

Doug Shulkind, Associate Editor
Nonfiction: war/military history, general history, popular culture, contemporary events.

John Thornton, Executive Editor
Science, nature, history.

Chuck Wall, Executive Editor, Arco Books
Careers and occupational guidebooks and reference dictionaries; study aids and standardized-test guides; technical film books; wide range of technical reference books for consumers and professionals.

Gail Winston, Editor
Parenting, child care, education, medicine.

Marilyn Wood, Editor-in-Chief, Travel Books
Travel books and series, such as the Baedeker and Frommer guidebooks.

PRENTICE-HALL PROFESSIONAL BOOKS DIVISION
(division of Simon & Schuster)
Englewood Cliffs, NJ 07632
201-592-2000

Acquisitions contacts and areas of interest

Ellen Coleman, Editor
Personal self-improvement books.

Ellen Kidin, Editor
Manufacturing, real estate.

Olivia Love, Editor
Human resources and personnel management, training, recruiting, occupational reference books and directories.

Jeff McCartney, Audiocassette Division

Produces multicassette audio albums relating to self-help business subjects. Tends to use authors published by the Prentice-Hall Professional Division.

Tom Power, Editor
General business books: self-improvement, public speaking, effective communications, trends, general management and marketing.

Betty Schwartzberg, Editor
Banking, finance, accounting, investing.

PRICE/STERN/SLOAN
360 North La Cienega Blvd.
Los Angeles, CA 90048
213-657-6100

Despite having recently published its first novel—Leslie Thomas's *The Adventures of Goodnight & Loving*—Price/Stern/Sloan remains primarily a nonfiction publisher of popular psychology, humor, children's books and audiocassettes (Wee Sing series), health, gardening, and cooking. *The Borderline Personality, Menopause, The Complete Garden Planning Manual,* and *The Fast & Easy Oat Bran Cookbook* are representative titles. It also does some photography, home improvement, and automotive titles.

Acquisitions contacts and areas of interest

Jeanette Egan, Editor
Cookbooks.

Vernon Gorter, Editor
How-to photography.

Ms. Spencer Humphry, Director of Business Affairs
Popular health, gardening.

Mike Lutfy, Editor
Automotive.

Lisa Ann Marsoli, Editorial Director, Juvenile Division

Illustrated fiction and game books for young children and pre-schoolers.

Doug Morrison, Editor
Health, fitness, exercise.

Helene Siegel, Editor
Cookbooks.

PRIMA PUBLISHING & COMMUNICATIONS
P.O. Box 1260
Rocklin, CA 95677
916-624-5718

The publisher of this book, Prima was founded in 1984, publishes general nonfiction titles with a focus on business and entrepreneurship, cooking, health, self-help, and music. Prima's books are distributed by St. Martin's Press. *Retin-A and Other Youth Miracles, Paddle to the Amazon, Native's Guide to New York,* and *Oat Cuisine* are recent titles. Prima may be the fastest growing of the independent publishers.

The acquisitions contact is
Ben Dominitz, Publisher.

PRINCETON UNIVERSITY PRESS
Princeton, NJ 08540
609-452-4258

One of the few university presses to own its printing plant, Princeton produces high-quality books, scholarly as well as a large percentage geared to the intelligent nonacademic reader. Princeton specializes in art history (*Esprit de Corps*); U.S. and European history (*The Liberals and J. Edgar Hoover*); political science (George Kennan); and philosophy (Joseph Campbell). Although most of its authors are of some academic repute, not all are necessarily currently affiliated with a college or university.

Acquisitions contacts and areas of interest

Cathie Brettschneider, Editor
Religion.

Robert Brown, Editor
Literature and poetry.

Margaret Case, Editor
Asian studies, Middle Eastern studies, Latin American studies.

Joanna Hitchcock, Editor
European history, classics, film studies.

Walter Lippincott, Director, International Relations
Anthropology, opera.

Elizabeth Powers, Editor
Fine arts, music (excluding opera), archeology.

Jack Repcheck, Editor
Economics.

Edward Tenner, Editor
Physical science, mathematics.

Gail Ullman, Editor
Political science, sociology, Soviet studies, social sciences, American studies.

Emily Wilkinson, Editor
Biological science, Bird Books series.

PROBUS PUBLISHING COMPANY
118 North Clinton Street.
Chicago, IL 60606
312-346-7985

This privately held company specializes in trade and professional business books, such as *Do It Yourself Investor* and *Professional's Desktop Guide to Real Estate Finance.* Areas of expertise include investment, real estate, banking, marketing, and other related subjects such as accounting, insurance, sales management, and manufacturing. Probus distributes its own books to the trade and also sells via direct response.

The acquisitions contact is

J. Michael Jeffers, Editorial Director.

PUTNAM PUBLISHING COMPANY
200 Madison Avenue
New York, NY 10016
212-951-8400

G. P. Putnam's Sons, which celebrated its 150th anniversary in 1988, has undergone enormous change in the past quarter century: In 1965 it acquired Berkley Books (see Berkley Publishing Group), and in 1975 the two were acquired by MCA, Inc., a communications conglomerate. Perigree Books, Putnams's trade paper imprint, was added in 1979; and in recent years, two new juvenile imprints were added: Philomel Books and Grosset & Dunlap. Putnam's fiction authors include Amy Tan, Robert B. Parker, Lee Smith, Paul Theroux, Dick Francis, Dean R. Koontz, and Robin Cook. Its nonfiction range is broad, with titles such as *The Six-Week Fat-to-Muscle Makeover, Greg LeMond's Pocket Guide to Bicycle Maintenance and Repair,* and *Incident at Howard Beach.*

Acquisitions contacts and areas of interest

Ms. Lindley Boegehold, Senior Editor, Special Projects
Wide range of commercial nonfiction, including humor, cartoonists, unusual ideas, relationships.

Eugene Brissie, Publisher, Perigee Books
Nonfiction: wide range of quality commercial paperback titles; how-to/self-help, popular business, cookbooks, health and exercise. Open to all popular subjects.

George Coleman, Senior Editor
Nonfiction: true crime, current events, popular and celebrity autobiographies and biographies, crafts and hobbies. Fiction: spy and mystery thrillers, popular frontlist fiction.

Stacy Creamer, Editor
Fiction: first-time novelists, thrillers, horror, medical thrillers. Nonfiction: true crime.

Ms. Adrienne Ingrum, Executive Editor
Popular, how-to business books; special-interest reference books.

Judy Linden, Senior Editor
Wide range of commercial nonfiction, including humor; travel guides; popular business; parenting; general self-help/how-to.

Lisa Wager, Senior Editor
Nonfiction: true crime. Fiction: commercial and serious literary fiction.

QUE CORPORATION
(division of Macmillan & Co.)
11711 North College Avenue
Carmel, IN 46032
317-573-2500

A division of Macmillan since 1986, Que is one of the leading publishers (mainly in trade paper) of computer books—specifically, corporate-sponsored user guides to computer software. Titles include *Using One-Two-Three: Special Edition, Using WordPerfect 5, MS-DOS User's Guide.*

The acquisitions contact is
Karen Bluestein, Technical Editor.

RANDOM HOUSE
201 East 50th Street
New York, NY 10022
212-751-2600

Owned by the Newhouse publishing conglomerate, the Random House empire's trade group includes the Random House adult line, the Villard hardcover imprint, the quality trade paper imprint Vintage Books, and the Fodor travel guides. (Also in the division but listed separately are Knopf, Crown, Pantheon/Schocken, and Times Books.) Random House's fiction authors include V. S. Pritchett, Robert Ludlum, and Ann Beattie. Its quality mainstream nonfiction includes Michael Holroyd's biography of Bernard Shaw, the memoirs of Nancy Reagan, and *America's Cottage Gardens*. Random House's juvenile division publishes books primarily for the preschooler, including the Dr. Seuss titles.

Acquisitions contacts and areas of interest

Susan Bell, Associate Editor
Nonfiction: politics, arts and culture, social history. Fiction: highly literary writing.

Robin Desser, Associate Editor
Fiction for Vintage Contemporaries line, a quality paperback series of modern fiction by new writers.

Joseph M. Fox, Senior Editor
Fiction: espionage thrillers, mysteries, suspense. Nonfiction: military and U.S. history, some sports, general current events, contemporary cultural issues.

Ellen Lichtenstein, Senior Editor
Trade-oriented, how-to business books; finance, careers.

Erroll McDonald, Executive Editor, Vintage Books
Literary fiction for quality paperback reprints. Nonfiction: political memoirs, current affairs, contemporary popular culture.

Charlotte Mayerson, Editor
Nonfiction: books with a strong backlist potential that can be kept current or revised frequently.

David Rosenthal, Editor
Current events, government and politics, contemporary biographies.

Becky Saletan, Editor
Nonfiction: journalism/media stories, women's self-help, health, parenting, popular science, personal travel memoirs.

Miranda Sherwin, Assistant Editor
Literary and commercial fiction. Nonfiction: personal travel memoirs, feminist/women's issues, current affairs. Not interested in popular self-help books.

VILLARD BOOKS
(division of Random House)
201 East 50th Street
New York, NY 10022
212-751-2600

Acquisitions contacts and areas of interest

Alison Acker, Editor
Fiction: mysteries, suspense, serious literary. Nonfiction: popular psychology, illustrated lifestyle, home care and gardening, general self-help.

Amy Bestler, Assistant Editor
General commercial fiction and nonfiction, especially in the self-help areas.

Peter Gethers, Editorial Director
Many interests, especially commercial fiction and nonfiction sports books.

Diane Reverand, Executive Editor
Nonfiction: parenting, child care, new age philosophy, metaphysics. Commercial and serious literary fiction.

RAWSON ASSOCIATES
(division of the Macmillan Publishing Group)
866 Third Avenue
New York, NY 10022
212-702-2000

Rawson Associates is a division of the Macmillan Publishing Group. When Rawson & Wade separated in 1981, Rawson joined Scribner Book Companies, which was acquired by Macmillan in 1984. Rawson is a nonfiction division, specializing in self-help, psychology, health, and lifestyle books. Titles include *Eat to Win* and *Letitia Baldridge's Complete Guide to a Great Social Life*.

The acquisitions contact is

Eleanor S. Rawson, Vice Chairperson.

FLEMING H. REVELL COMPANY
184 Central Avenue
Old Tappan, NJ 07675
201-768-8060

Revell, a subsidiary of Guideposts, Inc., is a religious publisher whose trade division, Wynwood Press, also publishes nonreligious personal-growth books. Among Revell's nonfiction titles are *Growing up with Your Teenager* and other parenting books; devotional guides; Gospel and Bible studies, such as *Notes on the Psalms;* and *Dare to Date Differently* and other books for young adults. Revell also publishes inspirational poetry and fiction, such as Grace Livingston Hill's Christian romance series.

The acquisitions contact is

Gary A. Sledge, Vice President and Editor.

RODALE PRESS, INC.
33 East Minor Street
Emmaus, PA 18049
215-967-5171

Rodale, which publishes *Prevention* and *Organic Gardening* magazines, specializes in health and gardening titles, such as *Positive Living and Health* and *The Square-Foot Garden*. Other areas of interest are psychology and self-help. The Good Spirit Press, its recently added mind/body imprint, has published *Alone, Live and Well, Climbing Toward the Light,* and *Making Miracles*. Rodale's books are distributed to the trade by St. Martin's Press and are also sold through direct mail.

Acquisitions contacts and areas of interest

Maggie Belitis, Editor
How-to crafts, hobbies.

Sharon Faelton, Editor
Health maintenance: avoiding and overcoming specific diseases.

Charles Gerras, Senior Editor
Popular psychology, spirituality, inspiration, sociology, healthful diets.

Bill Hylton, Editor
Woodworking, home repairs, building.

Deborah Tkac, Editor
Foods, nutrition, vitamins, diet supplements, general health advice.

ST. MARTIN'S PRESS, INC.

175 Fifth Avenue
New York, NY 10010
212-674-5151

Twenty years ago St. Martin's Press was a subsidiary of Macmillan Publishing, Ltd., U.K. (no connection with the U.S. firm of the same name), a small house of British imports and academic titles. But under the leadership of Tom McCormack, SMP has become one of the top ten New York houses. Today, it is known for an eclectic and very large list of books, including such best-sellers as *Silence of the Lambs, The Shell Seekers,* all the James Herriot titles, and *And the Band Played On*. In addition to best-selling fiction and nonfiction titles, SMP has several specialties, including mysteries and historical fiction, books on gay topics (Stonewall Editions), travel books, and celebrity biographies. St. Martin's Press has recently jumped into the highly competitive mass market area with great success. In addition, its Academy Editions imprint produces art and architecture books, and Scholarly Books publishes books on literature and the social sciences. (See also TOR Books.)

Acquisitions contacts and areas of interest

Barbara Anderson, Senior Editor
General nonfiction, including parenting, crafts, sewing and quilting, general how-to/self-help, popular psychology.

Ruth Cavin, Senior Editor
Fiction: mysteries, suspense, espionage. No science fiction or romance. Nonfiction: eclectic interests, especially popular science. Does not like self-help, how-to, or relationships books.

Hope Dellon, Senior Editor
Fiction: mysteries, romances.

Michael Denneny, Senior Editor
Gay interests; fiction mysteries; literary and historical biographies.

Thomas L. Dunne, Executive Editor (own imprint)
Wide range of fiction and nonfiction titles.

Kermit Hummel, Director, Scholarly and Reference Books
Nonfiction: social sciences and humanities, primarily for the academic and library market.

Jared Kieling, Senior Editor
Nonfiction: war and military-related subjects, psychology, health, general business, history and politics, investigative journalism, science and technology. Fiction: crime, suspense, espionage, technothrillers.

Ms. Toni Lopopolo, Executive Editor
Feminist books, biographies about women, diet books.

Maureen O'Neal, Associate Publisher, Mass market Division
Primarily mass market reprints.

Michael Sagalyn, Senior Editor
Fiction: serious/literary, espionage and military. Nonfiction: history, politics, current events, general business, popular science, Judaica.

Charles Spicer, Editor
Mysteries and suspense novels.

George Witte, Editor
Fiction: mysteries, mainstream fiction with Southern settings, first-time young novelists, thrillers, war stories. Nonfiction: sports, literary biographies, current events, investment guides, popular business, law-related subjects.

SCHOLASTIC, INC.
730 Broadway
New York, NY 10003
212-505-3000

Scholastic is one of the best-known publishers of children's general fiction and nonfiction titles, from *Clifford the Big Red Dog* for preschoolers through Walter Dean Myers's *Fallen Angels* for young adults. The Babysitters Club series offers fiction for children ages 8 through 12.

The acquisitions contact is

Regina Griffin, Senior Editor, Trade Group.

SCOTT, FORESMAN & COMPANY
1900 East Lake Avenue
Glenview, IL 60025
312-729-3000

Scott, Foresman, a subsidiary of Time, Inc., is the publisher of the well-known *Roberts' Rules of Order*. Its Professional Books Group produces computer and business books in management, investment, and finance. With the Association of

American Retired Persons, Scott, Foresman copublishes AARP Books, which are self-help and coping books for people aged 50 and above. Its professional and trade books are distributed by Little, Brown.

Acquisitions contacts and areas of interest

Amy Davis, Editor, Professional Publishing Group
Sales, marketing, management and general business self-help books, computer and software applications, user directories.

Ms. Jean Lesher, Editor
How-to and self-help books for people over the age of 50, primarily for the American Association of Retired Persons (AARP) imprint.

SHAMBHALA PUBLICATIONS, INC.
Horticultural Hall
300 Massachusetts Avenue
Boston, MA 02115
617-424-0030

Shambhala, one of the original publishers of new age books, is interested in titles in philosophy, psychology, religion, art, literature, and cultural studies. Recent titles range from *Secret Doctrines of the Tibetan Books of the Dead* to *Dreaming with an AIDS Patient.* Shambhala Dragon Editions publishes the sacred teachings of Asian masters; the New Science Library produces new age science titles; and Shambhala copublishes C. G. Jung Foundation Books with the C. G. Jung Foundation for Analytical Psychology.

The acquisitions contact is

Gary Doore, Editor
Holistic health, Eastern spiritual traditions, consciousness research, mysticism, deep ecology, environmental problems, psychology, shamanism, men's studies, sexuality, creativity, and the arts.

SHAPOLSKY PUBLISHERS, INC.
136 West 22nd Street
New York, NY 10011
212-505-2505

Founded in 1987, Shapolsky is a young company that publishes general-interest nonfiction. It has a strong Judaica line, as well as self-help, business, biography, and art titles. Shapolsky's *Contract on America,* a book about the JFK assassination conspiracy, was a best-seller.

The acquisitions contact is
Ian Shapolsky, Publisher.

SIERRA CLUB BOOKS
730 Polk Street
San Francisco, CA 94109
415-776-2211

The Sierra Club, which will celebrate its centennial in 1992, publishes books on nature, outdoor activities, mountaineering, health, gardening, and environmental issues. Recent titles include *Global Warming* by Stephen H. Schneider and *Whatever Happened to Ecology?* by Stephanie Mills. The Adventure Travel Guides, Naturalist's Guides, and Guides to the Natural Areas of the United States are among its series. Sierra Club Books for Children and Young Readers are copublished with Little, Brown.

The acquisitions contact is
Daniel Moses, Editorial Director.

SILHOUETTE BOOKS
300 East 42nd Street
New York, NY 10017
212-682-6080

Silhouette, owned by Harlequin Enterprises, has several romance lines, each with its own personality and set of writer's guidelines. Silhouette Romances, which describe sex only within marriage, emphasize the emotional complications of love. Silhouette Desires, in which sex takes place in serious committed relationships before marriage, stress the development of love. Silhouette Special Editions are sophisticated and modern, with steamier sex and a sharper focus on the characters. Silhouette Intimate Moments combine romance with other brands of mainstream fiction: adventure, suspense, melodrama, or even current issues such as surrogate motherhood. Silhouette Books are distributed by Simon & Schuster.

The acquisitions contact is

Karen Solem, Vice President and Editorial Director.

SIMON & SCHUSTER
1230 Avenue of the Americas
New York, NY 10020
212-698-7000

Acquired by Gulf + Western, Inc. in 1975 and the acquirer of Prentice-Hall in 1984, Simon & Schuster is a sprawling network of divisions, imprints, and groups, including Books for Young Readers. Simon & Schuster's trade division, encompasses Fireside, Poseidon, Touchstone, and Summit. Among its authors are Graham Greene and Larry McMurtry.

Acquisitions contacts and areas of interest

Maria Arana-Ward, Vice President and Senior Editor
Fiction: commercial hardcover, especially espionage themes. Nonfiction: general interests, especially general history; biography; true crime; popular science; public policy matters. Is not strong with business and lifestyle books.

Robert Asahina, Senior Editor

Social sciences, current issues, politics, history, biographies, CIA stories. No self-help or how-to categories.

Robert Bender, Vice President and Senior Editor
Nonfiction: many areas, including literary biography, health, popular psychology, natural history. No new age, music, or celebrity stories.

Fred Hills, Vice President and Senior Editor
Business-oriented titles.

Carol Lalli, Editor
Cooking, food, and wine books; investigative reporting; clinical child development. No politics or science.

Patricia Lande, Senior Editor
Female-oriented commercial fiction and mysteries.

Alan Mayer, Senior Editor
Primarily nonfiction: current affairs; politics; contemporary history; Hollywood and celebrity autobiographies, biographies, stories; gossip books.

Alice E. Mayhew, Vice President and Executive Editor
Politics, government, current affairs, memoirs; autobiographies and biographies relevant to the above.

Jeff Newman, Senior Editor
Sports-related titles.

Judith Regan, Editor-at-Large
Fiction: female-oriented themes, historical romances. Nonfiction: celebrity-oriented biographies and autobiographies, popular culture.

Alan Peacock, Senior Editor
Serious literary original fiction.

Laura Yorke, Editor
Serious literary fiction. Nonfiction: popular psychology, sociology, anthropology, travel.

SUMMIT BOOKS
(division of Simon & Schuster)

Acquisitions contacts and areas of interest

Dominic V. Anfuso, Senior Editor
Serious literary fiction. Nonfiction: politics, current events, recent history, biography.

Ileene Smith, Senior Editor
Nonfiction: classical music and musicians, psychology, human behavior, Judaica. Serious literary fiction.

FIRESIDE BOOKS
(division of Simon & Schuster)

Acquisitions contacts and areas of interest

Malaika Adero, Editor
Fiction: mostly reprints in quality paperback or originals with literary sociopolitical themes. Nonfiction: movie and TV tie-ins, film and moviemaking, African-American issues, health-oriented books, addiction, human sexuality, healthful cookbooks, popular business and careers.

Barbara Gess, Senior Editor
Popular new age, astrology and occult, cookbooks.

Cynthia Lao, Acquisitions Editor
Nonfiction: women's issues, relationships, travel, entertainment/leisure time.

Ms. Sydny W. Miner, Executive Editor
Parenting, family relations, child care, cookbooks.

Ed Walters, Editor
General popular how-to/self-help, medical and health, business basics, humor and cartoons, sports.

SOHO PRESS, INC.
One Union Square
New York, NY 10003
212-243-1527

Soho began publishing in the spring of 1987. It produces mainly fiction (largely suspense, plus some poetry and short stories) and some nonfiction (travel and autobiography, such as *O Come Ye Back to Ireland* and *Funny Business: An Outsider's Year in Japan*). Fiction authors include Jim Cirni, Maria Thomas, John Westerman, and Margaret Diehl. Soho's books are distributed by Farrar, Straus & Giroux.

The Acquisitions contacts are Laura Hruska, Associate Publisher, and Mr. Juris Jurjevics, Publisher.

THE SPORTING NEWS PUBLISHING COMPANY
1212 N. Lindbergh Boulevard
St. Louis, MO 63132
314-997-7111

Although this publisher specializes in sports statistics, some of its titles are by or about professional athletes; for example, *Strikeout* by Denny McLain and *Countdown to Cobb* by Pete Rose. Recent books have been on coaching and playing football and basketball.

The acquisitions contact is

Ron Smith, Director of Books and Periodicals.

STACKPOLE BOOKS
P.O. Box 1831
Harrisburg, PA 17105
717-234-5041

Stackpole, which publishes no fiction or juvenile titles, specializes in nature and outdoor books. These range from hunting and fishing to carving and woodworking how-tos, as well as guidebooks for amateur naturalists. Representative titles include *Fly Fishing in Small Streams, Wildlife Woodcarvers,* and

A Treasure of Outdoor Life. Stackpole's list is rounded out by cookbooks, history, military history, and guides for military officers. It handles its own distribution.

Acquisitions contacts and areas of interest

Sally Atwater, Editor
Gardening, outdoor sports, adventure, Alaska.

Judith Schnell, Editorial Director and Acquisitions Director
Entire range of list.

Judith Stolz, Associate Editor
Hunting.

Mary Suggs, Editor
Military books.

Stackpole anticipates the addition of an editor with a special interest in fly fishing books.

TAB BOOKS, INC.
Blue Ridge Summit, PA 17214
717-794-2191

TAB's eclectic line of nonfiction is represented by an array of recent titles: *Why Employees Do What They're Supposed to Do, Making Potpourri, Colognes and Soap,* and *Basic Electronics Theory.* Art and design books are published under the Design Press imprint; the International Marine Books imprint published *Bligh: A Chronicle of Mutiny Aboard His Majesty's Ship Bounty;* and the recently formed Wincrest imprint publishes an expanded computer book list. TAB and the Human Services Institute jointly publish books on substance abuse and recovery.

Acquisition contacts and areas of interest

David Conti, Editor
Business: trade and professional.

Jon Eaton, Editor

International Marine Books Series.

Nancy Green, Editor
Graphic design, graphic arts, architecture.

Stephen Fitzgerald, Editor
Electrical, mechanical, and civil engineering.

Larry Hager, Editor
Electrical, mechanical, and civil engineering.

Stephen Moore, Editor
Computer books.

Roland Phelps, Editor
Electronics, adult-level science.

Ron Powers, Editor
Computer books.

Kim Tabor, Editor
How-to, arts and crafts, general (el-hi) science, Human Services
Institute series.

Jeff Worslinger, Editor
Aviation, hobbies.

JEREMY P. TARCHER, INC.
5858 Wilshire Boulevard, Suite 200
Los Angeles, CA 90036
213-935-9980

Tarcher publishes mainly nonfiction and a few philosophical science fiction titles. Among its categories are personal
transformation, social transformation, creativity, health, nutrition, cooking, travel, and innovative business. *Sex in the For-
bidden Zone: When Therapists, Doctors, Clergy, Teachers and
Other Men in Power Betray Woman's Trust; The Memory Habit;
Your Mythic Journey* are titles from Tarcher's recent list. *Open
Secrets: A Guide to Tibetan Buddhism for Western Seekers* is a
part of the Library of Spiritual Classics series. Among its best-
sellers are *Drawing with the Right Side of the Brain,* and *Women*

Who Love Too Much. Tarcher titles are distributed by St. Martin's Press.

Acquisitions contacts and areas of interest

Rick Benzell, Editor
Humanistic business books regarding ethics and social policy, organizational behavior and interpersonal relations, creative learning and peak performance.

Dan Joy, Editor
Eastern philosophy and mysticism; humanistic business titles.

Ms. Connie Zweig, Editor
Spirituality, Eastern philosophy, female-oriented psychology, health, human sexuality, science, human behavior, books for writers.

TEN SPEED PRESS
P.O. Box 7123
Berkeley, CA 94707
415-845-8414

Ten Speed's most lucrative titles are *What Color Is Your Parachute* and *The Moosewood Cookbook.* They publish an extensive mix of career, health, and what can only be termed off-beat titles, such as *White Trash Cooking.* Ten Speed's first title, *Anybody's Bike Book,* continues to sell well and is an example of the general reference style that the press has become well known for. They are one of the most successful and respected independent presses in the business.

Submissions can be made to

Philip Wood, President and Editorial Director,
or
George Young, Editor-in-Chief.

TEXAS MONTHLY PRESS
P.O. Box 1569
Austin, TX 78767
512-476-7085

Texas Monthly Press, a subsidiary of Mediatex Communications, publishes general trade titles, in addition to some regional Texas and Southwest field and travel guides. It also produces true crime stories, some children's books for ages 9 and up, and one or two fiction titles a year.

The acquisitions contact is
Cathy Casey Hale, Director.

THAMES & HUDSON
500 Fifth Avenue
New York, NY 10110
212-354-3763

Thames & Hudson is an independent company that shares space with its distributor, W. W. Norton. It publishes fine art books in a wide range of subjects, genres, and media, ranging from photography to crafts, from ancient Greek art to Postmodernism. *Hockney Etchings and Lithographs, A Guide to Making Decorated Papers, Opera in Crisis,* and *Mummies, Myth and Magic* are some recent titles. Thames & Hudson books, although highly illustrated, generally contain a fair amount of text.

The acquisitions contact is
Peter Warner, President.

THUNDER'S MOUTH PRESS, INC.
93-99 Greene Street, #2A
New York, NY 10012
212-226-0277

Since its inception in 1980, Thunder's Mouth has been a publisher of literary and avant-garde fiction, quality non-fiction, poetry, and African-American fiction and theater. Books include a biography of Martin Scorsese, a history of the Merry

Pranksters and the 1960s, and poetry by Jayne Cortez and June Jordan. It also publishes Harry Dumas, Hubert Selby, Nelson Algren, and John A. Williams. Thunder's Mouth titles are distributed by Consortium Book Sales and Distribution.

The acquisitions contact is

Neil Ortenberg, Senior Editor and Publisher.

TICKNOR & FIELDS
(division of Houghton Mifflin)
1 Beacon Street
Boston, MA 02108
617-725-5000

TOR BOOKS
49 West 24th Street, 9th Floor
New York, NY 10010
212-741-3100

TOR Books, a wholly owned subsidiary of St. Martin's Press, specializes in category publishing: science fiction and fantasy, horror, mystery and suspense, and fiction. Among its recent titles are Paul Anderson's *The Boat of a Million Years,* Mark E. Rogers's *Samurai Cat in the Real World,* and Stephen Gallagher's *The Oktober Project.* It expanded into historical fiction with *High Freedom.* TOR also publishes the Just Say No series for young readers, as well as young adult classics and special activity books under the Aerie imprint.

The acquisitions contact is

Beth Meacham, Editor-in-Chief.

UNIVERSE BOOKS
381 Park Avenue South
New York, New York 10016
212-685-7400

Universe Books is primarily a fine arts publisher, producing hardcover and paperback books in the visual arts and art history. *Van Gogh's Flowers* and *The Pioneering Image* are two representative titles. The History of Art and Architecture series, written by academics in the field, is more textually oriented than most of its titles. Universe also produces graphic and fine arts products such as address books, generally in conjunction with museums. Its books are distributed by St. Martin's Press.

Send manuscripts to Adele Ursone, Senior Editor.

UNIVERSITY OF CALIFORNIA PRESS
2120 Berkeley Way
Berkeley, CA 94720
415-642-4247

The University of California Press is strong in classics, Asian studies, humanities, and the arts. About one-quarter of its list can be classified as trade, in areas ranging from Latin American studies to regional books such as the California Natural History Guides series. Its science titles, rather than being scholarly texts, tend to be for the general reader.

Acquisitions contacts and areas of interest

Ernest Callenbach, Editor
Film.

Jim Clark, Director
History, history of science, Japanese studies.

Alain Henon, Editor
Intellectual history.

Deborah Kretschmer, Editor

Literary criticism.

Mary Lamprech, Editor
Classics.

Sheila Levine, Editor
Asian studies, women's history, Slavic studies, French history.

William McClung, Editor
Humanities.

Naomi Schneider, Editor
Social sciences.

Los Angeles office:
405 Hilgard Avenue
Los Angeles, CA 90024
213-825-3018

Acquisitions contacts and areas of interest

Stan Holwitz, Editor
Anthropology, Judaica, history.

Elizabeth Knoll, Editor
Science.

Scott Mahler, Editor
Latin American studies, poetry in translation, contemporary art.

UNIVERSITY OF CHICAGO PRESS
5801 Ellis Avenue
Chicago, IL 60637
312-702-7700

University of Chicago Press, publisher of *The Chicago Manual of Style,* is primarily a scholarly house. Areas of interest include Japanese studies, women's studies, natural science, economics, linguistics, and critical theory. University of Chicago Press is also venturing into cognitive science titles (linguistics/computer science) and books that are directed to a more general audience, such as literary works and books on public policy.

Acquisitions contacts and areas of interest

Susan Abrams, Editor
Biological science, history of science.

T. David Brent, Editor
Anthropology, philosophy, psychology.

Gabriel Dotto, Editor
Music.

Geoffrey Huck, Editor
Economics, linguistics.

Douglas Mitchell, Editor
Sociology, history.

Alan Thomas, Editor
Literary criticism and theory, religious studies.

John Tryneski, Editor
Political science, law, education, geography.

Mary Wallace, Editor
Art; architecture, classics, women's studies.

UNIVERSITY OF OKLAHOMA PRESS

1005 Asp Avenue
Norman, OK 73019
405-325-5111

University of Oklahoma Press specializes in the history of the American West and regional topics. It produces an American Indian series, a Western biography series, historical atlases of the American West, and a series on ghost towns. Representative titles include *Hoover Dam, Route 66: The Highway and Its People,* and a biography of General Custer entitled *Cavalier in Buckskin.* University of Oklahoma Press aims for the general reader and is moving into literature and criticism with its Discourse and Theory series.

Acquisitions contacts and areas of interest

John N. Drayton, Managing Editor and Acquisitions Editor
Western history.

Thomas Radko, Acquisitions Editor
Literary criticism, classics.

UNIVERSITY PRESS OF AMERICA
4720 Boston Way
Lanham, MD 20706
301-459-3366

University Press of America is a scholarly and trade publishing group that produces monographs, textbooks, reference books, and trade titles in the humanities and social sciences. Under the UPA umbrella are Rowman & Littlefield, which specializes in scholarly social science books; Barnes & Noble Books, which copublishes with numerous British academic presses; and the trade division of Madison Books, Inc., which publishes current events, biography, history, and popular culture.

Acquisitions contact and areas of interest

James E. Lyons, Publisher
Academic books.

MADISON BOOKS
(division of University Press of America)

The acquisitions contact is

Charles Lane, Associate Publisher.

WALKER & COMPANY
720 Fifth Avenue
New York, NY 10019
212-265-3632

Walker & Company, founded in 1959, publishes mysteries, many of which are first novels; romances; Regency romances; Westerns, usually by established writers; and adventure novels. Nonfiction areas include science, self-help, business, travel, and marriage and family. Walker also publishes preschool picture books to books for young adults in its juvenile line.

Acquisitions contacts and areas of interest

Will Thorndike, Editor
General fiction and nonfiction.

Janet Hutchings, Editor
Fiction: mysteries.

Peter Rubie, Editor
Fiction: adventure, thrillers.

Mary Elizabeth Allen, Editor
Fiction: romances.

Amy Shields, Editor
Childrens books.

Jacqueline Johnson, Editor
Westerns.

Beth Walker, Editor
Large-print inspirational titles.

WARNER BOOKS, INC.
(subsidiary of Warner Publishing, Inc.)
666 Fifth Avenue
New York, NY 10103
212-484-2900

Part of the recently formed Warner Communications network, Warner Books publishes commercial fiction and non-fiction in mass market, quality paper, and hardcover original. Recent fiction titles include Andrew M. Greeley's *St. Valentine's Night,* Lynn V. Andrews's *Windhorse Woman,* and Sarah

Gilbert's debut novel *Hairdo*. Warner produces nonfiction in self-help, biography and autobiography, business *(Leadership Secrets of Atilla the Hun)*, sports, history, and current affairs. Warner Juvenile publishes fiction and nonfiction, mainly for preschoolers but with some books for young adults.

Acquisitions contacts and areas of interest

Charles Conrad, Editor
Fiction: thrillers, Westerns, men's adventure, mysteries. Nonfiction: military history, Vietnam history, general popular business, health, popular psychology.

Joanne Davis, Executive Editor
Nonfiction: all commercial popular self-help and how-to categories, including spirituality and new age.

Jim Frost, Vice President and Executive Editor, Hardcover Division
Business stories and commercial how-to.

Rick Horgan, Senior Editor
Fiction: suspense, thrillers, horror. Nonfiction: true crime, popular business, sports, popular culture, humor.

Ms. Leslie Keenan, Senior Editor
Nonfiction: new age, metaphysical, and spirituality books.

Beth Lieberman, Editor
Primarily fiction: mass market originals and reprints, some hardcover originals, women's commercial themes. Occasional nonfiction: education, popular psychology. No health or beauty books.

Alan Mahoney, Associate Editor
Fiction: science fiction and fantasy. Nonfiction: popular psychology, self-help, popular culture, film, TV, and theater.

Ms. Jamie Raab, Senior Editor
Fiction: contemporary women's themes. Nonfiction: popular culture, health-related books.

Brian Thomsen, Senior Editor

Fiction: mass market horror, science fiction and fantasy, cops and robbers. Nonfiction: violent true crime.

Jeanne Tiedge, Executive Editor, Popular Library
Fiction: hardcover, mass market originals and reprints; mysteries; general romance; women's themes; suspense and thrillers.

WARREN, GORHAM & LAMONT
1 Penn Plaza
New York, NY 10019
212-971-5000

Warren, Gorham & Lamont, which was acquired by the International Thompson Organization in 1980, is a specialist in professional books on banking, business, and real estate. Some representative titles are *Federal Banking Laws, Handbook for Business Strategy, Condominium Development Guide,* and *Estate Planning Law and Taxation.* Other categories include accounting, data processing, and engineering. Warren, Gorham & Lamont also publishes journals and newsletters in each of the above categories.

Acquisitions contacts and areas of interest

Alvin Arnold, Vice President
Real estate–oriented professional reference books.

John Boyd, Vice President, Business Publishing
Professional reference books for general business, law, and accounting.

SAMUEL WEISER, INC.
Box 612
York Beach, ME 03910
207-363-4393

Samuel Weiser, which began in 1956 in the back of a bookstore, specializes in oriental philosophy, with titles in meditation, metaphysics, alternative healing methods, magic, astrology, and astral projection, among others. Weiser publishes serious works by teachers and experts, with an emphasis on instructional books. *The Rays and Esoteric Psychology* and *Life Challenge Astrology* are among its recent titles.

Weiser buys only completed manuscripts, not proposals. Manuscripts should be double-spaced and single-sided; pages must be separated if printed on form-fed paper. Manuscripts should be boxed, not bound. Simultaneous submissions are unacceptable. Plan on two to three months for evaluation. Weiser may recommend another publisher if the manuscript is not right for its list.

The acquisitions contact is

Susan Smithe, Acquisitions Editor.

WESTMINSTER/JOHN KNOX PRESS
100 Witherspoon Street
Louisville, KY 40202
502-569-5000

The reunion of the Northern and Southern Presbyterian churches in the early 1980s resulted in the merger of their publishing houses at the end of the decade. Westminster/John Knox publishes scholarly books on theology, philosophy, pastoral counseling, and archeology, as well as books in these areas for general audiences. No children's books are currently produced. Past titles include *Westminster Dictionary of Church History,* the Interpretation series of Bible commentary, and the Environmental Theology series.

Acquisitions contact Davis Perkins, Editorial Director.

JOHN WILEY & SONS
605 Third Avenue
New York, NY 10156
212-850-6000

Founded in 1807, John Wiley & Sons publishes college textbooks, professional reference books, journals, and trade books in general business and business law. Areas of interest include computer/software, management, advertising and marketing, finance and accounting, and real estate. Wiley also publishes career, travel, science, and math books, and serious health and psychology books for the general reader.

Acquisitions contacts and areas of interest

Wendy Grau, Associate Editor
Investing, banking, finance.

Mike Hamilton, Editor
Career, real estate, small business and entrepreneurship, management.

Gwenyth Jones, Publisher
Marketing strategies.

John Mahaney, Editor
General Business and management, international business.

Steve Ross, Editor
Small business, careers, travel, tourism, personal finance, marketing, public relations.

Roger Scholl, Senior Editor
Popular science, 20th-century U.S. history, topical current events, business biographies.

Katherine Scholwalter, Executive Editor
Computer books.

David Sobel, Editor
Popular science, psychology.

Karl Weber, Editor
Finance and investing, consulting; banking.

Ms. Teri Zak, Editor
Computer books.

WILLIAMSON PUBLISHING COMPANY
Church Hill Road
Charlotte, VT 05445
805-425-2102

Williamson, which started in 1983 with its Success in Living series, publishes guides such as *Keeping Bees* and *Raising Poultry;* cookbooks and travel books; and parenting and education books, such as *Parents Are Teachers Too, Doing Children's Museums,* and *Public Schools USA.* Williamson publishes quality trade paperbacks exclusively.

The acquisitions contact is

Jack Williamson, Publisher.

WORD, INC.
5221 North O'Connor Boulevard, #1000
Irving, TX 75039
214-556-1900

An ABC/Capital Cities company, Word is a Christian publisher of inspirational, self-help, academic, and professional titles. Among its authors is Billy Graham. It offers preschool through young adult children's books, as well as Christian audiocassettes and music tapes.

The acquisitions contact is

Jim Nelson Black, Acquisitions Editor.
It's best, however, to write to Word first, who will send complete guidelines and stylistic rules.

WORKMAN PUBLISHING COMPANY
708 Broadway
New York, NY 10003
212-254-5900

Workman primarily publishes a variety of paperback nonfiction. With the 1988 acquisition of Algonquin Books of Chapel Hill (see separate listing) it has also become involved in fine fiction. Food and cooking, health, parenting, general reference, and humor are among its nonfiction categories, with titles such as *The Silver Palate Cookbook, What to Expect When You're Expecting, The Book of Questions,* and *The Preppy Handbook.* Workman has begun doing more children's titles, *The Bug Book and the Bug Bottle,* for example, and is well known for its calendars.

Acquisitions contacts and areas of interest

Sally Kovalchick, Editor
Humor; quirky popular science and history.

Ms. Carol McKeown, Editor
Americana; unique, family-oriented travel guides; humor; unusual cookbooks; social and environmental issues; general how-to.

Susan Rafer, Editor
Cookbooks, humor, family and children's activity books.

WRITER'S DIGEST BOOKS
(division of F&W Publications)
1507 Dana Avenue
Cincinnati, OH 45207
513-531-2222

Writer's Digest Books, which is a subsidiary of F&W Publications, produces guides and how-to books for writers in all genres: *Handbook of Short Story Writing, Fiction Writer's Market, Complete Book of Scriptwriting, Basic Magazine Writing, Poet's Market.* Additional titles are geared for writers of comedy, horror, mystery, and juvenile books, as well as titles such as *Writer's Block and How to Use It* for any brand of writer. Writer's Digest Books has also published several Don Aslett books including *Clutter's Last Stand* and *Is There Life After Housework?*

Acquisitions contacts and areas of interest

Ms. Jean Fredette, Editor
How-to books for writers.

Mr. B. Leslie Koch, Editorial Director
Desktop publishing.

Dianna Martin, Editor
How-to books for artists.

Kathleen Friel, Editor
How-to books for artists.

Judy Whaley, Editor
How-to books for musicians.

WYNWOOD PRESS

(Revell trade division)
264 Fifth Avenue
New York, NY 10001
212-889-4110

The acquisitions contact is

Bill Thompson, Editor-in-Chief
Primarily general nonfiction: biographies, history, business and management. Fiction: mostly mysteries.

YALE UNIVERSITY PRESS

302 Temple Street
New Haven, CT 06520
203-432-0960

Yale University Press, established in 1908, publishes scholarly books in the humanities, sciences, and social sciences. Areas of particular strength and interest are history, literary studies, political science, and art history. Yale sponsors the annual Yale Younger Poets Competition; the winning manuscript is published by the press. Its series include Composers of the Twentieth Century and Early Chinese Civilization. Yale handles its own distribution.

Acquisitions contacts and areas of interest

John Covell, Editor
Law, political science, economics.

Jeanne Ferris, Editor
Philosophy, archeology, music, primatology, psychology.

Mary Alice Galligan, Editor
Editions series.

Ellen Graham, Editor
Anthropology, classics, languages, literature.

Charles Grench, Executive Editor
History, Judaic studies, women's studies, religion.

Judy Metro, Editor
Art, art history, architecture and history of architecture, geography, landscape studies.

Gladys Topkis, Editor
Education, psychiatry, psychoanalysis.

Edward Tripp, Editor
Theater, science, reference books.

ZEBRA BOOKS
475 Park Avenue South
New York, NY 10016
212-889-2299

Zebra and Pinnacle Books, its 1987 acquisition, publish category fiction—historical romance, espionage, action/adventure, westerns, science fiction—as well as some humor, self-help, and autobiography titles. For representative historical romance, see the novels of Jeannelle Taylor and Sylvia Summerfield. For horror, see Ruby Jean Jenson, Rick Hautala, and William Johnstone. Zebra's books are distributed by Simon & Schuster.

Acquisitions contacts and areas of interest

Carin Cohen, Editor
Mass market romance line.

Wallace Exman, Editor
Men's action adventure and Westerns.

Wendy C. McCurdy, Editor
Mass market horror, suspense, and mysteries.

Michael Seidman, Editorial Director
Acquires in all above areas, including some nonfiction in paper and hardcover, especially Vietnam-oriented subjects.

ZONDERVAN PUBLISHING

1415 Lake Drive SE
Grand Rapids, MI 49506
616-698-6900

Zondervan, which publishes a variety of titles for evangelical Christian readers, has been a division of Harper & Row since 1988, which introduces its books to a broader readership. Topics include marriage and parenting, with such titles as *Love Life for Every Married Couple* and *Help Your Child Say No to Drugs*. It also produces books for writers, such as *Creative Writing for Those Who Can't Write* and *A Christian Writer's Manual of Style*. Zondervan publishes fiction that has a basis in Christian morals, as well as inspirational romance.

Acquisitions contacts and areas of interest

Joseph P. Allison, General Manager
Trade books.

Stan Gundry, Publisher
Academic and professional books.

Bob Hudson, Editor
General fiction.

David Lamser, Editor

Youth books.

Bruce E. Ryskamp, Vice President
Bibles.

Canadian Publishers and Editors

Special note on Canadian publishers: Most of these publishers have a special interest in Canadian subjects. Common sense will tell you that some titles—a book on U.S. tax law, for example—are not appropriate for the market north of the border. Furthermore, Canadian publishers receive subsidies for *Canadian* authors they publish from the Canadian Council to encourage the further development of Canada's national literature.

DOUBLEDAY CANADA, LTD.
105 Bond Street
Toronto, ON M5B 1Y3
416-977-7891

Doubleday Canada has a broad list that encompasses commercial and literary fiction, children's titles, and a range of nonfiction categories including politics, history, autobiography, current affairs, arts, sports, travel, and cooking. Doubleday Canada has a strong Canadian orientation, and will continue to emphasize Canadian authors, but is seeking more international titles and subjects.

Please note that Bantam Canada is a sales and publicity office only. Under the Seal Books imprint, it does publish a broad range of fiction and nonfiction, primarily as paperback reprints.

Send manuscripts to John Pears, Editor-in-Chief.

DOUGLAS & MCINTYRE PUBLISHERS
1615 Venables Street
Vancouver, BC V5L 2H1
604-254-7191

Douglas & McIntyre publishes fiction and nonfiction hardcover and paperback books with a Canadian—and often a British Columbian—emphasis. Their areas of interest in nonfiction include native art, history, and nature studies. Recent titles include *Caves in the Desert* by George Woodcock, *Wolves* by Candace Savage, and the novel *Midnight Twilight Tourist* by Sharon Reese. Douglas & McIntyre's Groundwood Press imprint publishes titles for preschoolers through young adults.

Send manuscripts to Saeko Usukawa, Senior Editor, or Barbara Pulling, Editor.

FITZHENRY & WHITESIDE, LTD.
195 Allstate Parkway
Markham, ON L3R 4T8
416-477-0030

Fitzhenry & Whiteside, which has a sizeable textbook list, specializes in nonfiction trade books. Its titles range from *The Monthly Epic: A History of Canadian Magazines* to *Ontario's Architecture*. Other areas of interest include biography, gardening, art, nature, and collectibles and antiques. Fitzhenry & Whiteside also publishes books for preschoolers and young schoolchildren.

Send manuscripts to Robert Fitzhenry, President (adult trade), or Sharon Fitzhenry, Children's Book Editor.

KEY PORTER BOOKS
70 The Esplanade
Toronto, ON M5E 1R2
416-862-7777

Key Porter, a publisher of nonfiction books with a Canadian orientation, produces titles in science and health, the environment, ecology, and politics, as well as coffee table picture books, sports books, entrepreneurial guides, and money books. Key Porter also publishes science books for children.

Send manuscripts to Phyllis Bruce, Editor-in-Chief, or Andrea Service, Assistant to the Editor-in-Chief (she actually screens all manuscripts).

LESTER & ORPEN DENNYS, LTD.

78 Sullivan Street
Toronto, ON M5T 1C1
416-593-9602

Lester & Orpen Dennys is a literary house that publishes modern fiction, literary biography, Judaica, and history. Recent titles include *The Struggle for Democracy, Chronological Atlas of World War Two, Leopard in the Afternoon,* the novel *Last of the Golden Girls,* and *The Illustrated History of Canada.* A children's version of this last title is one of the first books in its new juvenile division, which will also produce titles in fiction and science. Lester & Orpen Dennys books are distributed by Fitzhenry & Whiteside.

Acquisitions contacts and areas of interest

Louise Dennys, Publisher
All areas.

Malcolm Lester, President
All areas; a special interest in nonfiction and Judaica.

Kathy Lowinger, Editor
Children's books.

Catherine Yolles, General Acquisitions Editor
All areas.

MCCLELLAND & STEWART
481 University Avenue
Toronto, ON M5G 2E9
416-598-1114

Established in 1906, McClelland & Stewart, "the Canadian publisher," publishes literary fiction and nonfiction, as well as poetry, travel, history, and biography. They put special emphasis on Canadian topics. Recent titles include Margaret Atwood's *Cat's Eye,* Pierre Burton's *The Arctic Grail, The Green Consumer Guide,* and *Legacy,* an illustrated history of Ontario. Its juvenile list is small, consisting of several young adult titles and picture books. M&S, as they are known in the trade, has recently seen tremendous growth under the new ownership of entrepreneur Avie Bennet.
Send manuscripts to Linda Williams.

MCGILL-QUEEN'S UNIVERSITY PRESS
3430 McTavish Street
Montreal, PQ H3A 1X9
514-398-3750

McGill-Queens publishes academic titles and trade books with scholarly significance. Areas of interest include native studies, Canadian history, humanities, and social sciences—but no hard sciences. Although most of their titles are Canada-related, they do publish some European history and books on Latin America. Recent titles include *When Whalers Were up North,* an oral history of the Inuits, and *The Domestic Battleground: Canada and the Arab-Israeli Conflict.*

Acquisitions contacts and areas of interest
Donald Akinson, Editor
Canadian history and ethnic studies.
Peter Blaney, Acquisitions Editor

All areas.

Philip Cerconi, Director of Press & Acquisitions Editor
All areas

Peter Goheen, Editor
Canadian geography.

PENGUIN CANADA
2801 John Street
Markham, ON L3R 1B4
416-475-1571

Penguin Canada operates independently, although its list is similar to that of its American affiliate, Penguin USA. Penguin Canada's mandate is to publish Canadian authors, among them Robertson Davies and Peter C. Newman. Penguin Puffin and Viking Kestrel are its juvenile imprints. Penguin intends to publish more original hardcover mysteries; at present, it is the Canadian publisher of John LeCarre, P. D. James, and Stephen King.

Acquisitions contacts and areas of interest

Cynthia Good, Vice President and Editor-in-Chief
Mainly fiction, literary fiction, and mysteries.

Iris Skeoch, Executive Editor
Nonfiction: politics, biography, history, sports, sociology.

STODDARD PUBLISHING
34 Lesmill Road
Don Mills, ON M3B 2T6
416-445-3333

Stoddard Publishing is a division of General Publishing Company, a distribution house. It publishes a wide range of titles with a Canadian orientation. Subject areas include history, politics, biography, cooking, nutrition, business, and consumer information. Stoddard publishes some fiction, but nonfiction comprises the bulk of its list. Its children's books are for preschoolers through young adults.

Send manuscripts to Don Bastian, Senior Editor. Further inquiries may be addressed to Jack Stoddard, President.

UNIVERSITY OF BRITISH COLUMBIA PRESS
303-6344 Memorial Road
Vancouver, BC V6T 1W5
604-228-3259

This university press publishes academic books on Canadian subject matter. Recent titles include *Canadian Oceans Policy,* and *The White Man's Province,* which is a history of British Columbia. Other categories include political science; literary history and criticism; maritime, urban, and military studies; and, in the international areas, Asian studies and linguistics.

Dr. Jane Freedman, Senior Acquisitions Editor.

UNIVERSITY OF TORONTO PRESS
10 Saint Mary Street, Suite 700
Toronto, ON M4Y 2W8
416-978-2239

The University of Toronto Press, which produces no fiction or poetry, publishes books in Canadian studies, history, sociology, political science, science, literature and modern languages, women's studies, and music, among other fields. Representative titles include *Beyond the Vote: Canadian Women and Politics, Art History: Its Use and Abuse,* and *Atlantic Fishes of Canada.*

Acquisitions contacts and areas of interest

Joan Bulger, Editor
Art.

Virgil Duff, Managing Editor
Social sciences.

Gerald Hallowell, Editor
History and literature.

Ian Montagnes, Editor-in-Chief
All areas.

Ron Schoeffel, Senior Editor
Modern languages.

Kieran Simpson, Editor
Directories.

Prudence Tracy, Editor
Medieval studies.

WORLDWIDE LIBRARY
225 Duncan Mill Road
Don Mills, ON M3B 3K9
416-445-5860

Worldwide is a division of Harlequin Enterprises that publishes the Worldwide Mystery imprint, primarily reprints of soft-boiled mysteries, and Gold Eagle Books. The latter imprint produces a men's action/adventure series with paramilitary themes. The series includes *The Executioner, Able Team, Phoenix Force, Deathlands, Vietnam: Ground Zero,* and *Horn.* Gold Eagle also publishes *Super Books* for each series—longer novels with more fully-developed plots. Prospective authors should be familiar with the guidelines and regular characters associated with each series.

Send manuscripts to Mr. Feroze Mohammed, Senior Editor, Gold Eagle Books, or Randall Toye, Editorial Director, Gold Eagle–Worldwide Library.

Please note that Dianne Moggy, Editor of Worldwide Mystery, points out that she is not actively soliciting original mysteries at this time.

A P P E N D I X A

Literary Agent
Trade Associations

Unlike several other professions, such as law and
medicine, there are neither powerful centralized literary agent
organizations that require membership and speak for the industry as a whole nor any specific state or federal laws (to the best
of this author's knowledge) that in any way regulate this relatively small and specialized industry, other than usual common
law business practices and customs.

Anyone could put up a shingle and legally declare himself or
herself a literary agent, even without requisite background or
expertise. Therefore the buyer must beware. Chapter 3, An Introduction to Literary Agents, should serve as a useful primer
for both novices and veterans.

The industry does comprise two autonomous trade associations, the Independent Literary Agents Association and the Society of Authors' Representatives. A large number of practicing
agents belong to one or both of these groups. Neither group has
any policing or arbitrating powers, beyond controlling who is a
member.

The groups require members to attain certain performance
standards and not to violate stated rules of conduct. Agents who
have not achieved these standards are not granted membership,
and agents who are proven to have broken the rules can be
reprimanded or expelled from the group. Therefore membership
in either group does imply at least a minimal seal of respecta-
bility and good behavior. The groups' primary functions are to
serve as (1) networking communities, (2) information clearingh-

235

ouses, and (3) forums in which agents can act collectively regarding issues of importance to themselves and their clients.

This is not to imply that nonmembership is a black mark. Many excellent agents have simply chosen, for a variety of reasons, not to affiliate themselves with either group, though they are certainly qualified to be members.

Following are information and membership lists pertaining to both these groups.

Independent Literary Agents Association, Inc. (ILAA)
c/o Ellen Levine Literary Agency
432 Park Ave. S., #1205
NY, NY 10016

Founded in 1977, the ILAA is a nationwide trade association of more than 60 full-time literary agents who are located in New York, Boston, San Francisco, Washington, D.C., and other cities.

Through an active program of monthly meetings for members and special open seminars and forums, ILAA explores ways to improve author/publisher relations and cooperates with other literary agents' organizations on First Amendment matters and other issues of concern to the publishing industry.

Although most ILAA agents specialize in fiction and nonfiction trade books, members also work with textbooks; film, television, and play scripts; articles and short stories; poetry; and computer software.

BY LAWS OF INDEPENDENT LITERARY AGENTS ASSOCIATION, INC.

Agent Membership

Section 1. Qualifications for Agent Membership. Any person who is a literary agent and shall meet the criteria set forth in subparagraphs A through D shall be qualified to become an agent member of the Association.

(Printed with the permission of the ILAA.)

(A) A literary agent shall be deemed to be any person whose primary professional activity for the one year preceding application for membership in the Association has been an Author's representative for the selling of rights in and to Literary Works.

(B) A qualified literary agent shall have been the agent of record in connection with the contract or other appropriate document for the publication of ten (10) different literary properties in either hardbound or softbound editions during the 18-month period preceding application for membership. A single literary property published or contracted to be published in both hardbound and softbound editions shall be deemed to be one literary property for the purpose of this subparagraph.

(C) A qualified literary agent shall be one who shall meet the criteria set forth in subparagraphs A and B above and in addition shall be either (i) self-employed, or (ii) employed by an established literary agency.

(D) A qualified literary agent shall be one who shall meet the criteria set forth in subparagraphs A through C above and in addition shall conduct his or her business in such a manner as to avoid conflicts of interest in servicing his or her clients' professional needs.

(i) A qualified literary agent shall not permit his or her own business interests to be continually or frequently allied more closely with those of publishers or other purchasers of rights in and to literary properties than with those of the agent's author clients.

(ii) The agent shall not represent both buyer and seller in the same transaction unless both are notified prior to negotiations and either is offered the opportunity to select other representation for the transaction. The agent shall only receive compensation from one party to the transaction, and shall not receive compensation from purchasers of rights at the direct expense of agent's author clients.

(iii) The agent shall subscribe to all other canons of ethics and business practices as may be established by the Association during the full term of membership.

Section 2. Election of Agent Members.   A person may be elected as an agent member upon being nominated for membership by an agent member of this Association by written application to the Council. The nominee shall provide the Council a list of literary properties sold to the extent required by Section 1, subparagraph B above. The Council or its designee(s) shall review the application and obtain such further information as it may require to determine whether the proposed member shall meet the qualifications for agent membership. At the next scheduled Council meeting following the conclusion of the aforesaid review, if the Council or its designee(s) shall find that the proposed member meets the qualifications for agent membership, the Council shall vote to either (i) request that the proposed member furnish further information concerning his or her qualifications for agent membership or (ii) deny the application for agent membership or (iii) make such other ruling as may be fair and equitable under the circumstances. An applicant for membership in the Association who does not technically qualify for membership according to Section 1, but who, in the judgment of the Council, should be a member of the Association, may be accepted for membership if the application and supporting information be approved by a majority of the full Council. All votes for agent membership status, other than (iii) above, shall be decided by a majority vote of a quorum of the elected members of the Council. In the event that the Council cannot reach a majority decision in connection with the disposition of an agent's membership application after due diligence, the matter shall be put to vote by the entire agent membership at the next general membership meeting. At such membership meeting the proposed member shall be given an opportunity to address the general membership if the proposed member shall so request.

Section 3. Resignation.   Any member may withdraw from the Association after fulfilling all obligations to it by giving written notice of such intention to the Secretary, which notice shall be presented to the Council by the Secretary at the first meeting after its receipt.

Section 4. Suspension.   A member may be reprimanded, suspended for a period, or expelled for cause, such as violation of any of the Bylaws, Rules or Canons of ethics and business practices of the Association. Reprimand, suspension or expulsion shall be by two-thirds vote of a quorum of the Council, provided that a statement of the charges shall have been mailed by registered mail to the member under charges at his or her last recorded address at least 15 days before action is taken thereon. This statement shall be accompanied by a notice of the time when and place where the Council is to take action. The member shall be afforded an opportunity to present his or her position in connection with such charges, at the time and place mentioned in such notice.

INDEPENDENT LITERARY AGENTS ASSOCIATION

Full members

Carole Abel
Carole Abel Literary Agent
160 West 87th Street
New York, NY 10024

Dominick Abel
Dominick Abel Literary Agency, Inc.
498 West End Avenue
New York, NY 10024

Edward J. Acton
Edward J. Acton, Inc.
928 Broadway, Suite 301
New York, NY 10010

Richard Balkin
The Balkin Agency
850 West 176th Street
New York, NY 10033

Virginia Barber
Virginia Barber Literary Agency, Inc.
353 West 21st Street
New York, NY 10011

Amy Berkower
Writers House, Inc.
21 West 26th Street
New York, NY 10010

Meredith G. Bernstein
470 West End Avenue
New York, NY 10024

Andrea Brown
319 East 52nd Street, 2nd Floor
New York, NY 10022

Jane Jordan Browne
Jane Jordan Browne Multimedia
Product Development, Inc.
410 South Michigan Avenue, Room 724
Chicago, IL 60605

Martha Casselman
1263 12th Avenue
San Francisco, CA 94122

Maryanne C. Colas
Cantrell-Colas, Inc., Literary Agency
229 East 79th Street
New York, NY 10021

Nancy Colbert
The Colbert Agency, Inc.
303 Davenport Road
Toronto, ON M5R 1K5 Canada

Ruth Cohen
Ruth Cohen, Inc., Literary Agency
Box 7626
Menlo Park, CA 94025

Oscar Collier
Collier Associates
2000 Flat Run Road
Seaman, OH 45679

Robert Cornfield
Robert Cornfield Literary Agency
145 West 79th Street
New York, NY 10024

Richard Curtis
Richard Curtis Associates, Inc.
164 East 64th Street, Suite 1
New York, NY 10021

Liz Darhanshoff
1220 Park Avenue
New York, NY 10128

Patrick Delahunt
John Schaffner Associates, Inc.
265 Fifth Avenue
New York, NY 10001

Sandra Dijkstra
Sandra Dijkstra Literary Agency
1237 Camino Del Mar, Suite 515C
Del Mar, CA 92014

Joseph Elder
Joseph Elder Agency
150 West 87th Street, Apartment 6D
New York, NY 10024

Marje Fields
165 West 46th Street, Suite 1205
New York, NY 10036

Diana Finch
Ellen Levine Literary Agency, Inc.
432 Park Avenue South, Suite 1205
New York, NY 10016

Sarah Jane Freyman
Stepping Stone Literary Agency, Inc.
59 West 71st Street
New York, NY 10023

Lydia Galton
Lydia Galton Literary Agency, Ltd.
351 West 19th Street
New York, NY 10025

Jane Gelfman
John Farquharson, Ltd.
250 West 57th Street
New York, NY 10107

Peter Ginsberg
Curtis Brown, Ltd.
10 Astor Place
New York, NY 10003

Frances Goldin
305 East 11th Street
New York, NY 10003

Arnold P. Goodman
Goodman Associates
500 West End Avenue
New York, NY 10024

Elise Simon Goodman
Goodman Associates
500 Fifth Avenue
New York, NY 10024

Irene Goodman
Irene Goodman Literary Agency
521 Fifth Avenue, 17th Floor
New York, NY 10017

Francis Greenberger
Sanford J. Greenburger Associates
55 Fifth Avenue, 15th Floor
New York, NY 10013

Maxine Groffsky
Maxine Groffsky Literary Agency
2 Fifth Avenue
New York, NY 10011

Jeanne K. Hanson
Jeanne K. Hanson Literary Agent
5111 Wooddale Avenue South
Edina, MN 55424

Alexandria Hatcher
Alexandria Hatcher Agency
150 West 55th Street
New York, NY 10019

James B. Heacock
Heacock Literary Agency, Inc.
1523 Sixth Street, Suite 14
Santa Monica, CA 90401

Merilee Heifetz
Writers House, Inc.
21 West 26th Street
New York, NY 10010

Jeff Herman
The Jeff Herman Agency, Inc.
166 Lexington Avenue
New York, NY 10016

John L. Hochman
John L. Hochman Books
350 East 58th Street
New York, NY 10022

Bernice Hoffman
Bernice Hoffman Literary Agency
215 West 75th Street
New York, NY 10023

Sharon Jarvis
Sharnon Jarvis & Co.
260 Willard Avenue
Staten Island, NY 10314

Barbara S. Kouts
Barbara S. Kouts Literary Agency
788 Ninth Avenue
New York, NY 10019

Heide Lange
Sanford J. Greenburger Associates
55 Fifth Avenue, 15th Floor
New York, NY 10013

Vicki Lansky
The Book Peddlers
18326 Minnetonka Boulevard
Deephaven, MI 55391

Michael Larsen
Michael Larsen/Elizabeth Pomada
1029 Jones Street
San Francisco, CA 94109

Elizabeth Lay
Elizabeth Lay Literary Agent
Box 183
484 Lake Park Avenue
Oakland, CA 94610

Ellen Levine
Ellen Levine Literary Agency, Inc.
432 Park Avenue South,
Suite 1205
New York, NY 10016

Wendy Lipkind
Wendy Lipkind Agency
225 East 57th Street
New York, NY 10022

Peter Livingston
Peter Livingston Associates, Inc.
143 Collier Street
Toronto, ON M4W 1M2 Canada

Nancy Love
Nancy Love Literary Agency
250 East 65th Street
New York, NY 10021

Barbara Lowenstein
Barbara Lowenstein Associates, Inc.
250 West 57th Street
New York, NY 10107

Carol Mann
Carol Mann Literary Agency
55 Fifth Avenue, 15th Floor
New York, NY 10003

Janet Wilkins Manus
Janet Wilkins Manus Literary Agency, Inc.
370 Lexington Avenue, Suite 906
New York, NY 10017

Denise Marcil
Denise Marcil Literary Agency, Inc.
316 West 82nd Street
New York, NY 10024

Betty Marks
176 East 77th Street,
Apartment 9F
New York, NY 10021

Elaine Markson
Elaine Markson Literary Agency, Inc.
44 Greenwich Avenue
New York, NY 10011

Mildred Marmur
McIntosh & Otis
310 Madison Avenue, Room 607
New York, NY 10017

Evan Marshall
Evan Marshall Literary Agency
228 Watchung Avenue
Upper Montclair, NJ 07043

Margaret McBride
Margaret McBride Literary Agency
P.O. Box 8730
La Jolla, CA 92038

Martha Millard
Martha Millard Literary Agency
21 Kilsyth Road
Brookline, MA 02146

Howard Morhaim
Howard Morhaim Literary Agency
175 Fifth Avenue, Room 709
New York, NY 10010

Jean V. Naggar
Jean V. Naggar Literary Agency
336 East 73rd Street
New York, NY 10021

Ruth Nathan
Ruth Nathan Literary Agency
242 West 27th Street
New York, NY 10001

Bela Pomer
Bela Pomer Agency, Inc.
22 Shalimar Boulevard, Penthouse 2
Toronto, ON M5N 2Z8 Canada

Susan Ann Protter
Susan Ann Protter Literary Agent
110 West 40th Street, Suite 1408
New York, NY 10018

Roberta Pryor
Roberta Pryor, Inc.
24 West 55th Street
New York, NY 10019

Victoria Pryor
Arcadia, Ltd.
221 West 82nd Street, Suite 7D
New York, NY 10024

Helen Rees
Helen Rees Literary Agency
308 Commonwealth Avenue
Boston, MA 02116

Joseph Rhodes
Rhodes Literary Agency, Inc.
140 West End Avenue
New York, NY 10023

Jane Rotrosen
Jane Rotrosen Agency
318 East 51st Street
New York, NY 10022

Raphael Sagalyn
Raphael Sagalyn, Inc., Literary Agency
2813 Bellevue Terrace NW
Washington, DC 20007

Timothy Schaffner
Schaffner Associates, Inc.
264 Fifth Avenue
New York, NY 10001

Susan Schulman
Susan Schulman Literary Agency, Inc.
454 West 44th Street
New York, NY 10036

Arthur P. Schwartz
Arthur P. Schwartz Literary Agent
425 Riverside Drive
New York, NY 10025

Edythea Ginis Selman
14 Washington Place
New York, NY 10003

Charlotte Sheedy
Charlotte Sheedy Literary Agency, Inc.
145 West 86th Street
New York, NY 10024

Rosalie Siegel
Rosalie Siegel, International Literary Agent, Inc.
11 Murphy Drive
Pennington, NJ 08534

Irene Skolnick
Wallace & Sheil Agency, Inc.
177 East 70th Street
New York, NY 10021

Nikki Smith
Sanford J. Greenburger Associates
55 Fifth Avenue, 15th Floor
New York, NY 10003

Elyse Sommer
Elyse Sommer, Inc.
Box E
962 Allen Lane
Woodmere, NY 11598

Gloria Stern
Gloria Stern Agency
1230 Park Avenue
New York, NY 10128

Robin Straus
Robin Straus Agency, Inc.
229 East 79th Street
New York, NY 10021

Roslyn Targ
Roslyn Targ Literary Agency, Inc.
105 West 13th Street, Suite 15E
New York, NY 10011

Patricia Teal
Teal & Watt Literary Agency
2036 Vista del Rosa
Fullerton, CA 92631

Susan P. Ursadt
Susan P. Ursadt, Inc.
125 East 84th Street
New York, NY 10028

Maureen Walters
Curtis Brown, Ltd.
10 Astor Place
New York, NY 10003

Rhoda Weyr
Rhoda Weyr Agency
216 Vance Street
Chapel Hill, NC 27514

Audrey R. Wolf
Audrey R. Wolf Literary Agency
1001 Connecticut Avenue, Suite 1210
Washington, DC 20036

Susan Zeckendorf
Susan Zeckendorf Associates, Inc.
171 West 57th Street
New York, NY 10019

Albert Zuckerman
Writers House, Inc.
21 West 26th Street
New York, NY 10010

Ken Norwick (ILAA counsel)
Norwick & Schad
500 Fifth Avenue, 38th Floor
New York, NY 10110

SOCIETY OF AUTHORS' REPRESENTATIVES, INC. (SAR)

10 Astor Place, 3rd Floor
New York, NY 10003

In 1928, a group of literary and play agents organized the Society of Authors' Representatives, Inc. (SAR); a voluntary association of agents. The SAR regrets it cannot recommend individual member agents. Authors are advised to write directly to agents in the appropriate category (L = literary agent or D = dramatic agent if they wish to contact an SAR agent about their work.

Brett Adams, Ltd. (D)
448 West 44th Street
New York, NY 10036

Julian Bach Literary Agency, Inc. (L)
747 Third Avenue
New York, NY 10017

Lois Berman (D)
The Little Theatre Building
240 West 44th Street
New York, NY 10036

Georges Borchardt, Inc. (L)
136 East 57th Street
New York, NY 10022

Brandt & Brandt Literary Agents, Inc.
1501 Broadway
New York, NY 10036

(Reprinted by permission of Authors' Representatives, Inc.)

The Helen Brann Agency, Inc. (L)
157 West 57th Street
New York, NY 10019

Broadway Play Publishing (D)
357 West 20th Street
New York, NY 10011

Curtis Brown Ltd. (L)
10 Astor Place
New York, NY 10003

Knox Burger Associates, Ltd. (L)
39-1/2 Washington Square South
New York, NY 10012

Collier Associates (L)
2000 Flat Run Road
Seaman, OH 45679

Don Congdon Associates, Inc. (L)
156 Fifth Avenue, Suite 625
New York, NY 10010

William Craver (D)
Writers and Artists Agency
70 West 36th Street, Suite 501
New York, NY 10018

Joan Daves (L)
21 West 26th Street
New York, NY 10010-1083

Anita Diamant (L)
310 Madison Avenue, No. 1508
New York, NY 10017

Candida Donadio & Associates (L)
231 West 22nd Street
New York, NY 10011

Jeanine Edmunds (D)
230 West 55th Street
New York, NY 10017

Ann Elmo Agency, Inc. (L, D)
60 East 42nd Street
New York, NY 10165

John Farquharson, Ltd. (L)
Suite 1914
250 West 57th Street,
New York, NY 10107

The Fox Chase Agency, Inc. (L)
Public Ledger Building, No. 930
Independence Square
Philadelphia, PA 19106

Robert A. Freedman Dramatic Agency, Inc. (D)
1501 Broadway, No. 2310
New York, NY 10036

Samuel French, Inc. (D)
45 West 25th Street
New York, NY 10010

Graham Agency (D)
311 West 43rd Street
New York, NY 10036

Blanche C. Gregory, Inc. (L)
2 Tudor City Place
New York, NY 10017

Helen Harvey (D)
410 West 24th Street
New York, NY 10011

John W. Hawkins & Associates, Inc. (L)
(formerly Paul R. Reynolds, Inc.)
71 West 23rd Street, Suite 1600
New York, NY 10010

International Creative Management, Inc. (L, D)
40 West 57th Street
New York, NY 10019

JCA Literary Agency, Inc. (L)
242 West 27th Street, No. 4A
New York, NY 10001

Kidde, Hoyte & Picard (L)
335 East 51st Street
New York, NY 10022

Lucy Kroll Agency (L, D)
390 West End Avenue
New York, NY 10024

Pinder Lane Productions, Ltd. (L, D)
159 West 53rd Street
New York, NY 10019

The Lantz Office (L, D)
888 Seventh Avenue
New York, NY 10106

Lescher & Lescher, Ltd. (L)
67 Irving Place
New York, NY 10013

Ellen Levine Literary Agency (L)
432 Park Avenue South,
No. 1205
New York, NY 10016

Sterling Lord Literistic, Inc. (L)
1 Madison Avenue
New York, NY 10010

Elisabeth Marton (D)
96 Fifth Avenue
New York, NY 10011

Harold Matson Company, Inc. (L, D)
276 Fifth Avenue
New York, NY 10001

Gerald McCauley Agency, Inc. (L)
PO Box AE
Katonah, NY 10536

McIntosh & Otis, Inc. (L)
310 Madison Avenue
New York, NY 10017

Helen Merrill, Ltd. (L, D)
435 West 23rd Street, No. 1A
New York, NY 10011

William Morris Agency, Inc. (L, D)
1350 Avenue of the Americas
New York, NY 10019

Jean V. Naggar Literary Agency (L)
336 East 73rd Street
New York, NY 10012

Harold Ober Associates, Inc. (L)
40 East 49th Street
New York, NY 10017

Fifi Oscard Associates, Inc. (L, D)
19 West 44th Street
New York, NY 10036

Raines & Raines (L)
71 Park Avenue
New York, NY 10016

Flora Roberts, Inc. (L, D)
157 West 57th Street
Penthouse A
New York, NY 10019

Marie Rodell (L)
Francis Collin Literary Agency
110 West 40th Street Suite 2004
New York, NY 10018

Rosenstone/Wender (L, D)
3 East 48th Street
New York, NY 10017

Russell & Volkening, Inc. (L)
50 West 29th Street
New York, NY 10001

John Schaffner Associates, Inc.
264 Fifth Avenue
New York, NY 10001

Susan Schulman Agency (L, D)
454 West 44th Street
New York, NY 10036

The Shukat Company, Ltd. (L, D)
340 West 55th Street, No. 1A
New York, NY 10019

Philip G. Spitzer Literary Agency (L)
788 Ninth Avenue
New York, NY 10019

Roslyn Targ Literary Agency, Inc. (L)
105 West 13th Street,
No. 15E
New York, NY 10011

The Wallace Agency, Inc. (L)
177 East 70th Street
New York, NY 10021

The Wendy Weil Agency, Inc. (L)
747 Third Avenue
New York, NY 10017

Mary Yost Associates, Inc. (L)
59 East 54th Street, No. 52
New York, NY 10022

Author Organizations

Networking is an ideal way to keep up-to-date on virtually everything that's happening in the publishing industry. These contacts could prove invaluable to your career.

The following is a list of writers' associations reprinted from the *Literary Market Place*:*

The Academy of American Poets
177 E. 87th St., New York, NY 10128
212-427-5665
Pres.: Mrs. Edward T. Chase
Exec. Dir.: Henri Cole
Sponsor The Lamont Poetry Selection,
   The Walt Whitman Award, The Harold
   Morton Landon Translation Award,
   The Lavan Younger Poets Award, and
   annual college poetry prizes;
   workshops, classes, and literary-
   historical walking tours; award
   fellowships to American poets for
   distinguished poetic achievement.
Members: 2000
Publication(s): *Envoy* (semiannual);
Poetry Pilot (monthly)

*Reprinted with permission from R. R. Bowker

American Academy & Institute of Arts & Letters
633 W 155 St, New York, NY 10032
Tel: 212-368-5900
Chancellor: John Updike
Pres: Hortense Calisher
Sponsor awards in art, literature and
music (applications not accepted).
Members: 250
Publication(s): *Proceedings of the
American Academy & Institute of Arts
& Letters*

American Auto Racing Writers & Broadcasters
922 N Pass Ave, Burbank, CA 91505
Tel: 818-842-7005
Dir: Ms Dusty Brandel
Media people who cover auto racing.
Members: 475
Publication(s): Newsletter (members
only)

American Literary Translators Association (ALTA)
University of Texas, Dallas
Box 830688, Richardson, TX 75083-
0688
Tel: 214-690-2093
Exec Sec: Sheryl St Germain
Clearinghouse for translators; translation
library; other services for translators;
promotion of literary translation.
Members: 1000
Publication(s): *Translation Review* (3
issues/yr, $20/yr); newsletter
(quarterly)

**American Medical Writers
Association (AMWA)**
9650 Rockville Pike, Bethesda, MD
  20814-3928
Tel: 301-498-0003
Exec Dir: Lillian Sablack
Sponsor annual medical book awards
  and over 50 workshops at annual
  conference.
1989 Meeting: Lafayette Hotel, Boston,
  MA, Nov 15-18
1990 Meeting: Baltimore Hotel. Los
  Angeles, CA, Oct 31-
  Nov 3
Members: 2700
Publication(s): *Membership Directory*
  (annual); *AMWA Journal* (Quarterly);
  Freelance Directory (every 18 months)

American Poetry Association
Box 1803, 250 A Potrero St, Santa
  Cruz, CA 95061-1803
Tel: 408-429-1122
Outreach Mgr. Jennifer Manes
Anthology publication, poetry contest.
Publication(s): *American Poetry
  Anthology* (quarterly, $35)

**American Society of Journalists &
Authors Inc (ASJA)**
1501 Broadway, Suite 1907, New York,
  NY 10036
Tel: 212-997-0947
Pres: David W Kennedy
Exec VP: Tom Bedell
VPs: Elaine Fein; Dodi Schultz
Sec: Gloria Hochman

Treas: Nona Aguilar
Exec Dir: Alexandra S E Cantor
Service organization providing exchange
of ideas, market information. Regular
meetings with speakers from the
industry, annual writers conference;
medical plans available. Professional
referral service, annual membership
directory.
1989 Meeting: Writing to Sell '89,
Grand Hyatt Hotel, New York, NY,
May 6
1990 Meeting: Writing to Sell '90,
Grand Hyatt Hotel, New York, NY
Members: 750
Publication(s): *Annual Membership
Directory; ASJA Newsletter* (11 times/
yr); *Code of Ethics & Fair Practices
with Letter of Agreement*

**American Society of Journalists &
Authors (ASJA), Southern
California Chapter**
Box 35282, Los Angeles, CA 90035
Tel: 213-931-3177
Chpn: Isobel Silden
Exec Sec: Ruth Pittman
Professional freelance authors of
nonfiction; public workshops, annual
conference.
Members: 70
Publication(s): *Complete Guide to
Writing Nonfiction (Writer's Digest
Books,* $24.95)

**American Society of Journalists &
Authors, Midwest Chapter (ASJA/
MWA)**
Chicago, IL 60645
Tel: 312-943-7363

Pres: Hal Higdon, 2815 Lake Shore Dr,
  Michigan City, IN 46390
Members: 45

**American Translators Association
(ATA)**
109 Croton Ave, Ossining, NY 10562
Tel: 914-941-1500
Pres: Karl Kummer
Staff Admin: Rosemary Malia
Membership consists of those
  professionally engaged in translating,
  interpreting or closely allied work, as
  well as those who are interested in
  these fields.
1989 Meeting: Arlington, VA, Oct
Members: 2300
Publication(s): *ATA Chronicle* (10
  issues/yr, $25)

American Women in Radio & TV
1101 Connecticut Ave, Sta 700,
  Washington, DC 20036
Tel: 202-429-5102
Pres: Diane Sutter
For members of the radio & TV
  industries.
1989 Meeting: Orlando, FL, June
Members: 3000
Publication(s): *News & Views*
  (quarterly)

Arizona Authors' Association (AAA)
3509 E Shea Blvd, Suite 117, Phoenix,
  AZ 85028-3339
Tel: 602-996-9706
Pres: Dorothy Tegeler
Information and referral center for
  members; sponsor workshops and

seminars. Conduct annual writers conference.
Members: 200
Publication(s): *Authors Newsletter* (bimonthly); *Arizona Literary Magazine* (annual)

Associated Business Writers of America Inc
Div of National Writers Club
1450 S Havana St, Suite 620, Aurora, CO 80012
Tel: 303-751-7844
Exec Dir: James L Young
To help business writers and those seeking their services.
Members: 150
Publication(s): *Professional Freelance Writers Directory* (annual, $12)

Associated Writing Programs (AWP)
Old Dominion University, Norfolk, VA 23529
Tel: 804-440-3839
Exec Dir: Liam Rector
Newsletter, publications, directory, competitions for awards (including publication), advocacy for literature and education, annual meeting, job placement.
1989 Meeting: April
Members: 9000
Publication(s): *AWP Newsletter* (bimonthly, free to members, $12 nonmembers); *AWP Catalogue of Writing Programs* (irregular, $10)

Association of Professional Translators (APT)

Mellon Bank NA
3 Mellon Bank Ctr 2523, Pittsburgh, PA 15259
Tel: 412-234-5751 FAX: 412-234-0214
Contact: Josephine Thornton
Bimonthly meetings, translation instruction at University of Pittsburgh.
Members: 125
Publication(s): *APT Directory of Translators* (annual, $1); Newsletter (bimonthly)

The Jane Austen Society of North America (JASNA)

c/o Lorraine Hanaway, Box 252, Wayne, PA 19087
Tel: 215-687-4714
Pres: Lorraine Hanaway
Publications, annual conference, restoration of St Nicholas Church, Steventon, Hampshire, England.
1989 Meeting: Pride and Prejudice; Santa Fe, NM, Oct 13-15
1990 Meeting: Sense & Sensibility, Washington, DC, Oct 5-6
Members: 2000
Publication(s): *Persuasion* (annual, $5); *JASNA News* (newsletter, semiannual, free to members); *Persuasions: Occasional Papers* (2 vols in print)

The Authors League Fund

234 W 44 St, New York, NY 10036
Tel: 212-391-3966
Pres: Herbert Mitgang

1st VP: Robert Anderson
2nd VP: Samuel Grafton
Sec: Barbara W Tuchman
Treas: Richard Lewine
Admin: Susan Drury
Provide interest-free loans to
  professional authors in need.
Members: 1222

The Authors League of America Inc
234 W 44 St, New York, NY 10036
Tel: 212-391-9198
Cable: AUTHOLEAG NEW YORK
  FAX: 212-869-8237
Pres: Garson Kanin
Contact: Helen Stephenson
Pres, The Authors Guild Inc: Robert K
  Massie, Tel: 212-398-0838
Pres, The Dramatists Guild: Peter
  Stone, Tel: 212-398-9366
A national membership corporation to
  promote the professional interests of
  authors and dramatists, procure
  satisfactory copyright legislation and
  treaties, guard freedom of expression
  and support fair tax treatment for
  writers.
Members: 14,500

**The Authors Resource Center (TARC
  Inc)**
4001 E Fort Lowell Rd, Tucson, AZ
  85712-1011
Tel: 602-325-4733
Exec Dir: Martha R Gore
Serve writers and those needing their
  services; writer's research library and

consultations. Sponsor 50 workshops
and seminars held yearly at The
Authors Resource Center Building.
Literary agency services available to
members.
1989 Meeting: TARC Workshops,
TARC Bldg, 4001 E Fort Lowell Rd,
Tucson, AZ 85712-1011
Members: 300
Publication(s): *TARC Newsletter*
(monthly, $50/yr, free to members)

The Baker Street Irregulars
34 Pierson Ave, Norwood, NJ 07648
Tel: 201-768-2241
Wiggins: Thomas L Stix
Simpson: John Bennett Shaw, 1917 Ft
    Union Dr, Santa Fe, NM 87501
Devoted to the study of Sherlock
    Holmes & the Sherlockian scene.
1990 Meeting: New York, NY, Jan 6
Publication(s): *The Baker Street Journal*
    (quarterly, $15/yr), available from
    Fordham University Press, University
    Box L, Bronx, NY 10458

Before Columbus Foundation
1446 Sixth St, Suite D, Berkeley, CA
94710
Tel: 415-527-1586
Pres: Joyce Carol Thomas
Exec Dir: Gundar Strads
Provide information, research,
    consultation and promotional services
    for contemporary American
    multicultural writers and publishers. A
    nonprofit service organization that also

sponsors classes, workshops, readings,
public events and the annual American
Book Awards.
1989 Meeting: Washington, DC, June 4
1990 Meeting: Las Vegas, NV, June 3

Bilingual Educational Services Inc
2514 S Grand Ave, Los Angeles, CA
90007
Tel: 213-749-6213
CEO: Carlos Penichet
Focus on English as a second language.
Import Spanish-language books.

Brooklyn Writers' Network
2509 Ave K, Brooklyn, NY 11210
Tel: 718-377-4945
Dir: Ruth Schwartz
Seeks to improve contact between
  professional writers and publishing
  industry; newsletter; directory;
  conferences; workshops.
1989 Meeting: BWN: Writing &
  Publishing, Brooklyn Historical
  Library, 2nd Saturday in June
1990 Meeting: BWN: Writing &
  Publishing, Brooklyn Historical
  Library, 2nd Saturday in June
Members: 500
Publication(s): *BWN Directory*
  (Annual); *Pen in Hand* (Monthly, $25/
  yr)

The Byron Society
American Committee
259 New Jersey Ave, Collingswood,
NJ 08108

Tel: 609-858-0514
Exec Dir: Marsha M Manns
Annual seminar and tour in a country
  associated with Byron; annual meeting
  in conjunction with MLA Convention;
  book discounts.
Members: 2800
Publication(s): *Byron Journal* (annual);
  Byron Society Newsletter (biennial,
  both free with $12 membership dues)

California Writers' Club
2214 Derby St, Berkeley, CA 94705
Sec: Dorothy V Benson
Professional writers in the northern
  California area; conduct year-long
  workshops in fiction, nonfiction and
  poetry. Branches on Berkeley, San
  Francisco Peninsula, Santa Rosa,
  Sacramento, San Jose & Mount Diablo
  in northern California. Also San
  Fernando Valley Branch in southern
  California.
1989 Meeting: Asilomar, Pacific Grove,
  CA, July 14-16
Members: 700
Publication(s): *California Writers Club
  Bulletin* (monthly, free to members)

California Writers' Roundtable, *see*
  Women's National Book Association,
  Los Angeles Chapter

Canadian Authors Association
121 Avenue Rd, Suite 104, Toronto,
ON M5R 2G3 Canada
Tel: 416-926-8084

Exec Dir: Ginny Sumodi
Encourage and develop a climate
favorable to the literary arts in
Canada. Represent the concerns and
interests of members.
1989 Meeting: North York, Ontario,
June
1990 Meeting: Edmonton, Alberta, June
Members: 800
Publication(s): *Canadian Author &
Bookman* (quarterly, $20); *Canadian
Writers Guide* (occasional, $20);
Careers in Writing ($10)

**The Canadian Centre (English-
speaking) PEN**
The Writers Centre, 24 Ryerson Ave,
Toronto, ON M5T 2P3 Canada
Tel: 416-860-1448
Exec Dir: Jan Bauer
Pres: Graeme Gibson
Fight for freedom of expression on
behalf of writers in all nations; work
for the preservation of the world's
literature
1989 Meeting: PEN World Congress,
Toronto & Montreal, Sept 23-Oct 1
Members: 300

Canadian Copyright Institute
34 Ross St, Suite 200, Toronto, ON
M5T 1Z9 Canada
Tel: 416-595-9704
Chmn: John Irwin
1989 Meeting: Annual Meeting,
Toronto, ON Canada, Feb
Members: 61

Publication(s): *Newsletter* (irregular,
free)

**Lewis Carroll Society of North
America**
617 Rockford Rd, Silver Spring, MD
20902
Tel: 301-593-7077
Pres: Edward Guilian
1989 Meeting: New York, spring
Members: 300

Christian Writers Guild
260 Fern Lane, Hume, CA 93628
Tel: 209-335-2333
Chmn: Norman B Rohrer
Sponsor three-year home study course
and one-day "Write to Be Read"
workshops primarily for members of
the Guild and students but open to
everyone.
1988 Meeting: The Quill o' the Wisp,
260 Fern Lane, Hume, CA 93628,
July
Members: 3500
Publication(s): *Quill o' the Wisp*
(quarterly)

**Composers, Authors & Publishers
Association of Canada Ltd (CAPAC)**
1240 Bay St, Toronto, ON M5R 2C2
Canada
Tel: 416-924-4427
Gen. Mgr: Michael Rock
Repertory performing rights, seminars.
1989 Meeting: Toronto, Canada, April

Coordinating Council of Literary Magazines (CCLM)

666 Broadway, 11th fl, New York, NY 10012
Tel: 212-614-6551
Exec Dir: Eva Burch
Asst Dir: Robert Carnevale
A national nonprofit organization that provides services to noncommercial literary magazines, including cooperative advertising and promotion and several awards for literary magazines and writers.
Members: 435
Publication(s): *The Directory of Literary Magazines* (annual, $6.95 paper); *The CCLM News* (tri-quarterly, $6/yr)

Council of Writers Organizations

Box 341200, Los Angeles, CA 90034
Tel: 213-301-8546
Pres: Michelle Bekey
Treas: Isolde Chapin
Sec: Robert Scott Milne
Umbrella coalition of 25 professional writers' groups. Publish newsletter on tax, legal and other issues affecting writers, professional communication and cooperation; offer medical insurance, computer discounts and other services; hold periodic meetings.
1989 Meeting: White to '89, Grand Hyatt Hotel, New York, NY
Members: 35,000
Publication(s): *Word Wrap* (bi-monthly, to officers and directors of member organizations)

Dog Writers' Association of America Inc (DWAA)
9800 Flint Rock Rd, Manassas, VA
22111
Tel: 703-369-2384
Pres: Harold Sundstrom
Provide information about dogs (sport, breeding and ownership) and assist writers in gaining access to exhibitions.
1989 Meeting: New York, NY, Feb 5
1990 Meeting: New York, NY, Feb 4
Members: 300
Publication(s): *DWAA Newsletter* (monthly, free to members)

Editorial Freelancers Association (EFA)
30 E 20 St, Rm 305, New York, NY
10011
Tel: 212-677-3357
Mailing Address: Box 2050, Madison Square Sta, New York, NY 10159
Co-Execs: Elizabeth Burpee; David R Hall
Sec: Patricia M Godfrey
Treas: Sheila Buff
A professional organization of editorial freelancers: editors, indexers, writers, translators, proofreaders and researchers. Activities include program meetings, educational services, insurance programs, the gathering and dissemination of information on current business practices and trends.
Members: 750
Publication(s): Newsletter; Directory

Education Writers Association
1001 Connecticut Ave NW, Suite 310,
Washington, DC 20036
Tel: 202-429-9680
Exec Dir: Lisa J Walker
Conferences, seminars, newsletters,
publications, employment services,
freelance referral, workshops and
national awards.
1989 Meeting: Washington, DC, March/
April
1990 Meeting: Chicago, IL, March/
April
Members: 500
Publication(s): *Information Source
Directory* ($85); *Covering the
Education Beat* (occasional, $50);
Education Reporter (bimonthly
newsletter); *Lenses on Higher
Education in Indiana; Buskin Lecture*
(annual)

**Fédération Professionnelle des
Journalistes du Québec**
1278 rue Panet, Montreal, PQ H2L 2Y8
Canada
Tel: 514-522-6142
Pres: R Barnaby

Florida Freelance Writers Association
Cassell Communications Inc
Box 9844, Fort Lauderdale, FL 33310
Tel: 305-485-0795; 800-851-3392 (FL),
800-351-9278 (USA)
Contact: Dana K Cassell
Regular seminars throughout Florida;
computer data bank of Florida writers
by location and areas of expertise.

1989 Meeting: Florida State Writers
Conference, Orlando, FL, May 19-21
1990 Meeting: Florida State Writers
Conference, Orlando, FL, May 18-20
Members: 1500
Publication(s): *Freelance Writer's Report*
(monthly, $30/yr); *Directory of Florida
Markets for Writers* (annual); *Guide to
Florida Writers* (annual)

**Football Writers Association of
America**
Box 1022, Edmond, OK 73083
Tel: 405-341-4731
Exec Dir: Volney Meece
Select "All-America" team, Outland
Award winner, Coach of the Year &
national championship team (Grantland
Rice Trophy).
1989 Meeting: Annual Meeting, Hyatt
Regency, Dallas, TX, first Wednesday
in June
1990 Meeting: Annual Meeting, Hyatt
Regency, Dallas, TX, first Wednesday
in June
Members: 765
Publication(s): *Fifth Down* (monthly,
July-Dec, members only)

Freelance Editorial Association
Box 835, Cambridge, MA 02238
Contact: Daniel Marcus
An organization for full-time and part-
time editorial freelancers including
editors, writers, proofreaders,
indexers, researchers and translators in
trade, technical, scholarly, college, el-

hi, magazines and other print media.
Activities include monthly house
meetings, topic meetings, social
gatherings and various committees
whose purposes are to promote the
interests of editorial freelancers.
Publication(s): Quarterly newletter;
Yellow Pages

**Garden Writers Association of
America**
1218 Overlook Rd, Eustis, FL 32726
Tel: 904-589-8888
Exec Dir: W J Jung
Sponsor annual writer's contest.
1989 Meeting: Milwaukee, WI, Sept
14-17
1990 Meeting: Mobile, AL, Nov
Members: 1100
Publication(s): *Garden Writers Bulletin*
(bimonthly)

Golf Writers Association of America
Box 37324, Cincinnati, OH 45222
Tel: 513-631-4400
Pres: Joe Greenday
Exec Dir: Bob Rickey
To ensure good working conditions for
golf writers.
Members: 550

The Ibsen Society of America
DeKalb Hall 3, Pratt Institute,
Brooklyn, NY 11205
Tel:718-636-3794
Pres: Rolf Fjelde
Ed: Thomas Van Laan

Promote and study the reputation of
Henrik Ibsen and his writings and
stage performance in North America.
1989 Meeting: New York, spring and
fall
Members: 150
Publication(s): *Ibsen News & Comment*
(annual, free to members, lib subs $6)

Illinois Writers Inc
Box 1087, Champaign, IL 61820
Tel: 217-429-0117
Chpn: Deborah Bosley
Newsletter Ed: Barbara Lau
Dispense information to Illinois writers
and publishers and review Illinois
small press publications.
Members: 500
Publication(s): *Monthly* (10 issues/yr);
Review (semiannual)

Independent Writers of Chicago
645 N Michigan Ave, Suite 1058,
Chicago, IL 60611
Tel: 312-951-9114
Pres: J D Shults
Monthly meetings and six workshops
per year dealing with the business
aspects of independent writing.
Writers' line job referral; insurance.
1988 Meeting: Annual meeting, Oct 12
Members: 350
Publication(s): *STET* (monthly
newsletter, $20/yr); Membership
Directory (annual, $10)

**International Association of Crime
Writers Inc**
JAF Box 1500, New York, NY 10116
Tel: 212-757-3915

Exec Dir: Mary A Frisque
Pres: Roger Lary A Simon
Sec Treas: Thomas Adcock
Sec: Jerome Charyn
Promote communication among crime
  writers worldwide and enhance
  awareness and encourage translations
  of the genre in the USA and abroad.
Members: 200
Publication(s): *Border Patrol* (quarterly,
  free to members)

International Black Writers
Box 1030, Chicago, IL 60690
Tel: 312-995-5195
Pres: Mable Terrell
Sec: Rachel McMillan
Fiction, nonfiction, poetry, children's,
  media writing, inspiration, script-
  writing, legal protection.
1989 Meeting: Charlotte, NC, June 10-
  11
1990 Meeting: Chicago, IL, June 9-10
Members: 500
Publication(s): *Black Writer Magazine*
  (quarterly, $3/issue)

**The International Society of
  Dramatists**
Box 1310, Miami, FL 33153
Tel: 305-674-1831
Ed: Andrew Delaplaine
Publish script information resource
  books for dramatists; administer
  several playwriting awards annually,
  including the "Adriatic Award," to a
  full-length play produced or

unproduced. Writers Registration
Service available for novels, plays and
nonfiction works.
Members: 10,500
Publication(s): *The Dramatist's Bible*
(annual, $29.95); *The Globe
Newsletter* (monthly, $24, includes
dues); *Plays & Playwrights* (annual,
$29.95)

**The International Women's Writing
Guild (IWWG)**
Box 810, Gracie Sta, New York, NY
10028
Tel: 212-737-7536
Exec Dir: Hannelore Hahn
For women who wish to use writing for
personal &/or professional growth.
Services include manuscript referral
and exchange, writing conferences and
retreats, group rates for health and life
insurance, legal aid, regional clusters,
job referrals; annual award.
1988 Meeting: Late Fall Canadian
Goose Conference, Morristown, NJ,
Nov 12
1989 Meeting: "Open House/Meet the
Agents," New York, NY, Feb 26;
"Early Spring Berkshire Renewal
Conference," Sonoma, CA, March 3-
5; "Early Spring Berkshire Renewal
Conference," Canaan, NY, April 14-
16; "The Land of Enchantment
Conference," Saint Johns College,
Santa Fe, NM, May 19-24; "Annual
Summer IWWG Writing Conference,"
Skidmore College, Saratoga Springs,

NY July 28-Aug 4; "Open House/
Meet the Agents," New York, NY,
Oct 14
Members: 5000
Publication(s): *Network* (bimonthly,
$20/yr)

James Joyce Society
Gotham Book Mart Gallery
41 W 47 St, New York, NY 10036
Tel: 212-719-4448
Pres: Sidney Feshbach
Sec: Philip Lyman
Quarterly meetings.
Members: 200
Publication(s): *Newsletter* (annual,
$7.50, includes membership in the
Society)

League of Canadian Poets
24 Ryerson Ave, Toronto, ON M5T
2P3 Canada
Tel: 416-363-5047
Pres: Douglas Smith
Exec Dir: Angela Rebeiro
Tour Coord: Dolores Ricketts
Members: 278
Publication(s): *Poetry Markets for
Canadians* ($10); *When is a Poem*
($6.95); *Here is a Poem* ($7)

Literary Press Group
Subs of Association of Canadian
Publishers
260 Kings St E, Toronto, ON M5A
1K3 Canada
Tel: 416-362-6555 FAX: 416-361-0643

Dir: John Ball
Sales Rep Mgr: Lisa Alward
Promote Canadian fiction, poetry,
drama and literary criticism; sales
representation across Canada.
1989 Meeting: Annual General
Meeting, Saskatoon, SK, Canada,
April
1990 Meeting: Annual LPG Executive
Meetings, Jan, June & Sept
Members: 41
Publication(s): *Literary Press Group
Flyer,* (semiannually, free)

Literary Translators' Association
1030 Cherrier, Bureau 510, Montreal,
PQ H2L 1H9 Canada
Tel: 514-526-6653
Pres: Robert Paquin
Sec: Michel Buttiens
Promote and protect interests of literary
translators in Canada; provide legal
services, occasional meetings with
local universities and occasional
workshops.
1988 Meeting: Montreal, PQ, Canada,
May
Members: 90
Publication(s): *Transmissions* (3 issues/
yr, free)

Media Alliance
Fort Mason, Bldg D, San Francisco,
CA 94123
Tel: 415-441-2557
Prog Dir: Ida Jeter

Educational programs, medical plan and
referrals and job file; computer
training.
Members: 2500
Publication(s): *MediaFile* (bimonthly,
$25/yr); *Media How-to Notebook* ($5);
People Behind the News ($10);
Propaganda Review (quarterly, $20/yr)

The Melville Society
Dept of English
Glassboro State College, Glassboro,
NJ 08028
Tel: 609-863-6001
Sec & Treas: Donald Yannella
Annual and special meetings and
publications. Conferences in
association with the Modern Language
Association annual convention.
Members: 650
Publication(s): *Melville Society Extracts*
(quarterly, $7, $10 libs)

Miami Earth
Chapter of: Florida State Poets
Association Inc
Box 680-536, Miami, FL 33168
Tel: 305-688-8558
Pres: Barbara Holley
Sec: Florence Kahn
Meets every second Sat, Oct-June
Members: 300
Publication(s): *Quarterly Earth
Newsletter* (annual, $8); *Earthwise
Literary Calendar* (annual, $6.95,
$5.95 members)

Mystery Writers of America Inc
236 W 27 St, Rm 600, New York, NY
 10001
Tel: 212-255-7005
Pres: Tony Hillerman
Exec VP: Bruce Cassiday
Sec: Joyce Harrington
Exec Sec: Priscilla Ridgway
Treas: Elaine Budd
Membership open to professional
 writers in the mystery and other fields
 and to students and fans of mystery; to
 enhance the prestige of mystery story
 and fact-crime writing; sponsor
 workshops.
1988 Meeting: International Crime
 Writers Congress & Edgar Allan Poe
 Awards, New York, NY
1989 Meeting: Edgar Allan Poe Awards,
 New York, NY
Members: 2000
Publication(s): *The Third Degree* (10
 issues/yr); *Mystery Writers Annual* ($5)

**National Association of Science
 Writers Inc (NASW)**
Box 294, Greenlawn, NY 11740
Tel: 516-757-5664
Admin Sec: Diane McGurgan
Local meetings in seven cities.
1989 Meeting: Boston, MA, Feb 11-16
1990 Meeting: San Francisco, Jan 15-20
Members: 1350
Publication(s): *NASW Newsletter*
 (quarterly)

National Book Critics Circle (NBCC)
c/o Alida Becker, 756 S Tenth St,
 Philadelphia, PA 19147

Tel: 215-925-8406
Pres & Chmn: Nina King
VP & Treas: Eliot Fremont-Smith
VP & Sec: Alida Becker
Nonprofit professional organization
  whose purpose is to improve the
  quality of book reviewing throughout
  the country and help extend book
  review coverage. Sponsor awards
  honoring the best American works of
  fiction, general nonfiction, biography/
  autobiography, poetry and criticism of
  the year; annual citation for excellence
  in reviewing.
1989 Meeting: Annual Meeting, New
  York, NY, last Thursday in Jan
Members: 498
Publication(s): *NBCC Journal*
  (quarterly)

**National Coalition Against
Censorship (NCAC)**
132 W 43 St, New York, NY 10036
Tel: 212-944-9899
Exec Dir: Leanne Katz
Promote and defend free speech,
  inquiry and expression; monitor and
  publicize censorship incidents; sponsor
  public programs; assist in censorship
  controversies through advice, materials
  contacts with local organizations and
  individuals.
Members: 41
Publication(s): *Censorship News*
  (quarterly $25/yr); *Books on Trial; A
  Report on Book Censorship Litigation
  in Public Schools* (revised, $5); *Meese*

*Commission Exposed: Proceedings of a
NCAC Public Information Briefing on
the Attorney General's Commission on
Pornography, Including Kurt Vonnegut
Jr, Betty Friedan & Colleen Dewhurst*
($6)

**National Conference of Editorial
Writers**
6223 Executive Blvd, Rockville, MD
20852
Tel: 301-984-3015
Exec Sec: Cora Everett
Sponsor two annual seminars and
regional critique meetings and annual
foreign tour for members. Also
cosponsor the Wells Award for
exemplary leadership in offering
minorities employment in journalism.
1989 Meeting: 43rd Annual Convention,
St Paul, MN, Sept 12-15
1990 Meeting: 44th Annual Convention,
Orlando, FL Sept 11-14
Members: 575
Publication(s): *The Masthead* (quarterly,
$20/yr)

**National League of American Pen
Women**
Pen Arts Bldg, 1300 17 St NW,
Washington, DC 20036
Tel: 202-785-1997
Pres: Juanita Carmack Howison
Scholarships, letters, art & music
workshops.
Members: 6000

Publication(s): *Pen Woman* (9 issues/yr, $6/yr)

The National Society of Newspaper Columnists (NSNC)
Box 6955, Louisville, KY 40206
Tel: 502-426-3943
Pres: Richard Des Ruisseaux
PR: Patricia Kite
Treas: Bob Hill
Information exchange group for staff, syndicated and regular freelance newspaper columnists, writing on general interest, humor or "about town" topics.
1989 Meeting: Annual Conference, Connecticut, May
Members: 203
Publication(s): *NSNC Update* (quarterly, free to members)

The National Writers Club Inc (NWC)
1450 S Havana, Suite 620, Aurora, CO 80012
Tel: 303-751-7844
Exec Dir: James L Young
A nonprofit representative organization of new and established writers, founded in 1937, serving freelance writers throughout the world.
Members: 5000
Publication(s): *Authorship* (bimonthly, $25/yr); *Flash Market News* (monthly); *NWC Market Update* (bimonthly), *NWC Newsletter* (bimonthly, free to

members); *Professional Freelance Writers Directory* (annual, $12)

National Writers Union
13 Astor Place, New York, NY 10003
Tel: 212-254-0279
Pres: Alec Dubro
Exec Dir: Kim Fellner
Organizing for better treatment of freelance writers by publishers; grievance procedures; negotiate union contracts with publishers; health insurance; conferences.
Members: 2600
Publication(s): *American Writer* (quarterly); local chapter newsletters

Nebraska Writers Guild Inc
4111 Gertie, Lincoln, NE 68516
Tel: 402-488-9263
Pres: Harry A Dolphin
Sec: Steven Arts
Conferences held twice annually, April & Oct; regional study groups meet three to four times annually.
1989 Meeting: Nebraska Writers Conference, April, Oct
1990 Meeting: Nebraska Writers Conference, April, Oct
Members: 135
Publication(s): *Annual Bulletin* (members only), *President's Newsletter* (members only)

New England Poetry Club
2 Farrar St, Cambridge, MA 02138
Pres: Diana der Hovanessian

Honorary Pres: Robert Penn Warren
Sec: Mildred Nash
Society for professional published
poets. Sponsor various poetry contests
and workshops. Meet monthly at the
Harvard Faculty Club. Reading Series
first Monday of the month at Boylston
Hall, Harvard, open to the public.

Author–Agency Agreement

It is advisable for the agent and author to enter into a "plain-English" written agreement that clarifies the important aspects of their relationship. It's true that author–agent relationships tend to be more personal and friendly than the typical business association. Nevertheless, having the rules and expectations of the relationship codified in writing is helpful and avoids future problems.

Although there are substantial similarities among most agency agreements, none are exactly alike. What's most important for you as a writer is that you understand every aspect of the contract and are completely comfortable with it. Ideally, it will protect your interests as well as the agency's.

Here are some key aspects you should pay attention to:

Extent of the agent's representation.   Will the agent represent everything you write (book and nonbook)? Or will he or she be limited to just the project at hand? Will the agent have the option to represent your next book? It is not unethical or unusual for the answer to any or all of these questions to be yes, so long as you understand the ramifications and what your other options are.

Agent's commission.   —usually 10 to 15 percent.

Who pays for what? How are reimbursements for costs such as postage, messengers, long-distance phone calls, etc., to be made.

When, how, and what happens at the termination of the agent–author relationship?

The following boilerplate agreement of my agency provides an example of an author–agency contract.

Letter of Agreement

This Letter of Agreement between THE JEFF HERMAN AGENCY, INC. ("Agency") and ("Author") entered into on (date), puts into effect the following terms and conditions:

- The Agency is hereby exclusively authorized to seek a publisher for the Author's work currently titled (tentative working title), hereby referred to as the "Project." The terms and conditions of this Agreement will also fully pertain to any additional Projects the Author might explicitly authorize the Agency to represent subsequent to the execution of this Agreement, and separate Agreements will not be necessary for such subsequent projects, unless the terms and conditions differ from this Agreement.
- If the Agency sells the Project to a publisher, the Agency will be the Agent-of-Record for the Project's income-producing duration and will irrevocably keep (percentage) of all the Author's income relevant to sold Project. All Project income will be paid by the publisher to the Agency. The Agency will promptly pay the Author all due monies upon receipt and bank clearance, with full accounting provided. The Agency will not be required to return any legitimately received commissions. There will be an Agent's Clause in the Author–Publisher contract stating the Agent's status, the wording of which shall be subject to Author approval. These terms will be binding upon the Author's estate.
- The Agency will inform the author about all offers. The Agency cannot accept any specific offers or terms without

the Author's oral consent, and no deals will be binding upon the Author without the Author's signature.

- Unless otherwise agreed, the Agency will generally be responsible for all office-related expenses it incurs representing the Project (postage, telephone calls, office copying, etc.). However, the Agency will be entitled to be reimbursed for certain excessive costs such as overseas communications and overnight deliveries, etc., subject to the Author's prior approval. The Author will be responsible for providing the Agency with as many manuscript or, when lengthy, proposal copies as deemed necessary. Otherwise, the Author agrees to promptly reimburse the Agency for the manuscript/proposal copying costs.
- The Agency agrees to regularly forward to the Author copies of all correspondence received from publishers in reference to the Author's Project(s). Author is entitled to know, upon ten business days' notice, what parties Author materials have been submitted to, and what the status of such submissions are.
- This Agreement can be amended or expanded by attaching Rider(s) to it, if all parties concerned fully concur with the terms and conditions of the Rider(s) and sign them.
- The Agency's authorization to sell said Project can be terminated by the Author and/or the Agency can release the Author from this Agreement, upon written notice. But Agency will remain entitled to all due commissions relevant to any sales which result from Agency efforts implemented prior to any such termination and will be entitled to all other due monies as stated in this Agreement.

Signatures below by the parties named in this Agreement will indicate that all parties concerned fully understand and concur with the terms and conditions of this Agreement, and will endeavor to fulfill their obligations in good faith.

THE JEFF HERMAN AGENCY, INC.   Author
(signature)   (signature)

The Dos and Don'ts of Getting Published

Do: Query an editor or agent about your manuscript with a brief description and flattering, relevant information about yourself. Invite the editor/agent to write or call you requesting to see the manuscript or a portion thereof. Include a SASE.

Don't: Cold-call an editor or agent to describe in detail the novel you wrote, or perhaps are merely thinking about writing.

Do: Query the editor or agent first and give him or her the option to invite you to submit the material.

Don't: Send an unrequested manuscript to an editor or agent.

Do: If your query, proposal, or manuscript is rejected, accept the fact that the material wasn't right for that particular individual and move on to new prospects. If no progress is being made, reappraise your strategy and the quality of your material (including the query itself).

Don't: Write or call an editor/agent, arguing that he or she was wrong to reject your material.

Do: Personally address and print each letter.

Don't: Send photocopied To Whom It May Concern letters.

Do: Project yourself as being confident and fresh.

Don't: Complain in your query that everyone else has previously rejected you and how frustrating that is.

Do: Submit new and attractive-looking material.

Don't: Submit a tired, raggedy manuscript that looks as if it's been read (and run over) several times before.

Additional dos:

- Request the book catalogs of publishers that might be appropriate for your book (just call the switchboard and ask for one to be sent).
- Walk through several bookstores a month and observe what's being stocked, especially in your subject areas.
- Join local and national writers' groups. Network and learn as much as you can about the business.
- Remember that, in order to succeed, you must show that you can create value—$—for the publisher.

Model Nonfiction Book Proposal

[title page]
Proposal for:
"Cutting the Cord: How to Get Your Adult Children to Grow Up"

by
Dr. Janet Doe
Anywhere, USA
and
Richard Roe
Almost Anywhere Else, USA

Agent: The Jeff Herman Agency, Inc.
166 Lexington Avenue
New York, NY 10016
(212) 725-4660
[end title page]

OVERVIEW

"If you love your children, give them just two things—give them roots and give them wings." Sayings similar to this appear on cross-stitched samplers in nurseries across the United States. The ultimate goal of loving parents is to see their "fledglings" grow strong enough to fly away from the nest and successfully cope with life on their own. In this country, the normal growth and development process has recently and unexpectedly been thwarted.

Susan Littwin, in her recent book *The Postponed Generation: Why American Youth Are Growing up Later* (William Morrow, 1986), describes in detail the difficulties of young adults (ages 20–40) in separating themselves from their parents. Psychologists and psychiatrists across the country report an "epidemic"—countless parents coming for assistance with their dependent adult children. In the St. Louis offices of Health Science Services, a large mental health counseling center, the staff of 15 counselors estimates that they will handle 2,000 cases (of a total 2,700 cases) involving this problem in 1987 alone.

The problem goes well beyond the 22 million adult children estimated by the U.S. Census Bureau to be living at home. It includes children who continually turn to their parents for financial assistance, or who create crisis after crisis to continue an emotional dependency. The financial, emotional, and marital strain on the parents is enormous.

The number of young adults who do not live at home, but who are still dependent on their parents is difficult to estimate. But it would not be unreasonable to estimate that at least 40 percent of the current crop of young adults (20–40 years of age) are excessively dependent. This would mean that approximately 36 million young adults are taking longer than any prior generation to sever the ties of adolescence.

Cutting the Cord is designed for the parents of these young adults. Facing a problem they never expected, most parents blame themselves and make excuses for their children. This book is designed to break the useless guilt trap and allow parents to respond in a way that gently but firmly forces their children "out of the nest." It will be a practical, self-help book along the lines of *ToughLove Solutions* by York, York, and Wachtel (Doubleday, 1984). *ToughLove* addressed the difficulties of dealing with "acting out" adolescents and has spawned support groups across the nation as well as another book (*ToughLove: A Self-Help Manual*). We expect *Cutting the Cord* to have the same potential market.

MARKET ANALYSIS

Phyllis Feuerstein and Carol Roberts's book, *The Not-So-Empty Nest: How to Live with Your Kids After They've Lived Someplace Else* (Follett, 1981) is no longer in print, but it marked the first recognition of the delayed maturity trend. This book gave advice to parents on how to survive the time when young adults returned home—not on how to get them to stop being dependent. It addressed all the "needs" of the adult child, but not the fundamental adjustment. Since this only amplifies the guilt of the parent, the book was of no real help to the readers most likely to buy it.

There are several books currently on the market in this general area, but none is a self-help manual for parents designed to deal with the larger picture—the adult child who is dependent but may not live at home. Littwin's book *The Postponed Generation* shows the enormity of the problem, but does not offer any advice to parents dealing with it daily.

Released in October were two more books about the extended childhood of many of today's young adults. One is similar to *Passages,* but intended for the young adults themselves (*"Grown-Ups": A Generation in Search of Adulthood* [Putnam, 1987]). This book is clearly not competing for our target audience.

The second book, *Boomerang Kids: How to Live with Adult Children Who Return Home,* is written by two psychologists, J. D. Okimoto and P. J. Stegall (Little, Brown, 1987). *Boomerang Kids,* however, has as its primary emphasis kids who come home to live, not the greater problem of extended dependency, in all its varied forms. In addition, its emphasis is clearly on parents adjusting to the trials of children coming home again— not on ending their dependency.

Magazines have carried stories on this problem (*Woman's Day*, July 7, 1987; *Time*, May 4, 1987), and Regis Philbin recently addressed the issue on his show. The subject is highly topical, and *Cutting the Cord* is the book to fill the need for a self-help book that deals with the whole problem—not just one piece of it. But we cannot be alone in recognizing the opportunity. Rapid action will be needed to be the first such book on the shelves.

OUR APPROACH

We plan to write a 50,000-word book in simple terminology targeted toward the parents of adult dependent children. We will begin with an explanation of the problem and how healthy dependency and unhealthy dependency differ. This will be followed by a discussion of those feelings that tend to paralyze parents: guilt, embarrassment, confusion, the need to control, and so on. We will quote the viewpoints of parents and young adults enmeshed in this difficulty to demonstrate that the reader is not alone in this problem, and to give some perspective on the feelings of the dependent child. We will explain how parental behavior can either allow the situation to continue or work to correct it.

The book will then move to practical advice, itemizing typical situations and responses. Details from actual case studies will illustrate significant points. The reader will finish the book feeling that he/she now has some ideas to apply to his or her particular situation.

CREDENTIALS

As a writing team, we bring writing expertise as well as the perspectives of counselor and parent to this project.

Janet Doe, Ph.D., has been involved in the counseling field since 1961. She is currently the manager of the St. Louis office of Health Science Services (a counseling firm). She supervises 15 counselors and manages the Parsons Corporation Employee Health Advisory Program. She has been personally involved in counseling at least 500 families with adult child extended dependency problems, and is responsible for overseeing approximately 2,000 such cases at HAP in 1987 alone.

In addition to her counseling background, Janet has five graduate degrees to her credit, as well as an extensive list of university and government publications. She has traveled extensively, living and working in such remote places as Andahuaylas, Peru. Janet has developed a great sensitivity to the influences of various cultures and religions on human behavior and is uniquely qualified to advise American parents on this unusual phenomenon of extended dependency.

Richard Roe, a longtime writer, received his undergraduate degree in English, magna cum laude, from Tulane University. He received his master's degree in political science from Vanderbilt one year later with a 3.8 GPA. Presently working as an employee relations supervisor for a Fortune 500 company, Richard has two stepdaughters, ages 19 and 21. The older daughter's dependency problem has brought Richard closely in contact with the issue of delayed adulthood. In addition, similar problems with other members of his immediate family caused him to research this issue and discover the vast number of parents struggling with the same problem. Richard offers not only his writing experience to this project, but also his perspective as a parent trying to cope with the endlessly varied manifestations of this emotionally draining problem. He is very conscious of the ways a child can remain dependent although not living at home, and the impact that dependency has on other family members and on the parents' marriage.

OUTLINE

Chapter 1: Healthy and Unhealthy Dependency

Jane Goodall, in her multigenerational observations of a tribe of chimpanzees in Africa observed one dysfunctional family unit that surprised all animal behaviorists. Documented in her book *In the Shadow of Man,* and later in a television documentary, were Flo, an elderly female, and her second-to-last child, a son named Flint. When her last child was born, Flo was too weak to force Flint from the nest they had shared during his first two years of life. He was stubborn and strong and remained dependent until her death several years later. Following Flo's death, Flint refused to eat or to interact with the other chimps. Eventually he passed away, unwilling to take care of himself.

This story of an extended chimpanzee childhood has direct parallels in human behavior. But the lines between healthy and unhealthy dependency are rarely so clear. This chapter will help the reader understand the differences, using both narrative explanation and a self-diagnostic test.

To set the stage, healthy dependency will be explained. Such ideal parenting is called "egalitarian"—or "teaching self-dependency and trust." The normal development of a child into an adult will also be outlined. But how do parents know when they are not being "egalitarian" or the child is not developing normally? The authors will explain three common parental behavior traps: authoritarian behavior, demanding "blind" obedience; permissive/insecure behavior, allowing almost all behavior out of fear of loss of the child's affection; and overprotective behavior, meddling in all the child's affairs.

From the other side of the coin, How does a parent know when a child's dependency is "abnormal"? What is the difference between calling for advice and calling to get Mommy or Daddy to decide everything from which bank to use to what type of toaster to buy? When is it no longer reasonable for a child to expect financial assistance? The authors will explain several types of typical dependency behavior.

The chapter will conclude with a quiz that will allow the reader to evaluate his/her own behavior and that of the child. A scoring system will let the reader determine the severity of the dependency problem. (This quiz will also be designed for easy resale to magazines.)

Chapter 2: Is It My Fault?

The endless parental nightmare asks, Was it something I did? The Judeo-Christian culture is quick to blame the parents for the failings of the child. Yet few are the psychologists or behavioralists who would say that all behavior is the result of parental training. Genetics, instinct, or some other metaphysical influence may be equally important. But the nature/nurture argument is for philosophers, not for parents coping with a problem.

The authors will explain the other factors that go into a child's behavior; but regardless of the cause, searching for blame only wastes energy. What parents need is a way to respond now. Time can be given later to the philosophical questions.

The reader will be shown how to recognize unhealthy "guilt trips," whether they are self-inflicted or inflicted by others. Once identified, the reader can then use the steps outlined to break the paralyzing hold of such guilt and move on to positive thought and action.

The final section of this chapter will specifically address the greatest user of parental guilt: the child. A child learns at a very early age how to gain reactions from its parents. The toughest part for the parents is learning to stop their ingrained reactions, thereby thwarting the adult child's manipulation. This is essential if the parent is to stop anguishing over the problem at hand and act on it instead. Specific advice will show parents how to respond to statements such as, "Well, if we hadn't moved so much I'd be more settled by now."

Chapter 3: Encouraging the Problem

Both parents and adult children have needs that can cause them to subconsciously continue an extended dependency. Until those drives are recognized and defused, the subconscious needs will sabotage the best conscious intent to change things. This chapter will show parents how to recognize those drives in their own situation and work to eliminate them. The following specific parental desires will be addressed:

- "My kids should have it easier than I did."

- "Money can make up for the time I didn't spend with my kid."
- "My kids are a reflection of my success. What will the neighbors think if they don't succeed?"
- "I am the parent; I am in control. I will make my child meet my expectations."
- "My primary role is life as a parent. I am nothing without that" (empty-nest fears).
- "If we don't have the child to distract us, my spouse and I will have to look at our marriage for the first time in years."
- "But what if something bad happens to my 'baby'?" (over-protectiveness).
- "But if I refuse the requests, my child might not come to see me anymore."

Excerpts from interviews with parents will be included to give a real-life dimension to these feelings.

The authors will show how unrealistic and unhealthy these needs or fears are and show parents constructive ways to work out of their own "codependency."

Chapter 4: What's in It for Johnny/Mary?

Kids have their own reasons for wanting to continue the dependency, some of which may be quite surprising to parents. Understanding the motives that may be inspiring the reader's child will help that reader determine the best way to defuse his or her manipulative behaviors. This chapter will itemize the motives, which may not be conscious, that keep the child coming back again and again.

- Inability to cope with parents' divorce.
- Insecurity.
- Laziness.
- Fear of responsibility.
- Fear of failure as an adult/provider/employee/etc.
- Fear/dislike of independence (decisions were always made for them when they were younger).
- Peer pressure (others are getting money from their parents).

- "Mom and Dad owe it to me" (the entitlement syndrome, or what's yours is mine and what's mine is mine).
- "Mom and Dad can afford it."
- Anger/revenge for perceived injustices.
- Materialistic expectations that cannot be immediately met "on the outside."
- Enjoyment of dependency.

This chapter is not designed to make the parent feel that if they "only understood" their child's problem and could "communicate better" it would all go away. Chances are excellent that the adult child has no idea what his/her motives are. But even if he did, talk will not change behavior. Parents will have to act and react differently than they have in the past to cause different behaviors in the child leading to, hopefully, growth in his or her personality. But that is a separate question and not part of this book. The authors' goal is to get parents out of the philosophical realm and into dealing with the here and now. The child's motives are useful to understand only when they advise the parent on how to behave, or not to behave, in the present.

Chapter 4 will include excerpts of interviews with dependent young adults. The language and arguments they use will probably sound familiar to the reader. Chapters 5 through 9 will then deal with specific common situations and how to address them based on case studies.

Chapters 5–8: Case Studies

Chapters 5 through 8 will illustrate common dependency/codependency situations using case studies. The case studies selected will be those considered representative of the 2,000 client cases handled by Health Science Services in 1987. Each case study will involve in-depth interviews with the clients. The reader will be given a brief history of the situation and sample comments from the parents and the dependent child. These will let the readers know they are not alone in their feelings and problems. Those cases in which they can see themselves or their child will give them a more objective view of the unhealthy dependency behaviors being exhibited.

Chapter 5 will address the authoritarian parent and submissive child pattern. Chapter 6 will demonstrate a permissive/insecure parent and the child who takes advantage of that weakness. Chapter 7 deals with the overprotective parent and fearful child. Chapter 8 confronts the problem of chemically dependent children (drug addicts, alcoholics) and the way they tie their parents into codependency.

Chapter 9: Now What Do I Do?

Now that the reader has some idea of the nature of the adult child's dependency behavior and his/her own codependency, what can he/she do to end the cycle? This chapter will give specific advice to parents, first on how to stop participating in the problem. "What do I say when Johnny calls and asks me for money?" "What do I do when Mary drops by unannounced with her laundry?" These common, everyday problems will be addressed in terms that leave the reader feeling as though he/she has some concrete ideas on how to respond to his/her own particular situation.

Second, the authors will give advice on how to encourage the child to seek different behaviors, and reward him/her when they appear. When the child makes a decision on his/her own, what should the parent say? If Johnny decides to rent an apartment beyond his means, but takes on a second job to do it, should anything be said? Learning to reinforce the stumbling efforts to grow into adulthood takes time.

In the final portion of this chapter, advice will be offered regarding the formation of support groups. Sometimes even the strongest wills can falter when faced with the skillful manipulations of a son or daughter. Someone in a similar situation can provide invaluable support. Just knowing that others are struggling as well is sometimes all the support that is needed. But in some cases, professional assistance may be necessary. The reader will be told how to know when it's time to seek help from a professional counselor, and will be given a few tips on selecting one.

The reader will finish the book with valuable tools to assist in working out the problem with his/her child: how to get friends to help when needed and when to turn to professionals for assistance. Most importantly, however, the reader will know that he/she is not alone—that this is not a problem that should be hidden or denied, or one that should cause shame. The reader should feel some of the burden of guilt lifted and feel hopeful that a solution to the problem can be found.

Chapter 1 available upon request.

Glossary

Abstract Brief description of chapters in nonfiction book proposal; a point-by-point summary of an article or essay. Often appear with the articles themselves in scholarly journals.

Adaptation A rewrite or reworking of a piece for another medium; e.g., a novel for the screen.

Advance Money paid (usually in installments) against future royalties to an author by a publisher. If an author is given a $5,000 advance, for instance, the author will collect royalties only in excess of $5,000—after the advance has been paid. A good contract will protect the advance if it exceeds the royalties.

Advance orders The number of copies of a book ordered before the publication date.

Agents Persons acting for authors who present appropriate manuscripts to particular publishing houses. Writers pay 10 to 15 percent for their services.

Anthology A collection of stories, poems, essays, etc., with a unifying theme, by different authors or by a single author. Anthologies are compiled as opposed to being written; their editors (as opposed to authors) are responsible for securing needed reprint rights for the material used.

Auction Potential best-sellers sent by the literary agent for confidential bidding by publishing houses. Reprint, film, and other rights pertaining to a successful hardcover will also be auctioned off by the original publisher's subsidiary rights department.

Authorized biography A history of a person's life written with the authorization, cooperation, and, at times, participation of the subject or the subject's heirs.

Author's copies/author's discount The number of free copies of their books that authors receive. The exact number is stipulated in the contract, but it is usually at least ten hardcovers. In addition, the author can purchase the books at 40 percent off the retail price and resell them at readings, lectures, etc. If bought in large quantities, author discounts can go as high as 70 percent.

Author tour Travel and promotional appearances by an author on behalf of his or her book.

Backlist Books published prior to the current season and still in print. These titles are often a publisher's bread and butter. Some continue to sell briskly; some remain best-sellers. Although it may be difficult to find some backlist titles, they are easily ordered either through local bookstores or directly from the publisher.

Back matter Sections following the text, including the appendix, notes, glossary, bibliography, and index.

Best-sellers List of best-selling books based on sales by bookstores, wholesalers, and distributors. Lists can be local (newspapers) or national (*Publishers Weekly* or the *New York Times*). Fiction and nonfiction are usually listed separately, as are hardcover and paperback.

Bibliography A list of books, articles, and other sources, arranged alphabetically by author, that have been used in the writing of the text in which the bibliography appears. The format may vary according to house style rules. In more complex tomes, may be broken down into more detailed subject areas, such as General History, the Twentieth Century, or Trade Unions.

Book clubs Book-marketing organizations that regularly ship selected books to their subscribing members, sometimes at greatly reduced prices. Writers benefit from a book club sale since, though terms vary, the split of royalties between author and publisher is often 50–50. These sales are negotiated through the subsidiary rights department (in the case of a best-seller, they can be auctioned off).

Book contract A legally binding document setting the terms for the advance, royalties, subsidiary rights, advertising, promotion, publicity, and a host of other contingencies and responsibilities. Writers should be thoroughly familiar with the concepts and legal terms of the standard book contract.

Book distribution The method of getting books from the publisher's warehouse into the reader's hands—usually via a bookstore—by the publisher's own sales force, independent salespeople hired by the publisher, wholesalers, distributors, and/or direct marketing. Many large and some small publishers distribute for other publishers, which is a good source of extra income. A publisher's distribution network is extremely important, as it affects the visibility of its books.

Book producer or book packager An individual or company that conceives the idea for a book (usually, although not always, nonfiction), brings together the professionals needed to produce the book, and then sells the manuscript to a publisher. The book producer negotiates two kinds of contracts: one with the publisher; and another with the writers, editors, or illustrators contributing to the book.

Book reviews Before the public reads book reviews in the local and national print media, important reviews have been published in such well-respected trade journals as *Publishers Weekly, Kirkus Reviews, Library Journal,* and *Booklist.* A rave review from one of these journals will encourage booksellers to buy the book; copies of these raves will be used by the publisher for promotion and publicity and will encourage book reviewers nationwide to review the book.

Bound galleys Uncorrected typesetter's proofs, sometimes bound as an advance copy of the book. Bound galleys are sent to trade journals (see Book reviews) and to a limited number of major reviewers who have a long lead time.

Bulk sales The sale at a discount of many copies of a single title (the greater the number of books, the larger the discount).

Byline The author's name appearing on a piece, indicating credit for having written a book or article. Ghostwriters do not receive bylines.

Coauthor A joint author or collaborator with a byline. Each will share royalties based on his or her contributions to the book.

Collaboration A joint effort with professionals in other fields to produce books outside a writer's area of expertise (for example, with a doctor on a health book). The writer does not necessarily get a byline, and royalties are shared based on contributions to the book (for example, expertise as well as the actual writing).

Commercial fiction Novels or short stories written to appeal to as great a readership as possible.

Concept A general statement about the idea behind a book—most often used in nonfiction.

Cooperative advertising (co-op) An agreement between a publisher and a bookstore. The publisher's book is featured in an ad for the bookstore; the publisher contributes to the cost of the ad and is billed at a lower (retail advertising) rate.

Copublishing Joint publishing of a book, usually by a publisher and another entity such as a foundation, a museum, or a smaller publisher. An author can copublish with a publisher by sharing the costs and decision making and, ultimately, the profits.

Copyeditor An editor who reads for correctness of grammar, spelling, punctuation, and style.

Copyright An author's legal right to a work from the time it is completed. For legal recourse in the event of plagiarism, the work must be registered with the U.S. Copyright Office, and all copies of the work must bear the copyright notice.

Cover blurbs Favorable quotes from other writers, celebrities, or experts in a book's subject area, which appear on the dust jacket, and help sell the book to the public.

Deadline Author's due date for submission of manuscript to publisher. Can be a full year before publication date, unless the book is being produced quickly to coincide with a particular event.

Delivery Submission of the complete manuscript to the editor.

Dial-a-Writer Members of the American Society of Journalists and Authors can be listed with their referral service, which provides qualified writers-for-hire for most subjects.

Direct marketing Advertising that involves a "direct response" (the other term for it) from a consumer—for example, an order form or coupon in a book review section or in the back of a book, or mailings (direct mail advertising) to a group with a special interest in a particular book.

Distributor Any agent or business that buys books from a publisher to resell, at a higher cost, to wholesalers, retailers, or individuals. A large distributor can give a small publisher greater national visibility.

Dramatic rights Legal permission to adapt a work for the stage. Can be sold or assigned to another party by the author.

Dust jacket The paper wrapper covering the binding of hardcover books. Designed especially for the book by either the publisher's art department or a freelance artist.

Dust jacket copy Synopses printed on the flaps. Usually written by the book's editor, but sometimes by in-house copywriters or freelancers. Editors send advance galley proofs to writers, experts, and celebrities to solicit quotable praise to appear on the jacket (see Cover blurbs).

Editors Responsibilities vary from house to house (dividing lines are less clear in smaller houses). Generally, the duties of the editor-in-chief or executive editor are administrative: managing personnel, scheduling, budgeting, and defining the editorial personality of the firm or the imprint. Senior editors and acquisitions editors acquire manuscripts (and authors), conceive project ideas and find writers to carry them out, and may oversee the writing and rewriting of manuscripts. Managing editors have editorial and production responsibilities in the coordination and the scheduling of the book through different production phases. Associate and assistant editors edit; they are involved in most of the rewriting and reshaping of the manuscript. Copyeditors read the manuscript and correct for punctuation, grammar, spelling, etc. Editorial assistants, while laden with extensive clerical duties, have some editorial responsibility, often as a springboard to a more senior editorial position.

El-hi Books for elementary and/or high schools.

Epilogue The final segment of a book that comes "after the end." In fiction or nonfiction, it offers sweeter commentary or information.

Film rights Like dramatic rights, these belong to the author who may sell them to someone in the film industry—a producer or director, for example—who will try to convert the book into a film.

Footnotes Explanatory notes and/or attribution that appear at the bottom of the page. Footnotes are rare in general-interest books; bibliographies usually suffice.

Foreign agents Persons who work with their U.S. counterparts to acquire books from the United States for publication abroad. They can also represent U.S. publishers directly.

Foreign market Any foreign entity—a publisher, broadcast medium, etc.—in a position to buy rights. Authors share royalties with whoever negotiates the deal, or keep 100 percent if they do their own negotiating.

Foreign rights Translation rights or reprint rights that can be sold abroad. Foreign rights belong to the author but can be sold either country-by-country or en masse as world rights. Often the U.S. publisher will own world rights, and the author will be entitled to anywhere from 50 to 85 percent of the revenues.

Foreword An introductory piece written by the author or an expert in the given field (see Introduction). A foreword from a celebrity or well-respected authority is a strong sales tool for a book.

Frankfurt Book Fair The largest international publishing exhibition, held every October in Frankfurt, West Germany. Thousands of publishers, agents, and writers from all over the world negotiate, network, and buy and sell rights.

Freedom of Information Act Ensures the protection of the public's right to access to government records—except in cases violating the right to privacy, national security, or certain other instances. A related law, the Government in the Sunshine Act, stipulates that certain government agencies announce and open their meetings to the public.

Freight passthrough The bookseller's freight cost (the cost of getting the book from the publisher to the bookseller). It is added to the basic invoice price charged the bookseller by the publisher.

Frontlist New titles published in a given season by a publisher. Will usually receive priority exposure in the sales catalog, as opposed to backlist titles, which are previously published titles that remain in print.

Front matter Introductory material preceding the text, including the title page, copyright notice, dedication, contents, foreword, preface, acknowledgments, and (if not part of the text) the introduction.

Fulfillment house A company hired to fulfill orders for a publisher. A subscription card for a New York magazine, for instance, may be mailed to the Midwest. Although more common for magazine publishers, fulfillment houses also service book publishers.

Galleys Typesetter's proofs on long sheets of paper or made up as preliminary pages—the author's last chance to check for typos.

Genre fiction Mass market fiction that falls into a particular category: mystery, romance (including Gothic and Regency romances), Westerns, science fiction, and the like.

Ghostwriters Writers without bylines; often writers without the remuneration and recognition that credited authors receive.

Ghostwriters usually get a flat fee for their work; but even without royalties, experienced "ghosts" can receive quite a respectable fee.

Glossary An alphabetized and defined list of terms in a particular subject area.

How-to books An immensely popular category of books ranging from purely instructional (arts and crafts, for example) to motivational (popular psychology self-help) to get-rich-quick (real estate and investment).

Imprint A separate line within a publishing house with its own editorial department (which may consist of one editor), sometimes a certain kind of book (juvenile or paperback or travel), or its own personality (such as literary). An imprint's books often overlap categories with the publisher's other imprints, but help maintain a "small-house" feel to otherwise enormous conglomerates. They have the advantages of a small editorial department and access to the larger company's resources in publicity, sales, and advertising.

Index An alphabetical list at the end of a book detailing names and subjects discussed in the book and the page numbers on which they can be found.

Instant book A book produced quickly to appear in bookstores as soon as possible after a newsworthy event to which it is relevant.

International copyright Rights secured for countries that are members of the International Copyright Convention and using the copyright symbol, ©.

International Copyright Convention Those countries that are signatories to the various international copyright treaties. Since treaties are contingent upon certain conditions being met at the time of publication, an author should inquire before publication into a particular country's laws.

Introduction Remarks written by the author or an appropriate authority on the subject. If the book has a foreword and an introduction, the foreword is written by someone other than the author; the introduction is written by the book's author and deals more closely with the subject of the text.

ISBN (International Standard Book Number) A Ten-digit number that identifies the title and publisher of a book. It is used for ordering and cataloging books and appears on all dust jackets, the back cover of the book, and on the copyright page.

ISSN (International Standard Serial Number) An eight-digit number that identifies all U.S. and foreign periodicals.

Juveniles Books for children. They are divided into several categories: picture books (for the very young); easy storybooks (young schoolchildren); middle-grade books (elementary to junior high school students); and young adult.

Kill fee An amount paid by a magazine when it cancels an assigned article. The fee is only a certain percentage (no more than 50 percent) of an agreed-to payment for the article. Not all publishers pay kill fees; a writer should make sure to formalize this agreement in advance.

Lead The crucial first few sentences in which the writer must hook the reader, editor, or agent.

Letterhead Business stationery and envelopes imprinted with the company's (or, in this case, the writer's) name—a convenience and an impressive asset for a freelance writer.

Libel Defamation of an individual in a published work with malice aforethought, as contrasted to slander, which is defamation through the spoken word.

Library of Congress The largest library in the world. As part of its many services, it will supply a writer with up-to-date sources and bibliographies in all fields, from arts and humanities to science and technology. (Write to the Library of Congress, Central Services Division, Washington, DC 20540 for details.)

Library of Congress Catalog Card Number An identifying number issued by the Library of Congress to books it has accepted for its collection. The publication of those books, which are submitted by the publisher, are announced by the Library of

Congress to libraries, who use the Library of Congress numbers for their own ordering and cataloging purposes.

Literary fiction Works in which the quality and the art of writing are higher priorities than considerations of profit or general mass market appeal.

Literary Market Place (LMP) An annual directory of the publishing industry containing a comprehensive list of publishers, alphabetically and by category, with their addresses, phone numbers, some personnel, and the types of books they publish. Also listed are various publishing services, such as literary agencies and editorial and distribution services. (*LMP* is published by R. R. Bowker and is available in most public libraries.)

Logo A company or product identifier: for example, the company's initials or a drawing that is the exclusive property of that company.

Mainstream fiction Quality, nongenre fiction, excluding literary or avant-garde fiction, that appeals to a general readership.

Marketing plan The entire strategy for selling a book: its publicity, promotion, sales, and advertising.

Mass market paperback Less-expensive smaller-format paperbacks sold from supermarket and drugstore racks as well as in bookstores.

Mechanicals Typeset copy and art mounted on boards to be photocopied and printed. Also referred to as paste-ups.

Midlist books Generally, mainstream fiction or nonfiction titles forming the bulk of a publisher's list. They are neither explosive best-sellers nor distinguished and critically respected books with small print runs and select readerships.

Multiple contract A book agreement that includes a provision for a future book or books.

Mystery books An example of genre fiction that includes detective novels, thrillers, technothrillers, espionage novels, and horror stories. They rely on suspense as well as the usual literary techniques to keep the reader engaged.

Net receipts The amount of money a publisher actually receives for sales of a book: the retail price minus the bookseller's discount and/or other discount. The number of returned copies is factored in, bringing down even further the net amount per book. Royalties are sometimes figured on these lower amounts rather than on the retail price of the book.

New age An eclectic category encompassing health, medicine, philosophy, religion, and the occult presented from an alternative perspective (such as one influenced by Oriental or Native American traditions). Although the term has become well known during the 1980s, some publishers have been producing serious books in this category for decades.

Novella A work of fiction in a length between a short story and a novel.

Option clause/right of first refusal A clause in a book contract stipulating that the publisher will have the right to the author's next book. The publisher, however, is under no obligation to publish the subsequent book.

Outline A form used for both a book proposal and the actual writing and structuring of a book to let the writer (and the proposal reader) quickly see the development of ideas and the order in which they will be presented.

Out-of-print books Books no longer available from the publisher; rights usually revert to the author.

Package The book itself; the physical product.

Page proof The final typeset copy of the book exactly as it will appear, page for page, when printed.

Paperback originals Books published in paperback editions only, or simultaneous publications of hardcovers and paperbacks. Often mass market genre fiction (romances, Westerns, Gothics, etc.) as well as quality paperback fiction, cookbooks, humor, career, self-help, and how-to books, and other ever-expanding categories.

Permissions The right to quote or reprint published material, obtained by the author from the copyright holder.

Picture book Highly illustrated books with very simple, limited text geared for preschoolers and very young children.

Plagiarism The false presentation of someone else's writing as one's own. In the case of copyrighted work, it is illegal.

Preface An author's comments explaining the format of a book, or its genesis or purpose.

Premiums Reduced-price books sold to a bookseller who in turn is selling them as part of a special promotion.

Press kit A promotional package that includes a press release, tip sheet, author biography and photograph, reviews, and other pertinent information. It is put together by, for example, the publisher's publicity department and sent with a review copy of the book to potential reviewers and to media professionals responsible for booking author appearances.

Prices Several amounts applying to a single book: the invoice price, which is the publisher's cost to the bookseller; and the retail, cover, or list price, which is what the consumer pays.

Printer's error (PE) Typographical errors made by the typesetter or printer, not the publisher's staff. PEs are corrected at the typesetter's or printer's expense.

Proposal A detailed explanation of an idea for a book that is used to sell the book to an agent or publisher.

Publication date A book's official date of publication, set by the publisher to fall six weeks after the completed bound books are delivered to its warehouse. This date must be remembered when arranging advertising and publicity for the book so that a heavily advertised book is available in the stores.

Public domain Uncopyrighted material or material whose copyright has expired or is uncopyrightable. The latter includes government publications, jokes, titles and—it should be remembered—ideas.

Publicist The professional who handles the press releases for new books and arranges the author's publicity tour.

Publisher's catalog A seasonal sales catalog that lists and describes a publisher's new books; it is sent to all potential buyers, including individuals who request one. Catalogs range from basic to glitzy, and often include information on the author, print quantity, and the amount of money to be spent on publicity.

Publisher's discount The percentage by which a publisher discounts the retail price of a book for a bookseller, often based in part on the number of copies purchased.

Publishers' Trade List Annual A collection of current and backlist catalogs arranged alphabetically by publisher. Available in many libraries.

Publishers Weekly The publishing industry's chief trade journal. *PW* carries announcements of upcoming books, well-respected book reviews, author and celebrity interviews, special reports on various book categories, and trade news (such as mergers and personnel changes).

Query letter A brief written presentation to an editor designed to sell the editor on both the writer and the book idea.

Remainders Remaining stock of books that have not sold well (as well as unsold later printings of best-sellers). Purchased by bookstores from the publisher at a huge discount to be resold to the public.

Reprint Another printing of material that has already been published, especially in another format—the paperback reprint of a hardcover, for example.

Resumé An outline of an individual's employment experience and education. Sent to prospective employers and, when it contains vital author credentials, to prospective publishers or agents.

Returns Unsold books returned to a publisher by a bookstore, for which the store may receive full or partial credit (depending on the publisher's policy, the age of the book, etc.).

Reversion-of-rights clause A clause in a book contract stating that if the book goes out of print and the publisher fails to reprint the book within a stipulated length of time, all rights revert to the author.

Review copy Free copies of (usually) new books sent to print and electronic media to review for their audiences.

Romance novels Modern or period love stories, always with a happy ending, ranging from the demure to the torrid. They are not, however, sexually graphic, and they are moving away from the "helpless female" character to the modern woman of stronger character.

Royalties A percentage of the retail cost of a book paid to the author for each copy sold after the author's advance has been recouped. Some publishers pay a percentage against net receipts.

SASE A self-addressed, stamped envelope. Many editors and agents will not reply to submissions of author proposals and manuscripts unless an SASE is enclosed.

Sales conference A publisher's semiannual meeting for its editorial and sales departments and senior promotion and publicity staff members, to introduce the upcoming season's new books and to discuss marketing strategies.

Sales representative (sales rep) A member of the publisher's sales force or an independent contractor who, armed with a book catalog and order forms, visits bookstores in a certain area to sell the books to retailers.

Satisfactory clause In book contracts, a publisher's right to refuse publication of a manuscript that is deemed unsatisfactory. The specific criteria for publisher satisfaction should be set forth in the contract to protect the author, as the author may be forced to repay the advance if the complete work is unacceptable.

Science fiction/fantasy A genre that includes the hardcore, technological/scientific novel (fiction expanding on fact) and the novel concerned with magic, wizardry, and the supernatural (fiction transcending reality).

Screenplay A film script based on either original as previously published material.

Self-publishing An author pays for the costs of manufacturing and selling his or her own book and retains all profits from the book's sale. Although a risky venture, it can lead to distribution or publication by a larger publisher if successful.

Self-syndication Management of copyrights, selling, negotiation of the fee, and billing the newspaper or magazine by journalists or writers who sell their own columns to the periodicals that pick up their column.

Serial rights Reprint rights sold to periodicals. First serial rights include the rights for either the U.S. or wider market, whereby the periodical has the right to publish the material before anyone else. Second serial rights cover material already published, either in a book or another periodical.

Serialization The reprint of a book or part of a book in a newspaper or magazine prior to the publication of the book (first serial) or after publication (second serial).

Series Books published as a group either because of their related subject matter (such as Expressionist painters or World War II aircraft) or single authorship (a Dickens collection). This is a ready-made niche for an author who is up-to-date on a publisher's plans and has the qualifications to be a contributor.

Shelf life The amount of time an unsold book will stay on a bookstore shelf before the store manager will pull it to make room for newer incoming stock with greater or at least untested sales potential.

Short story A brief piece of fiction that is more pointed and more economical of character, situation, and plot than a novel. Short story collections often revolve around a single theme.

Simultaneous publication The coincidental publication of the paperback and hardcover editions of a book.

Simultaneous (or multiple) submissions Sending of the same material to more than one publisher. Publishers should always be made aware of this.

Slush pile Unsolicited manuscripts that sit indefinitely awaiting review at a publishing house.

Software In word processing, a program that allows the writer to write, edit, store, and print material. Some software packages are cumbersome and inefficient; care should be taken to find software appropriate to the individual's work and capabilities.

Special sales Sales of a book to appropriate retailers other than bookstores (for example, wine guides to liquor stores). Also includes books sold as premiums (to, for example, a convention group or a company) for promotional purposes. Depending on volume, per-unit costs can be very low, and the book can be custom designed.

Subsidiary rights The reprint, serial, movie, television, and other rights attached to a book. The division of profits between publisher and author from the sales of these rights is determined through negotiation.

Subsidy (vanity) publishing The author pays the publishing company to produce his or her work, and it may thus appear to have been conventionally published. Generally more expensive than self-publishing, since the subsidy house charges fees beyond the production costs.

Syndicated column Material published simultaneously in a number of newspapers or magazines. The author shares the profits with the syndicate that negotiated the sale.

Synopsis A summary, in paragraph rather than outline form. In fiction, a brief description of the manuscript that is part of a book proposal.

Table of contents A list of the book's chapters or a magazine's articles and columns, in the order in which they appear, with the page numbers.

Tabloid A smaller than standard size newspaper (daily, weekly, or monthly) often known more for sensationalism than for news reportage.

Terms The financial conditions agreed to in a book contract.

Theme The general concept of a book.

Tip sheet Information on a single book that presents general publication information (pub date, editor, ISBN, etc.), a brief synopsis of the book, information on competitive books, and other relevant marketing data such as author information and advance blurbs. Given to sales and publicity departments and included in press kits.

Title page The page at the front of a book that lists the title, subtitle, author (and other contributors, such as translator or illustrator) and, at the bottom of the page, the publishing house and sometimes its logo.

Trade books Books distributed through the book trade—bookstores—as opposed to, for example, mass market paperbacks that are sold at magazine racks and by supermarkets.

Trade discount A lower price than the cover or list price that a publisher gives a bookseller. It is usually in proportion to the number of books ordered (the larger the order, the greater the discount) and varies between 43 and 50 percent.

Trade list A catalog of all of a publisher's books in print with ISBNs and order information and sometimes descriptions of the current season's new books.

Trade (quality) paperbacks Reprints or original titles published in a larger format than mass market paperbacks, distributed through regular retail book channels, and often costing at least twice the price of mass market titles.

Trade publishers Publishers of books for a general readership—that is, nonprofessional, nonacademic books primarily distributed through bookstores.

Translation rights Rights sold to a foreign agent or directly to a foreign publisher by the author's agent or by the publisher.

Treatment In screenwriting, a full narrative description of the story, including sample dialogue.

Unauthorized biography A written history of a person's life published without the consent of the subject or the subject's survivors.

University press Generally a nonprofit university-subsidized publisher of noncommercial scholarly nonfiction books written by academics.

Unsolicited manuscript An unrequested manuscript sent to an editor or agent.

Vanity press A publisher that publishes books only at an author's expense—usually whatever is submitted and paid for (see Subsidy publishing).

Word count The number of words in a manuscript, rounded off to the nearest 100.

Work-for-hire Writing done for an employer, or writing commissioned by a publisher or book packager who retains ownership of the written matter.

Young adult books Fiction dealing with issues of concern to young readers ages 12 to 17.

Suggested Readings

Appelbaum, Judith, *How to Get Happily Published,* 3rd ed. (New York: Harper & Row, 1988). Beyond the "mere" acceptance of a manuscript, sensible advice on generating ideas, putting them into words, and maintaining control over the editing, sales, and marketing of one's work.

Appelbaum, Judith, Nancy Evans, and Florence Janovic, *The Sensible Solutions How to Get Happily Published Handbook* (New York: Sensible Solutions, Inc., 1981). Worksheets and additional information for authors of trade books, designed to be used in conjunction with the above-mentioned title.

Balkin, Richard, *How to Understand and Negotiate a Book Contract or Magazine Agreement* (Cincinnati: Writer's Digest Books, 1985). Essential reading for every writer who wants to make a sale.

Boswell, John, *The Awful Truth About Publishing: Why They Always Reject Your Manuscript . . . And What You Can Do About It* (New York: Warner Books, 1986). A view from the other side—that is, from inside the large publishing house.

Bunnin, Brad, and Peter Beren, *Author Law and Strategies: A Personal Guide for the Working Writer* (Berkeley, Calif.: Nolo Press, 1984). The ins and outs of publishing law, published by specialists in do-it-yourself legal guides.

Burgett, Gordon, *Query Letters, Cover Letters: How They Sell Your Writing* (Carpinteria, Calif.: Communication Unlimited, 1985). Essays by and interviews with 29 writers including Margaret Atwood, John Hawkes, Saul Bellow, and Hortense Calisher.

Fry, Ronald W., ed., *Book Publishing Career Directory* (Hawthorne, N.J.: The Career Press, published annually). Descriptions of the various publishing jobs by those who actually do them, plus advice on securing those jobs.

Gage, Diane, and Marcia Hibsch Coppess, *Get Published: Editors from the Nation's Top Magazines Tell You What They Want* (New York: Henry Holt, 1986). An extensive survey of dozens of national magazines—who they are and what they're looking for.

Gardner, John, *On Becoming a Novelist* (New York: Harper & Row, 1983). The late novelist's sympathetic and highly enjoyable account of the education, art, and survival of the beginning writer.

Goldberg, Natalie, *Writing Down the Bones: Freeing the Writer Within* (Boston: Shambhala Publications, 1986). Some thoughts and advice about the art of writing. The author is a Zen Buddhist and writing instructor.

Horowitz, Lois, *Knowing Where to Look: The Ultimate Guide to Research* (Cincinnati: Writer's Digest Books, 1984). An invaluable tool for anyone who has to dig up elusive facts and figures.

Judson, Jerome, *On Being a Poet* (Cincinnati: Writer's Digest Books, 1984). Thoughts on, and discussion of, the art of poetry—both the author's and that of other poets.

Judson, Jerome, *The Poet's Handbook* (Cincinnati: Writer's Digest Books, 1980). The art and mechanics of writing poetry by "rule" and example. Also included are tips on getting published.

Kilpatrick, James J., *The Writer's Art* (Kansas City, Mo.: Andrews, McMeel & Parker, 1984). An opinionated discussion of proper usage, style, and just plain good writing from one of the news business's most popular curmudgeons.

Klauser, Henriette Anne, *Writing on Both Sides of the Brain: Breakthrough Techniques for People Who Write* (New York: Harper & Row, 1986). How to refrain from editing while you write; how to edit, mercilessly and creatively, what you've just written.

Kremer, John, *101 Ways to Market Your Books—for Publishers and Authors* (Fairfield, Iowa: Ad-Lib Publications, 1986). Sensible, innovative, and inspiring advice on, first, producing the most marketable book possible, and then on marketing it as effectively as possible.

Larsen, Michael, *How to Write a Book Proposal* (Cincinnati: Writer's Digest Books, 1985). A clear and no-nonsense—even inspiring—step-by-step guide to the book proposal.

Literary Market Place (New York: R. R. Bowker, published annually). A huge directory of publishing houses and their personnel, as well as writing, editing, and publishing services nationwide.

Mann, Thomas, *A Guide to Library Research Methods* (New York: Oxford University Press, 1987). A practical guide to helpful, time-saving, and cost-effective information sources.

McCormack, Thomas, *The Fiction Editor* (New York: St. Martin's Press, 1988). How to fine-tune fiction. Every bit as helpful for writers as it is for editors.

Miller, Casey, and Kate Swift, *The Handbook of Nonsexist Writing* (New York: Harper & Row, 1988). Excellent guidelines for eliminating sexist terms and constructions from all writing.

Polking, Kirk, and Leonard S. Meranus, eds., *Law and the Writer,* 3rd ed. (Cincinnati: Writer's Digest Books, 1985). A collection of essays on legal issues that concern writers and their works.

Powell, Walter W., *Getting into Print: The Decision-Making Process in Scholarly Publishing* (Chicago: University of

Chicago Press, 1985). An eye-opening, behind-the-scenes look at the operations of two scholarly presses.

Poynter, Dan, and Mindy Bingham, *Is There a Book Inside You? How to Successfully Author a Book Alone or Through a Collaborator* (Santa Barbara, Calif.: Para Publishing, 1985). A thought-provoking series of exercises to help you determine your potential for publishing.

Provost, Gary, *The Freelance Writer's Handbook* (New York: NAL/Mentor, 1982). Invaluable advice, mainly for writers of magazine pieces.

Rivers, William L., *Finding Facts: Interviewing, Observing, Using Reference Sources* (Englewood Cliffs, N. J.: Prentice-Hall, 1975). A careful inquiry into the research process and the difficulties of achieving objectivity.

Roberts, Ellen E. M., *The Children's Picture Book: How to Write It, How to Sell It* (Cincinnati: Writer's Digest Books, 1981). A savvy and enthusiastic step-by-step guide by an established children's book editor.

Strunk, William, Jr., and E. B. White, *The Elements of Style,* 3rd ed. (New York: Macmillan, 1979). A highly respected, widely read, and well-loved classic.

Todd, Alden, *Finding Facts Fast* (Berkeley, Calif.: Ten Speed Press, 1979). Detailed basic, intermediate, and advanced research techniques; hundreds of ideas for those stuck in a research dead end.

Welty, Eudora, *One Writer's Beginnings* (New York: Warner Books, 1984). "Listening," "Learning to See," and "Finding a Voice"—three beautifully written essays (based on lectures given at Harvard) that trace Ms. Welty's influence and her growth as a young writer in the South.

Writer's Market (Cincinnati: Writer's Digest Books, published annually). A directory of thousands of markets and outlets. Best known for its listing of hundreds of consumer and trade periodicals, it also includes book publishers, book packagers, greeting card publishers, syndicates, and more.

Zinsser, William, *On Writing Well* (New York: Harper & Row, 1985). How to simplify nonfiction writing and deliver fresh, vigorous prose. An excellent book to keep in your library.

Index

A

A&C Black, 93
AARP Books, 200
ABA Book Fair, 95
Abbey, Edward, 158, 164
ABC/Capital Cities, 220
Abel, Carole, 239
Abel, Dominick, 239
Abingdon Press, 103–104
Abraham, Marilyn J., 187
Abrams, Harry N., Inc., 104
Abrams, Susan, 213
Abstract, 307
Academy Editions, 198
Academy of American Poets,
    The, 259
Ace, 120
Acker, Alison, 195
Ackerman, John G., 131

Acquisition process, 1–6
Acropolis Books, Ltd.,
    104–105
Acton, Edward J., 239
Acton, Edward J. Inc., 239
Adams, Alice, 162
Adams, Bob, Inc., 105
Adams, Brett, Ltd., 251
Adams, Chuck, 136
Adams, Deborah, 57–62
Adams, Elisa, 167
Adams, Robert L., 105
Adaptation, 307
Adcock, Thomas, 278
Ad-copy persons, 41
Addison, Herbert, 178
Addison-Wesley Publishing
    Co., Inc., 105–107
Aris Books, 109

331

Notes

Notes

Notes

Notes

Notes

Notes

Notes

Notes

Notes

Notes

Re: REQUEST FOR ADDITIONS
    DELETIONS/CORRECTIONS

Dear Reader,

The publishing industry is one of the most dynamic, with publishing companies emerging and disappearing with some frequency. The same is true of editorial personnel; the publishing industry is known for a certain amount of turnover. Additionally, in publishing this first-of-its-kind book, the author and publisher have done everything in their power to be accurate. Yet errors are bound to have slipped through.

We need your help. If you have any information concerning publishing/editorial changes, or if we have failed to include an important person or company, or if you find an error in this book, we would very much appreciate your bringing this to our attention. Please address all such comments to:

Prima Publishing & Communications
Department IGBEP
P.O. Box 1260
Rocklin, CA 95677

Thank you for your help.

Sincerely,

Jennifer Bern Basye
Project Director

SUCCESS TOOLS
FROM THE
WRITER'S BOOKSHELF

STANDING ORDER FOR:

*The Insider's Guide to Book Editors
and Publishers*
1991-92 edition
(*completely revised and updated every year*)

Be among the first to receive the next updated and expanded edition of *The Insider's Guide to Book Editors and Publishers.* As informative as the current edition is, the next *annual* edition will be fully revised and expanded to include over 50 more publishers. To receive your copy(ies) automatically, fill out the enclosed order form at the back of the book and mail today (with Visa/MC only). **Save Money!!** All standing orders will be charged at 1990 prices, in spite of anticipated price increase.

*TV/PR: How to Promote Yourself,
Your Product, Your Service,
or Your Organization on Television*
by Chambers and Asher

Authors, whether self-published or published by someone else, need to understand how to present themselves on television. One successful appearance on television can sell hundreds, even thousands of books. This fine book instructs the reader in every aspect of television promotion, from creating a media kit and getting booked to using visuals and giving a smashing interview. This one is a must! **$12.95**

How to Sell 75% of Your Freelance Writing
by Gordon Burgett

Gordon Burgett's seminar by the same name has been hailed by thousands of writers who have attended it. In this book he shows every writer how to use the same techniques he has perfected to place over 1,000 articles and *get paid for them.* A main selection of The Writer's Digest Book Club **$12.95**

The Complete Work-at-Home Companion
by Herman Holtz

Whether part time or full time, every writer has a business at home. In this definitive work here is invaluable information on overcoming distractions, best office-design ideas, choosing the best computer hardware and software, as well as advice on using on-line communication systems, and more! **$15.95**

How to Become a Successful Consultant in Your Own Field
by Hubert Bermont

This book shows you how to get paid for what you already know—regardless of your expertise. Consultants often make in one hour what they used to make in a day of working for someone else. This book will show you how to set up a profitable consulting business, how to get clients, and how to collect hefty fees. A selection of *both* the Fortune and Executive Bookshelf Book Clubs **$19.95**

FILL IN AND MAIL . . . *TODAY*

Prima Publishing & Communications
P.O. Box 1260, Dept. JH90
Rocklin, CA 95677

Use Your VISA/MC and Order By Phone
(916) 624-5718
Mon. Fri. 9-4 PST (12-7 EST)

Dear People,

Please add my subscription to your advance orders for the next annual edition of
The Insider's Guide to Book Editors and Publishers:

_____ copy(ies) of the hardbound edition at $27.95 for a total of $_____

_____ copy(ies) of the paperback edition at $15.95 for a total of $_____

I understand that this advance order is only available with Visa/MC.
This information I have included in the order coupon on the following page.

I'd also like to order copies of the following titles from the
Writer's Bookshelf:

_____ copy(ies) of ***TV/PR*** at $12.95 each for a total of $_____

_____ copy(ies) of ***How To Sell 75% of Your Freelance Writing*** $_____
at $12.95 each for a total of

_____ copy(ies) of ***Complete Work-At-Home Companion*** $_____
at $15.95 each for a total of

_____ copy(ies) of ***How To Become a Successful Consultant*** $_____
at $19.95 each for a total of

Subtotal	_____
Postage and Handling	$____3.00
Sales Tax	_____
TOTAL (U.S. funds only)	_____

(Continued on next page)

☐ Check enclosed for $_____, payable to Prima Publishing

   Charge my   ☐ Mastercard ☐ Visa

Account No. _____ Exp. Date _____

Signature _____

Your Name _____

Address _____

City/State/Zip _____

Daytime Telephone _____

GUARANTEE

YOU MUST BE SATISFIED!

You get a 30-day, 100% money-back guarantee on all books.

Thank you for your order.